MINGMING

& the Art of Minimal Ocean Sailing

ROGER D. TAYLOR

MINGMING

& the Art of Minimal Ocean Sailing

More Voyages of a Simple Sailor

F

Published by The FitzRoy Press 2010. Reprinted 2011, 2013.

𝓕
The FitzRoy Press
5 Regent Gate
Waltham Cross
Herts EN8 7AF

ISBN 978-0955803-512

A catalogue record for this book is available from the British Library

Publishing management by Troubador Publishing Ltd, Leicester, UK

To the memory of Mike Richey

In order to minimise the cost and ecological impact of this book, colour photographs have been omitted. Photographs and video clips linked to this text can be found at www.thesimplesailor.com

Contents

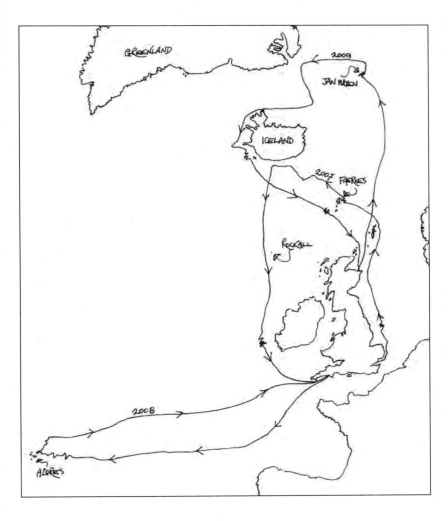

Mingming's *Voyages 2007-2009*

Preface

'This world, my boy, is a moving world; its Riddough's Hotels are forever being pulled down; it never stands still; and its sands are forever shifting.'

Herman Melville, *Redburn*

The first book in this series, *Voyages of a Simple Sailor*, which serves as an indispensable introduction to the present volume, enjoyed the longest of gestations and the most startling of births. It sprang into the world, fully-formed and raring to go, in just a matter of weeks. It rather took me by surprise; I had long discounted the arrival of any literary offspring.

Having got the taste for writing, I've been compelled to carry on. It's not been easier second time round; far from it. Inspiration has been replaced by dogged labour. Two thousand words of an early morning have shrunk to a hard-mined five hundred. It's been a tough task, but pleasurable nonetheless, for what greater pleasure could there be than to write about my little yacht *Mingming*? My affection for this tiny ocean-goer, and my gratitude to her for the adventures we have shared together, know no bounds. This book is a celebration of our partnership.

I have been driven too by another imperative: to show that

ocean sailing which is simple, harmonious, unaggressive and patient can bring the richest of rewards. The modern sailor is too often drowned in a technological morass. Overload obscures vision. Digital excess veils the real world. Constant hurry induces blindness. My own preference is to spar lightly and directly with the ocean in a soft and sensual combat that allows me to know it better. My task is to observe it in its minutiae and to report its every nuance.

I don't always like the sea; sometimes I loathe it. Nonetheless, I am hopelessly under its spell. It always draws me back. It is only by writing about it that I can start to fathom the lure of this final, fragile wilderness.

PART ONE

WHALES

Their goal was unmistakable; they were heading straight for
Mingming. *The lines of leaping heads, spread across nearly a*
mile of sea, some now closing us fast, others still dark and
intermittent smudges at the limit of my vision, were
converging on a single point as accurately and as purposefully
as if directed by some well-organised mission control. Perhaps
they were. Whatever was driving them on towards us was
unequivocal in its command; we were the focal point of this
approaching horde. I had never, ever, seen anything like it.
Wide-eyed, I watched them come.

1

I had long harboured a burning to sail north. It was the cold, the grey and the windswept that drew me. Bleakness exerted its charm. That I should want regularly to go to sea in an engineless yacht of *Mingming's* modest proportions already struck many friends as verging on madness. That my preferred destination was the far north confirmed me, in their eyes, in my insanity. I wasn't bothered. Sanity is an endless continuum; go far enough along the route to craziness and you are likely to meet good sense and mental rectitude plodding back the other way.

Whenever I pulled out my charts and ruminated on what might make a good voyage for *Mingming* for the summer of 2007, my eye was invariably drawn to the north. The cold and barren coasts of the Faroes, Iceland, Spitsbergen and the like exercised a magnetic attraction. The strangely euphonic Nordic names sprinkled sparingly in remote coves and deeply-carved inlets rang in my head like the dying clash of broadswords in some long-lost saga: Tjaldavik, Hvannasund, Tórshavn, Stykkisholmur, Seyðisfjördur, Husavik. They spoke of something angular, four-square, solid, uncompromising. This was a world where pretension would be stripped bare, where a man would be found out for what he was.

In contrast, I was unmoved by the yachtsman's more conventional dream of sailing, for example, to the warm and balmy waters of the Mediterranean. I had no desire to join the flotillas, the sun-worshippers, the sippers of sangria and spumante. The prospect of all that earnest pleasure-seeking left me cold.

No, what I needed was a tough and meaningful challenge. The constraints of my business life meant that I could allow myself six weeks. Evening after evening throughout the early winter I studied the pile of charts I had ordered. Is there any greater delight, when the nights draw in, than to sprawl in front of the fire, a heavy Admiralty chart unfolded on the rug? Now everything is possible. Every sea can be traversed with the run of a fingertip. Headwinds count for nothing. Rocky headlands can be skirted without fear. Storms melt away. The ice-pack too. Great and wondrous voyages can be accomplished in a single minute. It is a time to dream.

Little by little the dreams were tempered into a practicable project. Hour upon hour of studying, thinking, measuring, of laborious consultation of the pilot books, led to a synthesis of the improbably extreme with the dourly possible. My wildest and most unformed notions were rubbed down relentlessly with heavy grit paper until they took the shape of something do-able. Therein, perhaps, lies one of the pleasures of planning a voyage at sea. It is an odd side-show. Somehow that romantic urge to drive oneself on across the furthest horizons must be reconciled to the dull and the sub-lunary – the realities of time and distance and weather and boring worldly commitments and the not inconsiderable imperatives of survival. All is a finely balanced compromise. For months a great internal debate rages. The dreamer expounds his madcap schemes, his arguments rich in poetry and disdain for the bourgeois consideration. He would have us, if he could, sail non-stop to the moon. His restless imagination knows no bounds. The rationalist then steps in, implacable, unimpressed. He has every statistic to hand. He is the one that knows about wave heights and winds and weather patterns. He is an expert on victualling. He can calculate water consumption to the millilitre. He can tell you your average daily run from the year dot. He can shoot down every finely-turned but ultimately hair-brained point with a flurry of figures and boring, incontrovertible logic. To and fro the negotiations go. Bit by bit a deal is hammered out. Stalemate is not an option. For sail we must.

My plan took shape, therefore, and it was this. The primary objective would be to cross the Arctic Circle; this for no other reason than that it would keep me heading purposefully north. It would give me a latitudinal target of a whisker over 66°N. With reasonably fair winds it would just be attainable within my tight time-frame of twenty-one days outward voyaging and twenty-one days homeward. From my home base at Burnham-on-Crouch it meant running up just over fourteen degrees of latitude – a straight distance of a little less than nine hundred miles.

I did not, however, intend simply to sail due north. What a soulless, unimaginative project that would be, to do nothing more than to head northwards, to cross a wholly imaginary line of demarcation, a non-existent construct that of course has not a jot to show or say for itself, before turning tail to retrace my track south. Reaching the Arctic Circle may have been an objective, but not obsessively so. I have no interest in the modern cult, as prevalent in ocean sailing as any other activity, of the furthest, the fastest, the first to do this or that. It's a kind of puerile nonsense, ultimately self-defeating.

Given that I had limited time and could not in any way rely on a run of favourable winds, I finally decided on four possible routes for a good cruise. The first, the default option if the long haul up the east coast of the British Isles should take much longer than anticipated, was to sail round the northern tip of the Shetland Islands, then return south via the outside of Ireland. As with all the options, the planned end point of the voyage was Plymouth. If progress north were a little better, my trajectory would expand out to include the Faroe Islands and, for the hell of it, Rockall. An even faster run north would, I hoped, take me to the east coast of Iceland before I turned south to pass outside Rockall and Ireland on my way to Plymouth.

It was only a set of extremely favourable conditions that could get me to the Arctic Circle itself within the time available. To traverse it I would have to sail just a few miles north of the north-east tip of Iceland. I chose that area for a crossing point as it would give me the opportunity, with the right winds, of entering one of the mighty north-east Iceland fjords. The one that seemed most attractive from a navigational point of view was the Seyðisfjördur, the most northerly, one of the broadest, and only sixty miles or so from the Arctic.

In my mind's eye and with my restless fingertip, therefore, I constructed four possible ellipses, all starting at Burnham-on-Crouch and ending at Plymouth. They fanned out north from the Shetlands to north-east Iceland. Each had its own particular shape and satisfactions. I would be happy with any one of them as a voyage. They gave me a range of choices and options. They left me fancy-free. I could make it up as I went along. I would just set off and see what evolved. Too much pre-ordainment, an excess of cut-and-dryness, robs adventuring of its more delicious edges. I felt I now had a structure that could only in the most unfortunate and unforeseen circumstances fail to deliver a rewarding voyage, but a structure that was still loose and arbitrary enough to keep me finely balanced on the stimulating tightrope of uncertainty.

The winter evenings gripped tighter, darker, colder, but I cared little. I had work to do. I may well have been intending simply to set off and see what happened, but this did not in any way presuppose some sort of lax approach to the project. True freedom of the seas, especially for the sailor of a tiny, engineless yacht, can only be derived from the most rigorous preparation. More than fifty years of sailing had honed my wariness to razor sharpness. Having conceived the general shape of my intended journey, I now had to drill down into the smallest navigational details. Every aspect of the potential routes had to be explored. I had to think through every possible adverse situation to ensure that, in the worst case, I would not be putting myself and *Mingming* at risk.

At the micro-level, my planned voyage was fraught with dangers. I would have to negotiate, single-handed and without auxiliary power, the maze of shoals and sandbanks of the Thames Estuary and the coast of East Anglia. I had to plan a series of possible routes for different conditions. These already challenging waters are now overlaid with a grid of natural gas installations that further restrict and complicate the options for safe passage. There would be no respite once past the Norfolk coast, with the Wash and the shallow, ship-infested Humber Estuary to cross.

Past the Humber I could at last start to acquire some sea room by keeping on due north. The Yorkshire coast runs off to the north-west. It would not take long to have an offing of eighty miles of so. I would need it. In the event of a north-easterly blow there are no safe havens along that coastline. I had to remember too that in the North Sea I would always be in dangerously shallow water. My usual safety mantra – a minimum hundred miles of sea room and two hundred metres of depth – was unattainable. Further north I would have to run the gauntlet of another rash of energy platforms, oil this time. Once more I had to plan appropriate routes that would take me through with adequate margins of safety in all conditions. I would start to close the land again as I neared the Shetlands. To the west would be first the Pentland Firth, then the Fair Isle Channel. To be forced into either of these, two of the nastiest spots around the British Isles, in the wrong conditions, was an unthinkable prospect.

I spent many hours studying the charts and pilots for the Faroe Islands. My main chart was a delight, a gloriously old-fashioned Admiralty compilation, its data dating from Danish government surveys of 1895 to 1903. In these days of breakneck change it was curiously reassuring to have century-old numbers on which to rely. Heights were still in feet and soundings in fathoms. The rendition of the islands' steep slopes and tortuous contours was a masterpiece of lovingly detailed engraving. Pity the sailor who now derives all his information from a garish computer screen, ham-fistedly pixelated and devoid of all personality or sense of history. Just to open this chart, with its thick creamy paper and patient artistry, was enough to lift my spirits, to raise my pulse a fraction, to bring adventure to my very fingertips.

Apart from general familiarisation with the area I was, in essence, trying to determine whether, either in an emergency, or purely for pleasure, I could contemplate entering any of the islands' harbours. In the right conditions Tórshavn, the capital, seemed approachable, but I discounted anywhere else except in the case of direst need. Currents can run up to twelve knots between the most narrowly spaced islands. Fierce tide races abound. The coastline is mainly towering cliffs, some several thousand feet high. Whilst I was set on sailing in close enough for good views of this intriguing archipelago, I determined nevertheless to keep a good offing, should I get that far. As ever, my real refuge would be the wider sea itself.

On my researches ran, now to the north-east coast of Iceland. Viewed in large scale, Iceland seems little more than a huge and regular ink blot. Apart from a meaty and flamboyantly-shaped peninsular stretching out to the north-west, its coastline appears blandly uniform. As the scale decreases, though, the true Nordic character of the island reveals itself. Away from the straight contours of the south coast, scores of deep fjords pierce the mountainous terrain for most of the island's circumference. The south coast may be devoid of fjords, but it too has its own marvels – a series of monumental glaciers that rise almost sheer just a mile or two from the sea. On the north-east side I had chosen the northerly Seyðisfjördur as the most practicable fjord to enter, should I reach that far, but to the south of it were another five or so equally attractive and enticing deep and steep-sided indentations. Tides are modest here, and navigational hazards few. The biggest danger, in an area where storms can whip up quickly, and where there is a high prevalence of easterly winds, was the perennial lee shore. One over-riding message ran through all my studies of Icelandic navigation; the south coast is to be avoided. The shallow water, strong landward-setting currents and difficult visibility of the low-lying coastal fringe were stressed again and again. It would be no place to take little *Mingming*. It was a message I would have cause to remember.

I then had to consider the journey south to Plymouth. In keeping with my usual practice, I made a few rules of thumb to keep myself out of trouble. I would pass to the outside of Rockall, thus conferring on myself a modest circumnavigational honour, Rockall being, at two hundred miles or so to the west of the Outer Hebrides, the most remote and westerly outpost of the British Isles. I hoped against hope that conditions would be such that I could allow myself a close approach so that I could at least glimpse this tiny and totally useless hunk of granite. Why, I know not. I had no illusions that sighting a sixty-foot high rocky pinnacle would somehow prove a seminal moment in my life. Not being much given to boasting, I had no drive to acquire the rare bragging right of having seen the thing.

Whether I saw Rockall or not was of little relevance measured against the far greater and more general challenge of having taken a small yacht to the westward of it. Maybe it was the failing that afflicts us all; I was just plain nosey.

The west coast of Ireland would be given a wide berth. The summer depressions sweep in often enough through Sole and Shannon. I would keep myself well to the westward, off the continental shelf, so that I could ride out any heavy weather in long, pelagic seas and with a healthy margin under my lee. My closest approach to the Irish coast would be to the south-west, off Fastnet, as I angled in to cross the Celtic Sea. This is the point at which, I constantly stressed to myself, I would have to exercise maximum caution. This is the point at which every natural force can, in the worst case, combine to create a most difficult and dangerous sea state. The sea bed shoals rapidly, from a depth of four thousand metres to two hundred or less, within a few miles distance. The Atlantic Current drives the sea north-east. At the same time the land masses of Ireland and the English and Welsh coasts act as a great funnel, compressing the seas together. The tides grow stronger. All that is then required to stir up these ingredients into a right royal cocktail is a gale of wind from the south-west. The last thing I wanted was to be caught out in the mouth of this trap, to be forced to run to the north-east, deeper and deeper into the throat of the St George's Channel, the options for escape falling away as I went.

By now I was developing a sense of what this voyage might entail. In my imagination I had sailed every possible course under the most likely and unlikely conditions. I had tried to uncover every possible pitfall and make a mental provision for it. I knew well enough that there is a chasm, almost unbridgeable, between the imagined and the real. That does not, however, diminish the role of the imagined, or make it less necessary as a preparatory element.

The major determinant of the success or otherwise of my voyage, and the least predictable, was of course the weather. I had studied the northern wind roses and meteorological data in the Admiralty pilot again and again. In summer the Atlantic depressions move north, so I could expect a storm or two. There was a strong possibility of north or north-east winds too. Fog was likely in the vicinity of the Faroes.

In reality these expectations were partly fulfilled. I did indeed have a good deal of wind from the north and north-east. I was fog-bound many times near the Faroes. What I could not know or foresee, as night after winter's night I doggedly made my preparations, was that the summer of 2007 would bring exceptional weather conditions, that some pertubation of the jet stream would radically alter the usual summer weather patterns around the British Isles. As I made my plans I was blithely unaware that one of the worst and stormiest summers for many years was in prospect. A merciful and beatitudinous ignorance sheltered me from the fore-knowledge that the country, and the seas around it, would soon be hit by several of the most vicious and damaging storms for some time. These were real beauties. I would be sailing straight into them.

2

I could sail a thousand exemplary voyages in my head, but to execute even one in the unforgiving reality of the ocean itself required much more than mental preparation. I needed the right boat. Fortunately I had it. *Mingming*.

In a crowded anchorage *Mingming* would never attract a second glance from the casual observer. She would be dismissed as a little weekender, a starter boat for some impoverished family man or hard-up teenager desperate to get afloat, a tired and, with her low sheer and tiny portholes, rather out-dated hand-me-down. Her bilge keels, if seen, would reinforce the first impressions: here's an old boat good for little more than crawling round a shallow estuary on a fine summer's day.

Were this casual observer to take a second or third glance at her, and come a little closer to investigate, he may spot one or two surprising features. He may be puzzled and inclined to revise his initial assessment. Why would such a boat be equipped with such a robust ocean-going self-steering gear? How come the cockpit has been almost totally filled in? She has no washboards or sliding hatch! The only way in or out is via a watertight escape hatch! Why is she carrying what looks like a pair of oversized sweeps? What's that strange rig she's got? The mast seems to be un-stayed. There are control lines and cleats everywhere! What the hell *is* this?

Well, *Mingming* is a junk-rigged Mark II Corribee, just

under twenty-one feet in length, built in 1980. Prior to sailing her in the 2006 Jester Transatlantic Challenge (a voyage described, amongst others, in my book *Voyages of a Simple Sailor*) I had heavily modified her for ocean work. In addition to the exterior alterations that our casual observer may have noticed, I had made fundamental structural changes to the interior of the hull. The forward and after sections of the boat had been filled tight with flotation foam, sealed behind watertight bulkheads. More foam had been added under the cockpit floor. All my stores were carried in watertight containers, either lashed to the cabin sole or stowed in robustly-secured lockers. *Mingming* was unsinkable and, once the hatch and the single portlight were sealed, totally watertight.

In the summer of 2006 I had sailed *Mingming* well over two and a half thousand nautical miles, first from Burnham-on-Crouch to Plymouth, then on from Plymouth almost to the Azores, and finally back home to Burnham-on-Crouch. The main bulk of the sailing was a thirty-eight day non-stop voyage. That little adventure had confirmed my belief that the prettily-designed Corribee, conceived primarily for coastal sailing, could, with the right modifications, be transformed into an excellent and easily-managed ocean-going yacht. There were, however, a number of important improvements that I needed to make before taking *Mingming* to sea once more. Such are boats. There's always something.

Most crucially, I had to design and build a mechanism that would allow me to make infinitely fine adjustments to the self-steering gear without having to go on deck. The basic concept underpinning *Mingming's* rig and overall set-up was that she should be totally manageable from the hatch. The primitive system for controlling the self-steering gear, suggested by the manufacturer, that I had used in 2006, had been an unmitigated failure. As a result I had constantly to climb out on deck, at all times and in all weathers, and work my precarious and dangerous way to the stern of the boat whenever the gear needed adjusting. This had become an unbearable, and in heavy weather, dangerous chore. Something had to be done about it.

Second, I needed a lot more protection from spray and weather around the main hatch. The supposedly watertight hatch had an annoying tendency to leak in heavy rain, introducing into my haven below that least favoured of commodities – water. Keeping a good watch in heavy weather was wet and uncomfortable. The inability to keep the hatch open in even the slightest rain could make life annoyingly claustrophobic and robbed me of full headroom more often than I liked. I therefore determined to design and build a combination of fixed coamings, fitted with observation deadlights, with a folding spray hood on top.

Finally, I decided that *Mingming* deserved a proper bowsprit. For windward work in lighter weather I carry a small headsail. The tack for this has to be well forward. Up until then I had been using the loom of one of my long sculls as a bowsprit. This worked perfectly satisfactorily. However the sculls also double as emergency spars and steering oars. It seemed sensible to free them up from additional bowsprit duties, to give myself maximum flexibility. The bowsprit would have to be attached to the pulpit somehow, so yet another design and build project was added to my list.

My winter preparations for the voyage north were therefore of a dual nature. Contemplation was supported by carpentry. The kitchen worktops, ideal for heavy duty clamping requirements, particularly when it really was too cold to use my garage workshop, were littered with weird works-in-progress and their constituent parts, along with the saws, files, chisels, glues, screws and so on used to construct them. In the lounge and by the bedside the piles of charts and pilot books and almanacs grew steadily higher. To sail properly, and by that I mean to go to sea unequivocally and without compromise, for a month or two each year, is a year-round business. The preparatory ten months are as integral to the project as the weeks afloat. They are almost as satisfying too. The more time and effort that go into creating a successful modification, and indeed a successful cruise, the greater the pleasure of experiencing that success during the weeks at sea.

My new self-steering adjuster was a sturdy cross-shaped plywood structure that clamped to the main shaft of the steering gear with hose clips and was controlled by five colour-coded lines led to jam cleats on the bridge deck. Strong and simple, and more effective than I would have dreamed possible, it was about to transform my life at sea. The hatch coamings, with their inset deadlights on each side and forward, took many patient hours to construct. I laminated them from plywood and anchored them to the coach roof with substantial timbers made from oak salvaged from my old window frames. The framework for the folding hood was made in the kitchen from ordinary copper piping. I hand-sewed the hood itself from some leftover rescue orange cotton duck material. Total cost for the coamings and hood was about fifty pounds. Again, this addition to the boat would create a step change to my levels of comfort and relaxation at sea. The revolutionary bowsprit was laminated from old pieces of Douglas fir found in the garage and secured to the pulpit with stainless steel U-bolts.

All the new parts were painted in *Mingming's* signature grey, with some signal red highlights where appropriate. As winter reluctantly wound down and a hesitant spring occasionally made work on the boat itself possible, these singular creations were gradually fitted into place. They brought a smile to my face. More visible and defiantly idiosyncratic than any additions that had so far been made to

Mingming, they expressed better than anything what this yacht is really about. She is no more than an old geezer's realisation of a boyhood dream. Somehow she suggests, in the way I have rebuilt her, a wild amalgam of all those boats in all those tales and adventures that enthralled me as a child. *Mingming's* appearance has, on the face of it, a bath-tub quirkiness. As her odd appendages and bits and pieces proliferate, as she looks increasingly unlikely, the happier I am. A jaunty little yacht, provocatively unconventional, built to go anywhere, easy to sail, cheap to run; what more could man or boy ever want?

3

Sailors have always been a superstitious bunch. Perhaps the precariousness of life on the ocean develops an unhealthy obsession with signs and portents and a catalogue of little dos and don'ts designed to please and appease the watery deities. These superstitions are necessarily random and not a little irrational. Carrying bananas on board is not advised. To wear green is not simply a fashion *faux pas*, it is to wave a red rag, as it were, in the face of some short-tempered demi-god. If you'd like a little more wind, scratching the backstays will do the trick. Shipping a parson aboard will surely encourage disaster. And so on.

I have several times been told, in all seriousness and with an authoritative delivery, that it is bad luck to set sail on a Friday. Leave at one minute before midnight on Thursday and everything will go swimmingly. Cast off your mooring at one minute past midnight on Saturday and your voyage will be blessed. Anything in between is inviting trouble. My first instinct is immediately to ask whether the great arbiter whose wrath one risks incurring sets his watch to Greenwich Mean Time or British Summer Time. That technicality aside, I am not vain enough to think that any possible cosmic agency could have the slightest interest in my insignificant little timetables, still less be compelled to reorder the forces of nature in order to frustrate them.

I accordingly set my departure date for Friday, the

twenty-second of June. This was designed to give me a run of neap tides through the channels and sandbanks of the east coast, along with, further north, the optimum balance between short nights and favourable weather conditions. There was another important side-advantage. The following day would be my sixtieth birthday. It seemed appropriate to spend it alone at sea. I had been suitably treated in the terrestrial way a few days earlier. I could now turn seawards and with a clear mind get down to the business of creating a successful adventure.

Clutching a small rucksack stuffed with a few last-minute items, I jumped aboard the Rice and Cole launch just before nine in the morning. It was overcast and raining. As we puttered out to my mooring Pete the launchman and I exchanged the usual pleasantries and meteorological imprecations. Pete no doubt assumed I was off up the coast for the weekend. I preferred not to mention that, with luck, *Mingming* and I would have sailed to the Arctic before we next tied up anywhere. Pete put me aboard and with a roar, a swirl of foamy water and a puff of diesel smoke, his launch disappeared off along the trots.

I opened the hatch and squeezed my way down. I sat on my bunk and stayed there for a few seconds, immobile, my head empty of thought. I needed a quiet minute to savour the deliciousness of the moment. Once more I had managed to drag myself out of the rut of sensible workaday existence. Now, at last, I could sail off. I was free. I was alive. Anticipation coursed in my veins. My flesh tingled. Imminent adventure. The unknown. The wild ocean. Fear. Solitude. Ecstasy. Wonder. Discomfort. Despair. Joy. The thrilling cocktail of single-handed ocean voyaging. Once more I was there, on its very threshold.

I dragged myself out of my reverie and started preparing the boat for departure. She had been launched just a few days before, fully provisioned and stowed for sea. This would be my first and only sail of the year. With no conscious fore-thought I had slipped into the Tilmanesque habit of going sailing just once every twelve months. Six weeks of continuous time at sea totalled a thousand hours or so, the equivalent of several years' worth of normal weekend sailing. It was more than enough to satisfy my annual sea-going appetite. *Mingming* would be brought ashore as soon as our voyage was over.

Within a minute or two I had the sail cover off and stowed away, the boom support folded forward on the coach roof, and all the appropriate lines – mainsheet, main halyard, yard-hauling and luff-hauling parrels - uncoiled and ready for action. I went forward to throw off the mooring buoy lines, then aft again to raise a panel or two of the mainsail to give us some steerage way. With a light south-easterly breeze on the beam we moved slowly forward against the flood tide. It would soon turn and bear us quickly out to sea.

Framed only by a dreary sky, a deserted sea wall and the lines of yachts tugging gently at their moorings, I could not have wished for a more appropriate departure. Ordinariness has its own eloquence. These were the last close images of land that I would carry throughout the coming weeks. This was home; nothing special; nothing in particular; a little place by a muddy river; sometimes lively; often as not, as on this Friday morning, doing little more than existing beneath the leaden clouds. The quietness, the softness of the morning piqued my expectancy. This was how I wanted to leave. Forget the loud and grandiloquent farewells, the overblown fanfares. Give me rather the indifference of an empty shore, with no accompaniment save the distant bubbling of a lone curlew.

Once clear of the moorings I engaged the self-steering gear. It was the first time I had used my new mechanism to set and adjust it. Within a minute or two it was clear that it was going to work well. I could make the slightest alteration to our course merely by leaning out of the hatch and adjusting and re-cleating a couple of lines. For the first time I could use the self-steering, and stay comfortably below, within the confines of the river. The many hours spent making the adjuster were obviously well spent. It would take me a while to become fluent at using it, but the constant journeys to the stern were a thing of the past; I could stay warm and safe in the cabin. Moreover, the drizzle that was still occasionally falling no longer forced the closure of the hatch. My little orange spray hood was now earning its keep. Within ten minutes of setting sail I could appreciate how much these modifications were going to improve my life at sea.

The river widened as, with the full mainsail now set, and hugging the northern shore to keep out of the last of the flood, we moved smoothly seawards. As we neared Halliwell Point, the easterly extremity of the land, I noticed that we were not quite alone. A third of a mile to the south of us a little tan-sailed gaff cutter was entering the river. It was so tiny that at first I assumed that it was just a dinghy. It seemed an odd time and place for someone to be sailing an open boat, particularly from seawards. Once I had the binoculars on it I could make out a little cabin on the cutter's green hull. I was delighted. It was almost certainly the sixteen foot *Shoal Waters*, with, no doubt, Charles Stock at the helm. Charles has spent decades exploring every last inch of the east coast in *Shoal Waters*, covering many tens of thousands of miles in the process. He is a kindred spirit and an inspiration. He sails without an engine. He understands the pure and simple pleasures of the small yacht. He is his own man and has patiently forged a lifetime of unique sailing experience. I had met him a few years previously when he had spoken at our yacht club and autographed my copy of his book. I had never before seen *Shoal Waters*. We passed each other quickly, at distance. It was a happy coincidence, this brief encounter, that gave a final lift to my resolve as we cleared the land. I would not see another yacht for several thousand miles.

4

The sky cleared. The breeze freshened from the south-east. I dropped a couple of panels of the mainsail, a manoeuvre of just a few seconds' effort from the hatch, to keep us nicely balanced. The self-steering gear, now so comprehensively under my control from inside *Mingming*, settled into its unending round of correction and counter-correction. The tide turned. With every element in our favour we sped north-east, away from the low and featureless last vestiges of land, away from the repetitive and the humdrum, away from the contorted and the confused. By midday we were out of the Whitaker Channel and running up the outside of the Gunfleet Sand. Land now hovered low on the horizon to the west. Clacton. Frinton. Walton. All on-Sea. The Essex Riviera. Old friends, soon to be abandoned as we raced on, shaping our course ever more northerly. By five the Sunk lightship was abeam. With the wind now dead astern we ran peacefully on, troubled by no more than a gentle roll that told us yes, you really are off, you really are back at sea. The distant cranes and gantries of Felixstowe signalled the imminence of the soft contours of the Suffolk coastline and within the hour we were in new territory, venturing for the first time beyond the River Deben. The wind failed as we lay seven miles to seaward of a sleepy Southwold, but not for long. Within a few minutes a land breeze came up from the south-west, bearing with it the heady sweetness of wheatfield and woodland, faintly underscored with the dryer tones of summer's earth and coastal scrub. I breathed my fill and settled to a round of sleep and watch, sleep and watch as we moved slowly north against the tide, once more in flood.

By dawn we were enveloped in a light mist, the centrepiece of a milky-grey and otherwise featureless Lowry seascape. In the falling breeze and thickening murk I set the lightweight jib to keep us ghosting forward. Great Yarmouth lay somewhere on our port beam, invisible. A strange looking ship, its contours hard to determine in the fog, crossed our port quarter. An immature fulmar flew by. Two dolphins surfaced close by then disappeared, unimpressed by our slow progress.

On the morning's ebb I could still make some northing in what remained of the wind, now from the north-west and wintry. I knew that this forward motion and my control over it could not be guaranteed to last. We risked soon being becalmed, with the next flood tide carrying us southwards towards the Cross Sands, the outermost of the ring of shoals surrounding Great Yarmouth. My patient hours of familiarisation with the dangers and subtleties of the Norfolk coastline now began to pay off. This was just the sort of eventuality I had planned for. I abandoned any thoughts of taking the inshore route along the coast of north-east Norfolk. The Haisborough Gat and The Would form a passage six or seven miles wide between the coastline and the dreaded Haisborough Sand. This little area, innocuous enough on the chart, is the very epicentre of heroic lifeboatmanship, stormy derring-do and unlikely rescue. Old Henry Blogg, long-time coxswain of the Cromer lifeboat, is alone credited with a lifetime tally of eight hundred and seventy-three lives saved. If the level of caution accorded any coastal area were in direct proportion to the maturity and volume of its lifeboat statistics, as perhaps it should be, then this patch of water would probably top the scale. Whilst I still had wind with which to do it, I headed offshore, almost due east. If we were going to have fog and fickle winds then I wanted space, sea room, options. I could still find these beyond the Winterton Ridge, where another broad passage opens up to the north. This was by no means the end of the offshore shoals, with Smith's Knoll, the Lemon Bank and other assorted dangers still to seawards.

My caution paid off. By four that afternoon, the second of our voyage, we were comprehensively becalmed with a foul tide setting us southwards at a good rate. It was frustrating to be going the wrong way, but we were by now well clear of all dangers. The forecast was for strong south-westerlies, so this setback did not unnerve me too much. I found an army of sea-going spiders, evidently of good Burnham stock, stowed away around the boat. An athletic fulmar paddled twice round *Mingming* in the glassy water, squinting at her rig as he went. Several great claps of thunder heralded a heavy downpour that was itself the prelude to a perfectly formed and unbroken rainbow. The sky cleared and the light south-westerly resumed. We were now heading north-west for the Outer Dowsing Channel, the main commercial route through to the Humber, and still thirty miles or so distant. In the crisp evening air the north Norfolk coast trailed off westwards. A smartly painted blue and red ship, the *Weserstern,* overtook us on the starboard beam, heading the same way. We now had some respite from gas rigs and sandbanks. Night fell and I slept on and off. The lights of Norfolk faded below the horizon, giving way to those of a procession of ships in both directions. The traffic was widely spread, unthreatening.

The early morning weather forecast gave the first oblique hint of the trouble that lay ahead. It spoke of north-easterly winds, possibly Force 7, later. Apart from being uncomfortably close to a headwind, such a wind, if it eventuated, would put the shoals we had just negotiated, and the coast of north-east Norfolk, squarely under our lee. Some reconsideration of our optimum heading was called for. I determined to alter course due north. This would take us right through the next group of a dozen or so gas platforms, but was the fastest route to the deeper water that lay beyond. It would deliver a much greater margin of sea room than the more westerly course through the Humber shoals. The ideal tracks and their bearings were already marked on my chart. It was a quick and simple matter to switch from one to the other. The tide had just turned, so we would have six hours of ebb tide to help us. The wind was still fair on the port quarter.

In balmy conditions we ran quickly north, passing within a mile or two of the closest gas rigs. At least one was quite decrepit and abandoned. It looked as if it had been roughly cobbled together from a truckload or two of reclaimed timber. It was disconcerting to think that the nation's gas supply had once relied on such ramshackle structures. The more recent installations and the one I saw that was evidently still under construction were shinier, more futuristic, affairs, of much greater proportions. The platforms had all been accorded grand names plucked from the Arthurian legends, *Lancelot*, *Guinevere*, *Excalibur* and so on. I marvelled at the presumption of the energy marketing men. Amongst the gas rigs we were now well away from any commercial traffic. For the whole day as we sped north to safety we had the sea to ourselves, save for a single fishing boat and two odd craft evidently associated with the rigs. One of these was a small converted fishing boat, anchored in splendid isolation and bearing the word GUARD on a large sign on each side. The other, an orange ship announcing itself as the RESCUE ZONE, stood permanently off the platform under construction.

By late afternoon we were in clear water, the gas rigs no more than distant smudges on the southern horizon. We were by now north of the Humber entrance, about forty-five miles offshore. Mixed flocks of kittiwakes, fulmars, razorbills and guillemots wheeled and whirred in a noisy feeding frenzy. The sun still pierced a slightly hazy sky. The gentle south-westerly persisted. The weatherman nonchalantly dropped his little bombshell. A deepening depression was heading across the country. The forecast for Tyne and Dogger, just a little way to the north, was for north-easterlies Force 6 to 8, perhaps Force 9.

We had been at sea for two and a half days and had made good progress in generally favourable conditions. The worst of the east coast dangers were now behind us. Everything so far had been relatively benign. That was all about to change.

5

I have learned time and again not to place too much trust in weather forecasts, particularly where fast-moving and erratic low pressure systems are concerned. I was not inclined, however, to turn a deaf ear to this latest jolly pronouncement. The prospect of a severe gale whilst still relatively close to land and, worse still, with shoal waters and gas rigs under our lee, galvanised me into another close assessment of the charts and our options. What I needed was the best combination of sea room and depth. I decided that rather than holding my northerly heading I would strike even further seawards, to the north-east this time. If the forecast were correct, the twelve to eighteen hours or so that remained before the storm struck would give us enough time to reach the Skate Hole, by North Sea standards a deepish trench that runs on an east-west axis south of the Dogger Bank. It was by no means an ideal spot to ride out a bad blow, but it was the best I could rustle up in the time available.

There may be readers who ask why I did not simply head for the nearest harbour, with a view to tying up safe and sound and sampling the local hospitality until fair weather returned. The first reason for not so doing was generic. There are two types of sailor: those who on hearing the word *'gale'* immediately think *'shelter'*, and those who think *'sea room'*. I am of the latter, probably much smaller, group. Most well-found yachts, and I regret to say that excludes a good proportion of the modern production kind, properly handled, will survive any conditions the open sea can throw at them. What they cannot survive in storm conditions is contact with land. I had learned this the hard way as a young seaman. With the imminent possibility of an onshore Force 9 wind, the thought of heading landwards was, almost literally, unthinkable. The second reason for keeping the sea, if it were needed, was specific. There was no available safe haven that was not ringed about with shallow waters and sandbanks that reach their full potential for unmannerly behaviour in exactly the conditions forecast. The depressions that wing in across the British Isles can move very quickly and very unpredictably. To head landwards risked us being caught out, possibly terminally, in the no-man's-land between shelter and sea room. This is the belt that the summer day-sailor inhabits. This is the happy hunting ground of Henry Blogg and his sou'westered shipmates. This is not my kind of place. All I ever want is sea room and deep water.

The rogue weather forecast had come through just before six in the afternoon. By eleven that evening I had the sea room and depth I thought I needed and so, not being inclined to venture any further north towards the alleged centre of the depression, I hove to and waited. *Mingming* does not need much specific preparation for bad weather; she is on constant alert. Nevertheless I made myself feel better by re-stowing everything remotely movable, double lashing the anchor and headsails, and readying warps in the cockpit in case of need. The Skate Hole has a maximum depth of about eighty metres, too shallow to deploy my series drogue, one hundred and twenty metres' worth of last-ditch rope and cones.

For six expectant hours we lay bucking gently in the faintest of breezes that was working its way round from south-west to south-east. In my log I reflected on whether this was the calm before the storm, or a meteorological cock-up. It was both. The early morning shipping forecast gave a somewhat revised itinerary for the approaching depression. Its epicentre had apparently abandoned plans to visit the north and was now due to pass through Thames. The obvious sub-text was that nobody could really be sure what it was up to. I was resigned rather than surprised. The weathermen had at least been even-handed with their bounty; alerted to the approaching storm I had sought and found more sea room, but had just wasted six hours that may have been better spent heading on north.

In the steely dawn light, with a south-easterly wind that would soon reach that absolutely unwavering, relentless pitch that always presages the worst of weather, I made one final bid to find the best possible position to meet the imminent gale. The limitations of the Skate Hole were its narrowness and its proximity to the thirty metre depth contour just a few miles to the south. Moreover there were gas fields still relatively close to both the east and the west. I headed quickly north-west, more or less parallel with the Yorkshire coast about fifty miles away. Our course would bring us hard against the western side of the Dogger Bank. The point I was aiming for would give us clearances of fifty to sixty miles from land, forty miles from water shallower than thirty metres, and thirty miles from the nearest gas platforms, with the exception of the lone Kilmer rig twenty miles to the south. Dull statistics perhaps, but vital. At some point these dangers would all be under our lee, as the expected winds backed from east right through to north-west. We would have to meet the weather head on. What I could not know was whether, or how far, or how quickly, we would be driven to leeward if conditions deteriorated beyond a certain point.

With the wind backing and strengthening inexorably we raced on, taking increasingly bigger blows on the beam as the seas built. By ten that morning the moaning wind was up to half a gale out of the north-east. On we plunged at five knots under three panels. By midday we were sixty miles due east of Whitby and just three miles or so off the western extremity of the Dogger Bank, the North-West Riff. In my increasingly tired state I tried to work out how a dangerous patch of shoal water had earned a musical connotation in its naming. It was a while before I realised that 'riff' was probably a north-eastern variant on 'reef'. The momentary endearment that I had felt towards that triangular appendage to the main body of the Dogger Bank quickly evaporated. Not far to the east on the chart a terse little note - *Breaks in strong gales* – was another reminder that I was going to have to manage *Mingming* very, very carefully throughout the coming hours.

It was now three and a half days since we had set sail. All the expected initial navigational difficulties had been overcome. This was the point at which I had anticipated being able to unwind a little and catch up on sleep. Instead I had the prospect of a serious gale. I would have to drag up the last of my reserves to meet what lay ahead. By three that afternoon the storm was upon us in all its incipient fury.

6

On the twenty-fifth of June 2007 the County of Yorkshire suffered its highest daily rainfall since records began in 1882. In a single twenty-four hour period four inches of rain fell on Hull. Perhaps it deserved it. At Fylingdales in North Yorkshire the day's deluge totalled a mind-numbing, magisterial four and a half inches. The monsoon had finally come to the land of muck and brass. Gale force winds from the north-east and north severely exacerbated what was already a scene of total physical and social dislocation. Rivers five feet high flowed gurgling down grim village high streets; the City of Sheffield steeled itself against a carpet of noxious, noisome sludge; within a few hours the meadows of the valleys, low-lying and catchmental, were transfigured from lush herbage to ponds and lakes and green-fringed inland seas. Vehicles drowned, people too. It was not a good day to be in Yorkshire.

I knew nothing of this as the storm unleashed its first torrents of drumming rain on *Mingming's* decks and coach roof. I had my own business to attend to. In any case, once at sea, I am not inclined to tune in to the terrafirmaceous blather.

In what was now a full gale whipping spume and rain across the chastened wave-tops we soldiered on, still under three panels. It was a revelation to find that little *Mingming* could still carry her sail in these conditions; that she could plug gamely on, at the very least holding her position against the wind and waves battering at her. With the self-steering vane set at forty-five degrees to the apparent wind, and the mainsail eased until it was just feathering into the gale, she fore-reached comfortably along at a couple of knots, making good, by the time leeway and wave action and surface drift had all played their parts, a course of about ninety degrees to the blast. That was all I needed. As long as we were not being forced to leeward we could ride it out for as long as it took.

Slowly, then, and in a well-controlled configuration, we edged westwards towards land. By six that evening the wind had swung north and ratcheted itself up to a severe gale. I was near exhaustion, debilitated by a dearth of sleep and an excess of tension. Rain and spray scoured *Mingming* mercilessly. From time to time she would take a curling wave-crest amidships, forcing her sideways with a monstrous serpentine hiss. The temptation was to lay my head down and drift off, away from this elemental assault, away and into a cosy, down-filled amnesia. How sweet it would be, just to sleep and forget.

It was not yet the time. We had now sailed landwards as far as I deemed prudent. Whitby was now about forty-five miles ahead. With the wind backing it was the moment to go about and head back eastwards, towards the Dogger Bank.

Go about. It sounds so simple. *Ready about, lee-oh!* Ha! In the first place I would of course have to gybe her round; there was not the remotest possibility that *Mingming* could be brought through the wind in that maelstrom. The balanced lugsail of the junk rig produces a soft gybe, but I baulked at the prospect of gybing three panels in a Force 9. I would first have to lower a panel of the mainsail. In the increased wind the two remaining panels would probably then serve adequately for the next, offshore, board. I sat for a few moments and mentally rehearsed the sequence of what I would have to do. Swaddled in my yellow oilskins I opened the main hatch and pushed the folding spray hood forward. Standing on the companionway step I was about half out of the hatch. For the first time I could properly see and feel the ghastly seascape, the lowering sky, the sting of the rain as it drove horizontally in blinding sheets. An odd image swept obliquely through my head and was gone: trawlermen of old hauling nets in a North Sea storm.

I released the main halyard from its jam cleat. The mainsail was hard against the topping lifts but nevertheless worked its way down bit by bit until I was able to lean out and grab the bottom batten, pulling it down to the sail bundle. I quickly lashed the pendants attached to each side of the batten pocket around the whole sail bundle and boom. This is not normally necessary but in extreme conditions it guarantees that the sail bundle stays where it is. I hardened up the main halyard and yard parrel and cleated them.

With the sail reefed I could now turn to the trickier problem of gybing *Mingming* round. Using my new adjuster lines I reset the wind vane to forty-five degrees on the other tack, then, leaning out of the hatch, disengaged the self-steering chain from the tiller. I took over the steering myself, using the hand-steering lines permanently attached to the tiller and led through blocks to the hatch. *Mingming* was now under my direct control for the first time since leaving Burnham.

For half a minute or so I sailed her along, just getting a feel for the conditions and *Mingming's* reactions to them. I was facing aft, the wind and spray whipping over my left shoulder. I steeled myself to look to windward. I had to pick the right moment to bring the helm up and let *Mingming* run off then round. I did not want the moment when she gybed and rolled to starboard to coincide with the arrival of a steep wave crest. I turned my head to face the storm. I have seen plenty of grim scenes at sea and this was as grim as any, icily monochromatic, the day's palette not venturing beyond a few tints of pewter, as sky and rain merged seamlessly into spray and spume and sea, hypnotically awful, wild, searing, magnificent.

A flatter patch arrived and I brought the tiller to windward. *Mingming* bore quickly off and for a few seconds we had the relative calm of running downwind. It was tempting to run on, the storm at our back, but round we came. I hauled quickly on the mainsheet and after the usual hesitant moment the boom and sail crashed across to the other tack. I let out the mainsheet until we were once more nicely balanced and re-attached the self-steering chain to the tiller. Relieved and elated at having managed the manoeuvre entirely from the safety of the hatch, I reset the spray hood and returned to my haven below, sealing the hatch behind me.

I rubbed my streaming face with a towel and cleaned my glasses. The reaction to that final effort of body and will now set in. *Mingming* was now set fair on her offshore tack. She would work her way slowly back towards the Dogger Bank, sashaying defiantly through the tumult. There was nothing more I could do. It would be ten hours at least before another manoeuvre was needed. Relieved of any short term task, knowing that I could now relax, I just unravelled. The determination and raw necessity that had been holding me together for the previous day or so evaporated, almost in an instant. Within a minute or two I felt terrible, worse than I have ever felt at sea. This was not seasickness, though there was nausea mixed in there somewhere. The component parts of my body, my heart, my head, my limbs, somehow became separate organisms. I felt as if I were falling apart, literally. My chest seemed on the verge of exploding. My thoughts whirled uncontrollably. I could scarcely remember where I was, or why. I lay my head down, wondering if I would ever wake from the sleep about to overtake me. I was still wearing sea boots and all my oilskins. I didn't care. I scarcely knew. My little yacht, a ridiculous affront to the forces assaulting her, an absurd contrivance pushing to the very limits of possibility, sailed on and on and on, whilst I, I slept the sleep of the dead.

7

My ship's log has no entry for the whole of that night. The record is blank for a twelve hour span. My memory too. I can remember nothing except a deep and uneasy blackness as I fought to re-gather my wits and strength.

By seven thirty the next morning, with the gale now backed to north-west and throwing up a confused sea that had us bucking and rolling without let-up, I was evidently revived. My entries in the log resume with their normal tone and rhythm. During the night we had moved twenty miles east and were now four miles off the Dogger Bank. Our holding pattern had worked perfectly. *Mingming* had excelled herself. By ten we were once more skirting the North West Riff and I repeated the manoeuvre of the previous evening, more confidently this time, to bring us back on to our shore-wards tack. An easing of the rain and a perceptible lifting of the cloud base suggested that maybe the worst was over. I dozed on and off all day, rebuilding my strength, reconstructing my resolve. We had only been at sea for four days. Our voyage had scarcely begun. I was going to have to get my shattered self back on track pretty quickly to have any chance of success.

The storm had set up a strong surface drift that was now setting us to the south, but with the wind now just a little less ferocious I was unconcerned. The sea room that we had sought had served its purpose. The barometer started to rise. The odd patch of blue raced by aloft. The forecast was for a moderate westerly, an ideal wind to help us north. By seven that evening we were in sight of the Kilmer platform, the most northerly of this region, and within an hour or two the gale was gone.

Is there anything sweeter for the seaman than the aftermath of a storm, especially if, as on this occasion, he is graced with perfect conditions? *Mingming* and I had never before faced anything remotely as severe. We had been lucky to have had enough time to find a good position to ride it out. I had chanced on a combination of self-steering and sail settings that had enabled us to sail aggressively into the gale and hold our position. *Mingming* had taken many a thundering blow, and been put on her beam ends at least once, but had shrugged it all off. It was fortunate that just at the point where I had reached the limit of my reserves I was able to sleep long and deeply.

I felt pleased with the way we had handled the conditions, but not complacently so. I had learned a whole new chapter in the textbook of junk rig heavy weather sailing, a chapter I scarcely knew existed. It had been a revelation that would increase immeasurably my levels of confidence for meeting future storm conditions in *Mingming.* But I was acutely aware too that we had had our share of good fortune. Despite all the rational analysis, the lessons learned, the pleasure at having seemingly got it right, my overwhelming emotion as the storm abated, as it always must be for the realistic sailor, was an expansive, heart-warming relief. How could it be otherwise? In the worst of weather any yacht is only ever a chance rogue wave away from a rolling and possible dismasting, or from being picked up and thrown back on to the rudder, destroying the boat's steering, or from any number of similar mishaps. That I was as prepared as I could be for any misfortune did not in any way lessen my relief at having avoided having to cope with one.

And so as the wind came round into the west, moderating so comprehensively that I soon had the full mainsail set, and *Mingming* and I, now battle-hardened, storm-tempered, thoroughly sea-toughened, resumed our track north, I glowed once more with the unbounded atavistic happiness of the survivor, brazenly revelling in the oldest and crudest instinct of them all. We were still here and, it seemed, in one piece. What could be better?

Come-uppance, though, was ready to pounce. Later that evening an untypical flogging of the usually peaceful junk sail led to the discovery that the whole leech of the next-to-top panel had split. I lowered and lashed down the sail and armed with needle, sailmaker's palm and a good length of waxed thread, set to re-sewing the three-foot tear. There was still a massive swell running from the north, and with no sail set we rolled horribly. It was a severe physical effort to lean far out of the hatch and hold and sew the after end of the sail. The westerly wind was unaccountably wintry but I was soon sweating hard as we lurched back and forth and I battled to force each stitch through the double thickness of the leech tabling. After a ghastly hour or so I tied off the last stitch and retched long and uninhibitedly over the side, or more likely the side deck, which was as far as I could reach from the hatch. It was an ignominious comedown for the great survivor of storms and a timely reminder that there is no more effective and impartial leveller than the wide ocean.

It was another day before the nausea and accompanying lethargy that had got a hold on me cleared, by which time we were sixty miles east of Newcastle, occasionally sailing well, occasionally becalmed in the left-over slop of the storm. For the second consecutive night we ran on due north in a cool westerly that by now had freshened a little. I was once again my usual self, thoroughly revived and optimistic. Nothing could stop us now.

Within a few hours, on a chilly and unwelcoming Thursday morning, I was once more repairing the rig. Heavy weather will always have the final say. In the first light of dawn I chanced to look aloft and my heart lurched. Oh no! Weakened by the strains of sailing in a severe gale and, no doubt, by the accumulated bangings and endless slattings of the previous year's ocean calms, the top batten had fractured, creating an ineffective and unsightly deep V shape in the top sail panel. Once more I was forced to lower the sail, this time to sew a line of lanyards along the batten pocket. These were used to lash my wooden boathook alongside the fracture, splinting the broken batten. Like most hastily improvised repairs at sea it was rough-and-ready, but it did the job and that's all that mattered.

After the first misgivings of having to deal with a broken batten it was strangely heartening to look aloft and see my boathook up there, doing unanticipated service twenty-five feet above the deck, contributing gamely to the effort to keep us moving on. Heartening, that is, until later that same day when I checked upwards that all was well and found that the next batten down had also snapped midway along its length. I was dismayed. Were the battens going to disintegrate one by one? Had they suddenly and simultaneously reached the end of their useful life? I could cope with one fracture, but two, or three? As ever I had a good supply of materials for concocting repairs, but every repair reduced the efficiency of the sail. Every repair weakened our chances of a successful voyage.

Rather than splinting this next casualty, I decided to use the other junk rig expedient of simply lashing it to the batten below. This would take one panel of the sail out of service, but given my general expectation of heavy weather during this cruise, that did not concern me too much. I reasoned that two battens lashed together would be stronger than one, reducing the chance of further breakage. How wrong I would be.

Despite these setbacks and the refusal of this voyage to settle in to a steady sea-going rhythm, we had the first intimations that some progress was being made; we were now a hundred miles due east of Edinburgh. Scotland! It wasn't quite the Arctic, but it had a slightly more wild and windblown ring to it than Frinton-on-Sea.

8

There are those who would say that it was my own wretched fault for having set sail on a Friday. I was inviting trouble and trouble I got. As we approached the end of our first week at sea, a week in which we had managed to rack up a mere five degrees of northerly latitude, three hundred painstaking miles in all, a week that had left us battered and limping, a week that had pushed us close to the edge of our capabilities, the crackling voice at the other end of my long wave receiver announced that more gale force winds were on the way. With our newly distressed and as yet untried rig I was less than enthusiastic about immediately meeting more heavy weather, but when you go to sea you get what you get and that's that. I was wilfully seeking out the cold and the bleak, so could scarcely complain if it arrived a little earlier and more energetically than anticipated.

Compared with our recent Dogger Bank interlude the blow, when it swept icily in from the north-west, well-laced with self-important rain squalls that had the halyards all a-shiver and beating post-modern tattoos on *Mingming's* long-suffering mast, was a second-rate, almost benign affair. Not wanting to over-stress *Mingming's* convalescent rig without good cause I simply lay-to for twelve hours with no sail set, fore-reaching gently to the north-east.

We were soon sailing again, though, with Aberdeen slipping alongside sixty miles to the west and the first of the oil platforms ahead. Late on that Saturday afternoon, our second at sea, with a reticent south-westerly zephyr to edge us north and, for once, a hint of sunshine and warmth to lift my spirits and, more practically, to help dry and air *Mingming's* interior, now dank from confinement and condensation, we skirted the west side of three closely-spaced oil fields: Triton, Gannet, and Teal & Guillemot. Monuments to the power of the black gold, they dwarfed their gaseous cousins from further south. A large ferry, possibly plying from Norway to Aberdeen, crossed our bow a few miles ahead, silhouetted romantically against the low evening sun. A pod of ten or so dolphins paid us a fleeting visit. To the east the exuberant flare of the Gannet oil rig flamed bright yellow, garishly luminescent against the deepening violet of the dusk sky.

I sat happily in the hatchway and watched the world. Nothing could mar the contentment of the moment. It had been a tough first week, but I would go through it all again just to be here, still pressing gently on, still thrilling to the slap and gurgle of the bow wave, still testing the limits of the unknown and the unexpected. The myriad dazzling lights of the oil rigs shone ever more stridently as the northern twilight darkened in the east to a deepest purple. To the north-west the sun, reluctant to quit the scene entirely, hung on and on behind a low and fiery haze that only slowly transmuted through a thousand gradations to the dullest of oranges and reds. A kind of night eventually came, but with the sun now ranging round not that many degrees below the northern horizon it was an unconvincing, half-hearted affair. From here on north there would be no more solid, coal-black darkness, not even in the smallest hours.

By early morning we were once more swept up in the filthiest of weather. A nasty, rain-laden breeze, trying its best to become a half-gale, had got up from the south-east. Just half a panel of sail was all that was needed to keep us running quickly on, heading slightly west of north. A set of ship's lights dead ahead refused to budge. It happens sometimes, usually with fishing boats. Whatever course shift you apply to give yourself some clearance, the damn thing always ends up dead ahead. Fishing boats mooch back and forth, so this is understandable. The ship I had in my sights for several hours was clearly not a fishing boat, but it was nonetheless a moocher. Sometimes it appeared to be heading off. Then there it was again, as dead ahead as it's possible to be. It simply would not go away. It kept me awake all night and as we closed it I took over the steering myself, using the tiller lines. We passed close by at first light. It was a small black ship of several hundred tons displacement, flying a German ensign, and with the word 'Küstenwache' painted prominently on its sides. It was a German Coast Guard vessel, standing watch over the distant beaches of the Federal Republic from a stationary position sixty miles to the east of the Moray Firth.

On we ran, now just under the sail bundle as the wind successfully wound itself up to Force 7. The rain was now furious, keeping up a low-pitched and incessant drum roll on the coach roof. Once more I was confined to quarters; even my new spray hood could not protect the hatchway from this assault from astern. The forecast for Fair Isle, now not far ahead, was for gale force winds. Another low was about to wing in across the Hebrides and all points east. It was a familiar litany. We risked an awkward lee shore as we ran up the east side of the Orkneys and Shetlands, closing the land as we went. Once more I dawdled a little to let the worst of the weather pass ahead, or at least to give myself the impression that I was letting it pass ahead. It was unlikely that a knot or two of difference in my speed would have any material effect, but with a couple of days of critical navigation ahead as we skirted several danger spots I was determined to weight even the smallest factor in our favour.

By mid afternoon, in a south-easterly that had eased a little, we had passed to the west of the Goldeneye oil rig, the last in our path. The oil and gas platforms that so crowded my charts, creating in theory a nightmarish obstacle course, had in reality proved surprisingly unthreatening. I was nevertheless glad to see the last of them; they tainted the seascape, robbing it of its nobility, its wildness; they spoke too brazenly of man's helter-skelter plundering of the earth's riches, of myopic greed on the grandest industrial scale.

We were now in clear water but the weather continued damp and murky. Heavy rain had given way to what I suppose was a Scotch mist that shrouded the horizons and restricted our view of the world to a corridor perhaps half a mile wide. We passed close by a lumbering trawler or two, gear deployed and straining. Otherwise the seas were now empty of traffic. There were puffins, though, rouged up like Montmartre streetwalkers and as flight-ready as a squadron of festive plum puddings. They seemed to be heading up an evolutionary cul-de-sac, unlike the great skuas we were also starting to meet. If any seabird were to rank as the tough guy on the block it is the great skua. Unattractively plumaged, ugly of build, nasty of nature, it is hard to find a redeeming feature for this mugger of the high seas. It is, though, supremely fit for purpose. It shows no fear, not the slightest hesitation in attacking and harrying any bird it happens across, even the mighty gannet. Endowed with the unwavering self-belief of the natural-born bully, it is unlikely ever to go hungry.

The Pentland Firth was now behind us and somewhere to the west lay the Orkneys. Whether tracing the meridians east or west, every mile of latitude brought with it another evocative name to roll around in my head; to the west Scapa

Flow, Stronsay Firth, the Brough of Birsay, the North Sound; to the east Flekkefjord, Egersund, Stavanger, the Boknafjorden. There was no question about it: we were now leaving one kind of world behind and finding our way into something of a wholly different nature. The transition was not abrupt; it took a number of days, starting perhaps as we approached the first oil rigs off Aberdeen. As each day passed and we made our northing I felt lighter, more buoyant. The land was falling away. Now there were just islands. Soon there would be nothing; nothing, that is, save the boundless sea and a clear passage to the far north.

9

The Shetland Islands lie somewhat to the north-east of the mainland, as if drawn back towards the Nordic landmass with which they share so much history. Keeping on due north, then, would bring us in to the Shetland coast without any need to alter course. A fresh south-easterly urged us on at a good pace and by first light on the third of July, after just under eleven days at sea, we were lying sixteen miles to the east of Sumburgh Head, the Shetlands' southernmost headland. It was by far the closest we had been to land since leaving the Thames Estuary, but with the heavyish mist continuing, there was nothing to be seen. The only intimation of land was the increased bird activity. It was frustrating to have come so far and be denied any sight of the islands. What a landfall that would have been, with the steep and wind-sculpted contours of Fair Isle perhaps still looming on the south-western horizon.

Around breakfast time, in a faltering breeze that had persuaded me to exit the hatch for the first time in well over a week in order to un-gasket and set the light weather headsail, a faint shoulder of coastal cliff, that I took to be the easternmost extremity of the isle of Bressay, insinuated itself momentarily through the mist, proving, at least, that land was indeed there. But it was soon gone and the thickening fog and occasional drizzle even hid the Out Skerries, the rocky outcrops that protruded almost into our path. We had the sea to ourselves, these waters being an 'Area to be Avoided by Shipping of Over 5000 Gross Tonnage'. Aloft it was a different matter, with low-flying helicopters plying their trade between Lerwick and the oilfields to the north-east. Despite that, and the single intrusion of a noisy fishing boat that crossed our stern at distance heading west, I felt charmed, bewitched. It was magical, to be here, in this place, with *Mingming*. Little yachts had no doubt gone before, others would come after, but this was our day. We had sailed the whole length of the British Isles; we were actually here, just a few miles off the Shetlands. Within a few hours we would take our departure north, with ten days or so of outward sailing still in hand.

To add to my elation the haze finally lifted a little and an indistinct sun pierced through from time to time. At four in the afternoon I handed the light weather jib as the breeze freshened and we altered course to the north-west. This would bring us in close to the Holm of Skaw, the north-eastern tip of Unst. With a fair wind from astern I was ready and determined to come in close. I was not going to bid farewell without a sight of this mythical headland.

Then, at last, as if it were a grudging reward for our persistence, the mist cleared a little and there to the west was the isle of Fetlar, about seven miles distant. In the early evening light the island was dark and murky and featureless but it was solid land that we were now closing fast. Before long the most northerly of them all, the isle of Unst, a long charcoal razorback capped with a halo of motionless cloud, was abeam. The heavy moisture-laden air softened every edge and contour. The island just hung there, ethereal, silent. We were moving forward easily through the smallest of wavelets, the breeze from dead astern. We were not alone. Sea and sky were alive with the cut and dash of gannets and fulmars and puffins and guillemots and terns and skuas.

Closer we came, enough for the monolithic sombreness of the land to separate out into the merest hints of greens and browns and purples. Still we closed the shore, until I could just make out the chalky line of waves breaking softly against the cliffs.

We were now only two miles off, but the end of land, the end of the kingdom itself, was rushing up on our port side. The open sea was already beckoning. With a fortuitous tide still under us we raced on and there, opening up to port, were the buildings of the Holm of Skaw lighthouse and the headlands and indentations of the northern coast of Unst. I could not have wished for a finer, more atmospheric evening on which to pass this remotest edge of Scotland. The several northern headlands of the island, huge natural battlements, rose steeply from water's edge higher and higher until lost in a mantle of wispy cloud. How many millenia had they stood here, squared up to the sub-arctic seas, unseeing, indifferent? Further to the west I could now make out Muckle Flugga lighthouse. We were clearing the land and slanting across this final stretch of coastline. The deep-cut sound to the east of Muckle Flugga disappeared darkly into the mountains, fjord-like. There was in any event a Nordic edge to the silent broodiness that tinged the scene. It would not have taken much imagination to have called up longships and horn-helmed warriors. The lingering clangour of battle-axe on bronzed shield shimmered in the air, just the slightest inclination of the ear beyond audibility.

As twilight settled in we pulled away into open sea. It had taken us eleven and a half days to range the whole length of the British Isles. The difficult first leg of our voyage was over. The first option for our cruise, the rounding of the Shetlands only, could be discarded. The Faroes were now just a couple of hundred miles away to the north-west. If this south-easterly wind held we could be there within three days. To reach north-east Iceland was possible within the ten days left. Most importantly, the Arctic Circle was still, just, within our reach.

A great joy seized me as we sailed out into the Norwegian Sea. The wide ocean, at last! How I had craved it! We were now free of the North Sea corridor and the constraints and technicalities of its navigation. Behind lay an exercise in seamanship; ahead, adventure. Within a few miles the tone of our voyage had been transformed. To sail west would now bring us to the coast of Greenland; due north lay nothing but the Arctic ice-pack. This changing geography invigorated my senses. What a privilege it was to be here, a lone sailor in these Viking seas. The wink and loom of the two lighthouses were quickly lost astern as we foamed forward with a quartering wind and a placid, welcoming sea. For half the night I sat in the hatchway, chilled by the breeze on my neck, too elated to sleep.

It was scarcely credible: we wafted on throughout the next morning under a warming sun that drew blinding sparkles from a million tippy-toe cat's-paws, while the weatherman intoned a mantra of gloom for the world we had abandoned: gales for Humber, gales for Thames, gales for Dover, gales for Wight, gales for Portland, gales for Plymouth, gales for everywhere and everyone, it seemed, save *Mingming* and me. To be thus excluded from a general rout was not our usual fate. For the moment our lives were charmed. I had no expectation that it would last.

For a while the breeze deserted us completely, leaving us to a glassy calm that allowed me the leisure to study our guard-of-honour at close quarters. Deprived of an uplifting wind, and reduced therefore to common-or-garden flapping, the fulmars that were now our constant companions had taken instead to the water. They lay just off the stern, twenty or thirty, establishing their pecking order, as it were, with noisy displays of gaping and croaking. The bolder ones, perhaps showing off a little, paddled close alongside and we stared at each other, they and I, in mutual unfathomability. Occasionally one deserted its post, flying off low over the water after a splashy take-off. But the traffic was generally inwards; curiosity soon swelled our after-guard; even a gannet or two took up position, lying a little further off, less trusting, less inquisitive.

For two days we edged our way across the Faroes-Shetland Channel in the most hesitant of weather. Long periods of calm were broken by a succession of little breezes from here and there. Each one brought a contribution to the growing accumulation of fog that now beset us. From time to time the thickening mist turned to drizzle, but never for long. A little black coaster, the *Laxfoss,* passed astern early one morning, heading south-east. I shed my sea boots, worn for much too long, unnecessarily, and replaced them with soft thinsulate bootees, my usual sea-going footwear. Beneath us we had, for the first time on this voyage, a proper depth of water as the continental shelf dropped away to fifteen hundred metres or so.

Despite the insubstantial winds we were making fifty miles a day. The crosses on my chart advanced towards the Faroes with a modest but satisfying regularity. I was now engrossed once more in the pilot books that had occupied me for so many winter's evenings. I knew the salient facts by heart, but still came back to check and recheck every last detail on the approaching archipelago. The Faroe Islands. Føroyar. Literally translated, and a shade disappointingly, the Sheep Islands. Enigmatic, marginal, difficult to grasp, impossible to define. The islanders kill whales and send unlikely football teams to international tournaments. They fish. They have, presumably, a lot of sheep. They have, too, landscapes and seascapes of an unsurpassed scale and beauty, towering headlands, vertiginous bird cliffs. The islands, in the main rising sheer out of the water for several thousand feet, are sliced to a tight-fitting julienne, creating deep cuts, long and narrowly-spaced canyons between the islands that spawn unimaginable tidal rushes. Forbidding, monumental, as bleak and enticing as anywhere on this earth, they now lay just a day or so's sail beyond the north-west horizon.

10

Leaving the Shetlands we had basked for a day in an all-encompassing blue worthy of the Cap d'Antibes; now, with the weather closing in and an increasing northerly influence in the gyrating zephyrs, there was no doubt about it – it was starting to get cold. Confirmation of this, if any were needed, came from my personal and infallible bellwether; my knees were starting to ache. I was still in the early stages of adaptation to my startling new status as a sexagenarian, still trying to decide whether it is knowledge of one's age that subtly sows the seeds of incipient decrepitude, thereby reaping its own harvest, as it were, or whether the body just gets on with it anyway, fed up with all that tiresome maintenance and renewal. What was not in doubt was that my poor old knees, wrecked from a lifetime of shuffling around on decks and floors and cold concrete, had developed an aversion to the slightest hint of chill. Nor were they the least bit reticent in throwing a fit of pique should a drop in temperature take them out of their wimpish comfort zone. In perfect collusional harmony, port and starboard, they set up a constant complaining ache just below the knee-cap. I often resorted to comforting them with a five-minute massage, but they were stubbornly inconsolable. I would just have to put up with it.

I had the rest of myself to keep warm, too, and my swaddling ballooned out in direct proportion to our increase in latitude. I was not yet quite Michelin Man, but started to notice a tightness-of-fit when pushing my torso through the hatchway. Below the waist I was now sporting four layers of assorted protection: first underpants, then thermal long-johns, then tracksuit bottoms and over all that the sealing *pièce de résistance* – my padded ski trousers. My top half, often thrust out into the sub-arctic wintriness, boasted up to five or six layers, depending on the severity of the weather: first long-sleeved thermal vest, then a polo shirt, then a woollen guernsey, then a woollen polo-necked sweater, then a fleece, and then, if that were not enough to maintain a tolerable body temperature, my heavy snow-boarding jacket. My feet were kept warm with a pair of ordinary socks overlaid with thick woollen ski socks and my thermal bootees. Atop I was now permanently decked out in a Russian-style imitation fur hat. I had even moderated my disdain for wearing gloves at sea and occasionally pulled on a pair of ski gloves to rescue my fingers from frozen stiffness. I was well trussed up, then, but by no means always warm; the sedentary nature of life aboard *Mingming* and the speed and ease with which any normal sailing manoeuvre could be carried out gave little call for warming physical exertion. At night in particular, when the drop in air temperature meant that there was no counterbalance to the chill creeping through *Mingming's* hull from the increasingly icy sea water, I could only keep reasonably warm by forcing my bloated form, snow-boarding jacket and all, into the confines of a cruelly misused high-altitude sleeping bag.

It is not a straightforward matter to adapt to such a baroquely multi-layered entourage of clothing. Skills and techniques have to be learned and honed. Lack of well-founded scientific management of the various strata of bodily protection can lead quickly to unforeseen consequences and failure of the system to achieve its ends. The meticulously-assembled swaddling can never remain in place for more than an hour or two; the ineluctable and regular demands of a fully-functioning organism see to that. The sad fact is that after a careful ten minutes or so of rigorous padding-up, the traitorous body may well immediately demand, with a fist-thumping urgency, the immediate unpacking of the whole works.

The dismantling and reassembling of this complex corporeal protection is therefore a never-ending chore. The temptation is to skimp, to rush, to do it any old how. Bitter experience soon teaches the inadvisability of a slap-dash approach. This is a serious business. The crux of good technique in this admittedly arcane area of clothing adjustment lies at the level of the 'tuck-in'. I have devoted large chunks of my life to its detailed study. There are two fundamental truths that must be understood by the tyro in these matters. The first is that poorly arranged clothing will always, always be found out. The slightest unevenness of layering, or worse still, an exposed patch of skin, however miniscule, will come to haunt and harry the careless dresser, usually at the worst moment: on that dreamy threshold before deep sleep comes, for example, or just two minutes after putting the whole lot back on. That little cool patch, usually in the small of the back, chilling kidney and spine, rapidly transforms from a minor irritation to a full-blown and intolerable physical crisis. Second, it must be understood that it is impossible, where so many layers of clothing are concerned, satisfactorily to rearrange a poorly executed tuck-in whilst lying down, sitting, or even standing up. There is simply no alternative but to restart the whole process from scratch. One soon learns that it is extremely unpleasant to have to stand in the open hatchway at, say, three in the morning on a freezing sub-arctic night, for no reason other than an earlier lack of attention to fine detail, and shrive one's shortcomings by first pulling down over-trousers then trousers then long-johns then underpants, and then pulling up jacket then fleece then sweaters then vest, thereby exposing oneself brazenly from knee to navel to the icy caresses of the night air and risking innovative forms of frostbite. This is why I take obsessive care over the tuck-in and have in fact developed, through years of patient experimentation, what I call the *Mingming* patent tuck-in.

The *Mingming* patent tuck-in has several variants, depending on the amount and nature of clothing being worn at the time. Here is an example of how to deal with the main under-layers. Having suitably prepared yourself as described above, that is to say separated top and bottom layers by a clear margin that negates any chance of a mix-up, and ensures the possibility of a good overlap for each stage, the drill is:

1. Up with underpants.
2. Down with thermal vest.
3. Up with thermal long-johns.
4. Down with shirt *and* sweater.
5. Up as high as possible, to the armpits if possible, with tracksuit bottoms.

The subtlety and success of the *Mingming* patent tuck-in lies at the double-tuck at Stage 4, followed by the clinching master over-tuck at Stage 5. This provides for maximum grip, total ergonomic inter-layer compatibility, and fully optimised thermodynamics. I believe that this may well be the first time that the principles of three scientific disciplines have been combined and applied simultaneously to the delicate question of how to adjust one's clothing. I have created a very fine cut-away illustration showing the application of the *Mingming* patent tuck-in in uncompromising detail, but will not reproduce it here, in deference to reader sensibilities.

Finally, a word of warning. This is purely a sea-going rig. Do not be seen sporting a *Mingming* patent tuck-in on land; you may experience a rapid and mystifying decline in your social acceptability. In fact I would strongly advise you never, ever to wear tracksuit bottoms, let alone tuck your sweater deeply into them, other than at sea,. No man, sailor or otherwise, thus attired ashore can confidently be judged to be of sound mind.

11

At four on a Friday morning, a few hours less than two weeks since setting sail, we crossed the outer edge of the Nolsø Bank, bringing us once more back on to soundings. Almost on cue, two Faroese fishing boats chugged out of the encircling mists, passing close by, their deck lights eerily diffused in the moisture-heavy dawn air. These were chunky, serious-looking craft, high-prowed, wide-bridged, ocean-ready. *Mingming,* a stark Lilliputian contrast at every level, except perhaps for her own particular and fierce style of ocean-readiness, was scarcely moving, just ghosting forward in a provisional zephyr from the south-east. The two trawlers, evidently working in tandem, mooched within sight for a while and we lay there, the three of us, the oddest of trios, a grossly unbalanced two-against-one, strangely bonded by our occupation of that same little stretch of grey and placid water in the middle of nowhere. My VHF radio remained well-stashed in its waterproof container, so I was not privy to the streams of rough Danish that no doubt hurtled from one skipper to the other. I doubt whether their comments were kind; I have no delusions about the average fisherman's opinion of the normal yacht, let alone an outrageously-rigged foreign minnow interloping out of the gloom into such a remote and personal fishing fiefdom. Their invective and incomprehension no doubt burst steaming and writhing from the depths like the very Kraken itself.

Our paths drifted apart, and in a freshening breeze that was once more backing towards the north, *Mingming* closed the islands. The wind continued to strengthen, and maliciously hauled on round almost to the north-west. We were now forced due west, straight along latitude sixty-two degrees north, with land somewhere dead ahead. My plan of skirting the north-east tip of the islands looked increasingly forlorn, with a brisk headwind kicking up a sea, and our options to sail either further and further in towards the approaching crescent-moon of islands, or further offshore and away from the land I had not yet seen, away towards the north-north-east and the depths of the Norwegian Basin. I decided to stand on in for the time being. With an offshore wind I felt reasonably secure. My priority was a view of the islands; to sail through their protective mists and carry on northwards without even a sight of those great buttresses was too wretched to contemplate. After my usual lunch of black bread and cheese I took a short nap. Refreshed, I took up position in the hatchway at about two-thirty. The cloud base had lifted a little and there they were, the Faroes at last, ranged along the full length of the western horizon, some partially veiled, others in clear, unblemished profile. With hand-bearing compass and chart it was only a minute or two before I had them off pat and laid out in my mind like a row of miscreant Nordic children: Suðurø, Sandø, Nolsø, Streymø, Eysturø and...there I faltered, for the most northerly islands, the most dramatic, the ones I dearly wanted to see, were still wrapped in persistent but shifting cloud that fell right to sea level. Occasionally a black shoulder showed through for a second or two, but whether it was Borðø or Svínø or the great bird-cliff of Fuglø itself was impossible to say. Although we were still almost twenty miles to seawards, the loom and presence of that fragmented amphitheatre of cliffs and headlands spoke of something beyond the ordinary, something savagely momentous and long-lasting, something profound and tantalising, impenetrable to puny mortal ken. Despite intimations of the crushing ephemerality of it all, my heart sang with the happiness of the moment and my outstretched fingertip once more traced the curve of the islands, not this time on the velvety flatness of a chart spread before a winter's fire, but through the three dimensions of the landscape itself. We stood in for another hour, enough for the shape and pattern and rhythm of the islands to be stamped indelibly on my memory, then, lashed by frequent rain squalls and a north-westerly now up to Force 6, turned once again seawards.

The fog came down again. A cold and nasty wind blew nonetheless. I dropped a couple of panels of the mainsail. We edged back offshore, making good a track to the north-east. The islands were now lost behind us. I hoped to make another pass across the northern end of the group. There lay the island of Viðø, and the highest headland in the world. It was not to be; I would not sight the Faroes again, on this voyage at any rate.

By five the next morning, after an unpleasantly chilly night made worse by the frustrations of being forced well off our track, we had reached the perimeter of the Fuglø Bank. Fortunately I was awake, busying myself with something or other, otherwise I may well have missed the sudden hum and vibration that signalled an engine somewhere close. I rushed to the hatch. Emerging from the grey murk, and just fifty yards away, the rampart bows of a chunky, serious-looking, wide-bridged and ocean-ready Faroese fishing vessel were bearing down on us. In a few seconds' time Danish welded steel would cut its teeth, as it were, on Dorset glass-fibre lay-up. There was little doubt which pairing would carry the day. Evasive action was, I suspected, called for, and quickly. By the grace of Neptune, the fishing boat had its trawl set, and so was labouring forward at just a couple of knots. In a flashing two-second whirl my hands had the self-steering chain disengaged, the tiller lines operational and the helm up. A figure raced across the bridge of the trawler. We had at least been seen. The ship's hooter belched a throaty blast at us, far too late, for we were already running quickly off the wind away from that devilishly sharp-looking blade of a bow, and back on to our previous heading. A few seconds more and we were lost to each other in the fog, but not before a second chunky and serious-looking doppelganger had materialised ghost-like further aft and as quickly vanished. I just had time to make out the number of my would-be destroyer – TN350.

For many hours afterwards I reflected on the near miss. Had we been a minute later on that heading, and I a little less alert, we could well have sailed between the fishing boat and its trawl. Only cute timing had saved us from ending our days as a constituent part of a consignment of finest Nordic fish-paste. There are probably worse fates, but not many. I resolved then and there to send the skipper of the trawler, via the harbourmaster at Tórshavn, a box of cigars, as a memento of our brief encounter. Like most resolutions made in the flush of holiday fever - tactical proposals of marriage to Fuerteventuran waitresses, for example - it soon lost its urgency and to this day remains disgracefully unfulfilled.

On we plugged, for a while heading more towards Spitsbergen than Iceland. For a whole fifteen minutes around breakfast time a lifting of the fog brought brilliant sunshine, sunshine whose jollity and hail-fellow-well-met brashness seemed suddenly out of place in the general pallid sombreness we were adjusting to; but fog, and plenty of it, is the byword for these parts as the warming summer airs sweep north over a frigid sea, and my eyes had scarcely adjusted to the excess of lumens flooding into the cabin before we were once more wrapped up in the habitual veil of miserable grey. The returning gloom came, though, with a compensating wind shift in our favour. An easterly! Within a minute or two we were settled on starboard tack with the wind free and the north-east tip of Iceland no more than three hundred miles ahead. Six days sail in moderately favourable conditions. Twenty-one days out from Burnham. It was tight, but still possible.

My optimism was tempered by the last shipping forecast I bothered to listen to. A crackly and ethereal voice that came and went and could just as well have been broadcasting from Alpha Centauri gave the impression, if I had decoded the broken syllables correctly, that strong north-westerly winds were expected in Faroes and South-East Iceland. I did not take this altogether too seriously, as I have often suspected that the shipping forecast is based on the meteorology of some heavenly body other than Planet Earth, but it did nevertheless throw a twinge of alarm into my generally up-beat mood. My margin of extra time had all been used up with a succession of storms and calms. There was no more fat on the bone. From here on I needed fair winds. A north-westerly was the unfairest of them all. I need not have worried too much. A wind from the north-west would put paid to our most far-flung aspirations, for sure, but then so would a full cast of other checks and setbacks. They were all waiting in the wings, preening and powdering themselves, ready for their grand entrance.

12

The subtlety of the Chinese junk rig is hard to convey; to be appreciated it has to be experienced, to be lived with, and at length. Enlightenment advances slowly. It is a process of gradual and piecemeal absorption. To an extent it starts, for the occidental, as an act of faith. Too many built-in, scarcely recognised prejudices militate against easy acceptance. Without acceptance, understanding is not possible. The western sailor is, in the main, too impatient. His leaning is for the quick and the obvious. He wants results, and now. Peremptory rejection, scornful dismissal, delivered in double-quick time, is the usual verdict on this most elegant of rigs.

Born of two millenia of infinitely patient trial, error and sinuous inventiveness, graced with a score of tiny details whose relevance hover, like Columbus' egg, just the other side of comprehension until the penny drops with an obvious and embarrassing clunk, infinitely forgiving to mast and sail and hull, supremely easy to manage, the junk rig is a perfect manifestation of the oriental genius. It expresses as well as anything the salient characteristics of the eastern worldview. It is a non-confrontational rig, soft, relenting. It absorbs rather than resists. It turns the other cheek, feinting gently away, while calmly appropriating the forces directed against it. It advances quietly, without thrash or bang. It sets up no strains on the hull it drives. The mast wants to fly, to rise up through the partners and take to the air, rather than drive itself through the keel below; it yields to the wind, curving gently, the pressure of the sail ranged evenly along its height through the regular spacing of the battens and parrels. The sail delivers its power at the slightest of angles to the breeze, its fan-like configuration ready to be closed up in a second or two when reefing is called for. No junk-rigged craft need ever be forced on its ear. The sailing is upright, sedate, unstressed. It strives for a simple non-aggressive harmony with wind and wave.

The contrast with the bar-taut, hard-edged and, until recently, cumbersome rigs of the West is as good a metaphor as any for the great divide between the eastern and the western psyche. The modern occidental rig seems to set itself up in opposition to natural forces. It attacks them, brutally. Its aim is to overcome them rather than to work with them. The principle is to create ever stronger materials then stress them to the limit in a triumph of myopic engineering machismo. It is a hotbed of high tension. Every bit of kit is wound up to within a fraction of its breaking point. Everywhere winches, levers, turnbuckles and multi-blocked tackles are ratcheted up to deliver tons of opposing tensile and compressive forces on mast and hull. This is the finest and dandyest of set-ups, go-fast and gung-ho, until a shroud or a swage or a thread or a rivet or a humble pin gives up the ghost and the whole edifice comes tumbling down in a mess of alloy and astonishment.

The aerodynamics of the junk rig are still poorly understood. Advanced scientific analysis, wind tunnels and all, has not yet come up with a definitive theory as to exactly how it works. The rig seems to defy comprehension. Forget smooth air flow. Forget aerofoils. The disturbances and vortices set up by the battens seem to be a positive attribute. The saggy luffs so hated by the western sailor seem to enhance performance. Everything is arse-about, counter-intuitive, typically bloody foreign.

No sail is easier to cut and more forgiving of its material than the junk sail. The cloth, and it can be virtually anything you like, even old hessian sacking if that's all you've got, is simply laid out flat and cut to size. No fancy cambers or curved seams are necessary. The sail-maker's skill is redundant. Any Tom, Dick or Ha Jin adept with a sewing machine or a needle and thread can knock up a sail between breakfast-time and happy hour. Once made the sail will last and last. *Mingming's* mainsail, as we left the Faroes astern, was in its twenty-seventh year. Supported at every point by close-spaced battens and their multipartite sheeting, the material is seldom stressed. It never flogs. Holes and patches have little adverse affect on performance.

The sail battens are traditionally made from bamboo or tree branches. Just cut to size however many lengths you need and hey presto! A few spares are usually carried on board in case of breakage. In the West the repertoire of materials used has inevitably expanded to include aluminium, plastic, fibreglass. No doubt somebody somewhere is using carbon fibre or kevlar or whatever is the latest space-age compound. Each material has its ardent advocates and its indignant detractors; each has its good points and its not-so-good points. In the arcane world of junk rig specialism the debates and arguments and experimentation continue year after year, with little sign of agreement or resolution.

I was still using the five sail battens, each one twelve feet long, that came with *Mingming* when I had bought her two years previously. Although somewhat unusual, they were well thought through and carefully constructed. Until the two recent fractures, they had performed more than adequately for several thousand ocean miles. Fundamentally they were made of thirty-two millimetre plastic waste pipe, the sort of grey piping that takes the dishwater away from the U-bend under the kitchen sink. It's bendy and cheap, but could not be used without modification for the higher battens that have to cope with heavier weather. The three upper battens had been fitted with wood cores, softwood for most, but hardwood for the top one. Each of these cores had a section of flexible narrow-gauge plastic piping incorporated. The finished battens, although strong, therefore still retained some flexibility.

The battens are enclosed in long pockets sewn into the sail, and are fed into the pockets from the forward end. This is why I do not carry complete replacement battens aboard. The almost physical impossibility, not to mention the danger, of trying to manhandle an awkward and fairly heavy twelve-foot length of batten, most of which would initially have to project out over the bow, then feed it into a tight pocket, all from *Mingming's* tiny fore deck, in even the slightest seaway, ruled that out. The conditions in which such a manoeuvre would be remotely viable probably obtain on about one day in thirty. A splinting repair made from the hatch is not as effective as a total replacement, but it can be made at any time, in any conditions, in total safety.

Twenty-four hours after our brush with the Faroese trawler, on a similar early morning that had us bound up in mist and light rain, our northerly progress almost ended for good. A third batten fractured, the third batten down, in fact, that was supporting the already broken second batten. Only the two lower battens now remained intact. My heart pounded at the sight of the sail, broken and misshapen yet again. For an hour or so I lost the will and the confidence to carry on. How could we keep on pushing further and further north with a rig that was steadily falling apart? I improvised a splint for the new fracture out of my aluminium boat hook and the handle of the deck brush, gaffer taped together and lashed in place. The upper part of the sail now looked a sorry mess, a sagging bird's nest of repairs. I felt that we had crossed the threshold of what was reasonable; we were now pretty much under a jury rig, with at least fifteen hundred miles of sailing still ahead. Every additional mile that we sailed north would add to that distance. We were now well past the Faroes, so could still complete the second of our projected options. That would have to do.

With the repair in place I put up the helm and we ran off to the south-west, bound for Rockall, pushed seductively on by the fresh north-easterly. We might have an easy run. *No, no!* Within a second or two everything in me rebelled at this capitulation. *No, no! What the hell am I doing?* It was unbearable, absolutely hateful, to be heading southwards. *No, no, no! We've come so bloody far! Please, please don't give up!* Suddenly shocked at how quickly I had allowed my resolve to evaporate I leaped to the hatch and hauled us back on to the wind, resetting our course to the north-west and Iceland. Our southerly retreat had lasted scarcely a minute. It was a minute too much. I was dismayed at this lapse of will.

We settled back under just two panels. Well supported by the topping lifts the sail still functioned adequately. There was no question that our windward ability would be adversely affected from here on, and that I was going to have to nurse us along even more solicitously than usual. We had now crossed latitude 63°N. The Arctic Circle lay just two hundred miles or so further on. It was so close. Surely, surely we could make it.

13

On we plugged, a chastened skipper under a hang-dog rig. I had been seeking out the bleak and the solitary, and now found it with a vengeance. The wind had for several days been flirting with the idea of setting in from the north; now it steadied itself up and let loose a persistent blast, icy and uncompromising, straight down from the Pole itself. We pitched on into a short and uncomfortable sea, a sea as deathly grey and as featureless as the low dome of cloud that pressed down upon us. Even the whitecaps that were forcing us to the west were devoid of glint or shine or sparkle; all was dull pallor, bland frigidity. We had left the fishing grounds well astern and so, apart from the faithful fulmars in never-ending wheeling attendance, had this seascape to ourselves.

Our target on the Iceland coast slipped further and further south, as the contrary wind forced a constant revision of my plans. The north-east cape, Langanes, was no longer a viable goal. Then the Seyðisfjördur, the most northerly of the fjords, and the focus of so much of my winter dreaming, dropped out of contention. For a while it looked as if we could still lay the Reyðarfjördur, further to the south. That in its turn was abandoned as the northerly got up to a good Force 7, at the same backing a little to the west, and I saw with dismay that we were now losing ground, making good a course slightly south of west. The row of crosses that advanced across the Iceland-Faroes Rise now started to loop round like a great question mark. The outlying shoals of south-east Iceland lay just a hundred miles to the north-west, less than a hand's span on my chart. These were waters to be avoided. For the first time a treacherous thought edged into my mind: if this wind continues for much longer we may have to try for south-west Iceland, rather than the north-east. In any event time was running out; in three days my twenty-one day outward time allowance would be up. Our voyage had reached a kind of deadlock. We badly needed a wind shift, any wind shift, to make the most of these last few days.

Such is small-boat ocean sailing. Frustration piles upon frustration, setback upon setback, compromise upon compromise. Expectation is constantly modified; aspiration endlessly recalibrated. It is a kind of siege warfare. Every conceivable engine of war encircles the optimistic spirit, lobbing rocks and firebrands and nasty explosive devices into the battered citadel. Towering scaffolds are run up against the defensive battlements, disgorging hordes of screaming mercenaries intent on mayhem. Hulking squads run battering rams into the gates of the barbican. Spears and lances and a thousand sharp-tipped arrows rain down from the skies. The air is thick with the rumble of artillery. The single-handed sailor must constantly repel these attacks, damp the fires, rebuild the crumbling brickwork. The running battle is never over.

We had taken our fair share of assaults and reversals during this voyage, though nothing beyond the expected norm. These had been more than adequately counter-balanced by a handful of moments of a beauty and a poise so intense, so crystalline and so unattainable other than through the toughest rite of passage, that I still felt favoured rather than beleaguered. In sum, I had nothing to complain about.

The rig was still giving me trouble, though. At every available opportunity the topping lifts were finding their way between the sail and the ends of the rough-fangled splints that supported the broken battens. It was impossible to lower the sail fully on starboard tack. There was a risk of the sail becoming permanently jammed up there; a nightmarish scenario. The seas were still too lively for me to undertake improvements, but I planned a series of counter-measures to keep the topping lifts and the splint ends well segregated. In the meantime, if for any reason I had to get the sail down in a hurry, I would first have to put us on to port tack. I was not particularly happy with this state of affairs – it might just complicate matters at a critical moment – but it provisionally solved the problem and allowed us to keep on sailing as best we could.

By the morning of Tuesday the tenth of July we were commencing our nineteenth day at sea. Our rhythm was by now well established; each day ran seamlessly into the next; we were now well beyond the intrusions of forecasters and newsmen; our universe was once again comfortably defined by the hazy encircling horizons and the press of cloud-blanket bearing down from above; there was nothing else. To have the world thus simplified and reduced, to have all noise, the white noise and febrile babble of our over-connectedness, that is, and all distraction and all temporal complication filtered out, was, as ever, a kind of liberation. We were back to the pure business of sailing the ocean, nothing more, nothing less. Overlaying this was the delicious knowledge that by now it would be impossible for even the most skilled and assiduous of trackers to have the slightest clue as to where we were. We were now well beyond the scent of any ocean bloodhound, our geography no more definable than 'somewhere at sea'.

By then it seemed as if we had been on starboard tack – my 'non-sleep' tack - for ever. On *Mingming* I don't really have one proper bunk, let alone a port and starboard bunk for each tack. I sleep as best I can on a pallet composed of the forward end of the starboard quarter berth, the narrow midship seat, just fifteen inches wide, and the aft end of what was the starboard forward berth. There are no lee boards or cloths. On starboard tack I therefore sleep on the uphill side of the boat. *Mingming* does not heel much, but the slightest roll to leeward will still try to pitch me off my makeshift couch and on to the cabin sole, or across the divide into the galley or, on the most violent occasions, in particular a good broadside from a breaking crest, clear across what remains of the forward double berth and into the shelving against the port side of the hull. Many a time an airborne dream has turned out to be just that, ending in the rudest of awakenings with a forceful thump into some part of the boat. But on *Mingming* the distances that one can travel, even in astral flight, are severely limited, so the damage is more to continuity of sleep than to flesh and blood. In those northern waters my thick and multi-layered clothing acted as a good shock absorber if I was flung off my bunk. I have in any case developed a varied and ingenious repertoire of curlings and bracings and contortions that resist the leeward impetus and more or less keep me where I should be. I am often surprised by how well I sleep in the most uncongenial of positions. It may seem that I am needlessly ascetic in not organising a nice deep and comfy cot for myself, but the self-denial and deliberate discomfort serve the vital purpose of making sure that I am always within a whisker of wakefulness. Sleep is by design a shallow and fitful affair.

By noon we had, despite the poor conditions and our patched-up rig, notched up a twenty-four hour run of about eighty nautical miles. But it was to the west rather than the north. The nearest land, in the region of Stokksnes, lay just a hundred miles to the north-west. With a fair wind the Arctic Circle was two days' sail away. I tacked to see if we could make some northing on the other board, but it put us straight into the left-over swells from the north-east, stopping us dead. The wind dropped. I raised the small jib and a couple of panels of the main, but we were by now lolling about, unable to make a worthwhile heading on either tack. We were, as the artist once said, stuck, stuck, stuck. There was nothing to be done except to wait. I sat in the hatchway under a slatting mainsail that was barely moving us and tracked the flight of the fulmars. The usual crowd of thirty or so kept us close company, weaving a skein of complex flight paths around and around and along and up and down and round again, straight-winged, soft-eyed, incomprehensible. For the whole afternoon I watched them wheel against the gun-metal sky, calmed by the simple inevitability of their ceaseless pattern-making.

Around six I cooked a quick one-pot meal, then stretched out on my bunk. Within a minute or two I was back at the hatchway, drawn by the quick *pphoooff!* of a cetacean exhaling. *Mingming* hung there, a grey ship on a grey ground, rolling in the smoothing swells. Only the outlandish orange of her sun insignia disturbed the all-encompassing shades of silver and pewter and iron and lead that bound us below and above. A shapely fin broke the surface a few yards away. Then another. Dolphins! My senses, lulled to dullness by the hours of empty contemplation, suddenly sharpened. There were splashes to port and to starboard and then astern. Fins now came and went all around, quick flashes of crescented black. Occasionally a striped flank showed and was gone. It seemed somehow unlike the usual visitations; something about the rhythm and the encircling behaviour of the dolphins struck an odd note. Within a few seconds the sea astern, to the very horizon, erupted. The day changed. My world changed. Our little voyage was about to reach a kind of apotheosis. If there was any point or meaning to our nineteen-day struggle to get this far, it was about to be revealed. Whales, hundreds of them, a vast army of glistening flesh, ton upon dense and graceful ton of muscle and sinew and raw killing power, fruit of the depths, outriders of the underworld, were coming helter-skelter to join us.

14

Globicephala melas. The long-finned pilot whale. Squads of five or six or ten, each group close-packed and synchronised in its undulating pattern of breathe and dive, were homing in on us from a wide arc across the north-eastern horizon. Their goal was unmistakable; they were heading straight for *Mingming.* The lines of bulbous leaping heads, spread across nearly a mile of sea, some now closing us fast, others still dark and intermittent smudges at the limit of my vision, were converging on a single point, as accurately and as purposefully as if directed by some well-organised mission control. Perhaps they were. Whatever was driving them on towards us was unequivocal in its command; we were the focal point of this approaching horde. I had never, ever, seen anything like it. Wide-eyed, I watched them come.

The first unit of five or six whales, angling in off the port quarter, seemed to pause for a moment at about thirty metres' distance. Their surfacing lost its urgent athleticism. They advanced gently, a little warily, their surface rolls slowed down to give them a half-second more to assess their strange target. For the first time I could get a sense of their bulk and, seen from ahead, the curvature of their profile: broad head narrowing just a shade at the neck, then a widening at mid-body before the long narrowing to the transverse fluke. The pod was pressed in close together, flanks almost a-rub, crowded in familial or social or defensive bonding. Their quick, explosive exhalations came in sporadic bursts as they broke the surface in unison.

This advance guard evidently found nothing untoward and cruised easily past us ten metres off the port beam. The rest, or at least the start of the rest, began to arrive. From straight astern, from the quarters, from the port and starboard beams, group after group after group of whales came bounding in, their outrageously swollen black brows and meaty dorsal fins creating a moving patchwork of chiaroscuro against the unrelenting grey of sky and ocean. Still they came, and as they squeezed in closer all reticence was lost. Within a few minutes we were absorbed into the herd. We were scarcely making a knot of speed in the faint breeze, far too slow for an equal advance with our new entourage. The whales therefore made passes down each beam, then circled round to repeat the manoeuvre again and again. I thought they would soon tire of our slow progress and be quickly gone, but no, they stayed, and I gradually realised that this strange and mismatched communion in the sub-Arctic seas had more about it than a mere crossing of paths.

The whales settled into a rhythm of endless progress along our flanks. As they grew in confidence the distance they kept reduced; before long they were crowding in right alongside, with *Mingming* accorded a convivial proximity that suggested honorary membership of the herd. This may sound like an exaggeration, inclined towards cuddly anthropomorphism, but bear with me: our story is by no means told.

The whales settled into a rhythm, then, and in that ghostly northern twilight delivered a mesmerising ballet, a supremely controlled and graceful rise and fall and turn and twist as they streamed past for hour after hour in an endless round of gentle surfacing, breathing and rolling forward to regain their station just a foot or two below the surface. Round and round they went, on and on, tirelessly, several hundred of them, their ranks stretched out a quarter of a mile on each beam. With so many now so close their breathy exhalations formed a continuous background accompaniment to their gyrations, a constant wheezing rat-a-tat that was more than just aural – each expulsion of air brought with it a cloud of misty spray as fishy as it was fine, and before long *Mingming* and I and all my clothing were doused in a film of moisture that had us stinking like the Grimsby fish dock in the days when there were still catches to be caught. After nearly three weeks of perching on an inert ocean, I was overpowered by this sudden explosion of movement and sound and smell. More than that, though, it was the scorching physical charisma exuded by these great creatures that knocked my senses askew.

Amidships *Mingming* has about twelve inches of freeboard. The closest whales were passing no more than five or six feet from my vantage point in the hatchway – almost within touching distance. The big males, each weighing several tons, were as long as *Mingming*. But the herd was a composition of family groupings, close-knit and faithful. Young whales just a few feet long, but no less fast and athletic than the full-grown adults, were tucked in at their mothers' sides. They must all have been there: grandmothers, toddlers, teenage jack-the-lads, uncles and aunts and cousins, hoary old bulls and little princesses looking for love. We had somehow fallen in with a whole tribe of nomadic predators and I longed for some real wind so that we could range along with them at full speed ahead, as it were. The wind was still easing off, though, and the silvered water was now throwing up reflections of the fins and long backs as they broke the surface, fins and backs that showed an infinite range of subtle variation in their colouring. Up close the whales belied their old-time whalers' name of 'blackfish'. They were mottled in intricate patterns of slate-blues and greys and milky-browns. Scratch marks described pale insignia at obtuse angles. Many of the fins had half-moon gouges in their after edges. One had its topmost section missing entirely. After a while individuals became recognisable as they passed again and again.

It would be untrue to say that I did not from time to time feel somewhat anxious at having hundreds of tons of burly and dynamic flesh crowding closely around us. It would have been a small matter for one of those giant cannon-ball heads to have stove in *Mingming's* hull. Now and then a fluke was flicked at us, sending a great cloud of spray across the boat. Just once or twice we got a mild slap on the sides. I don't think the intent was aggressive; it was, I suspect, more a kind of inquisitive provocation, a testing out.

I went below to fetch my camera and discovered a new and startling aspect of this visitation; the whales were talking to each other. *Mingming's* fibreglass hull, usually so acoustically hard-edged, now redeemed itself as a perfect sounding board for the seamless warblings radiating through the water. The whales were not communicating with clicks or squeaks or grunts. They were singing. Extraordinary high-pitched cadences ran on and on, blackbird-like phrases transposed up and elided into an endless stream of haunting and unworldly melody. The lines criss-crossed in aleatoric counterpoint as my ears picked out more and more voices piercing the aqueous depths. A whole symphony was going on out there! I sat on my bunk, an audience of one, enchanted. Mahler Five, Bruckner Eight, yes, but this, this was something beyond art, beyond artifice. This was the un-modulated voice of nature itself: matter turned flesh turned music. These sinewy brutes were advancing in a cloud of dainty coloratura; it was as incongruous as a burst of Handelian counter-tenor from an ensemble of East London doormen. For half an hour

I listened hard and tried to discern some sense or pattern in these messages, but it was beyond me. I imitated the phrases with third-rate whistling, imprinting the pitches and cadence and intonation into my inner ear. Then, feeling more and more shattered by this surfeit of stimulation at every level, I returned to the hatch and resumed my vigil.

It was by now approaching midnight. Our sole source of light, now somewhere just below the northern horizon, set up a faint and diffused glow that robbed the scene of any sense of shadow or relief or dimension. This flat suspension added to the unreality as the whales crowded closer and closer. The wind had given up entirely and we just lay there, scarcely moving, the hub and centrepiece of this great mass of restless flesh. I would have thought our immobility the signal for the herd to move off, but it drew them in tighter, transforming their configuration from phalanx to circle, and infecting them too with a lazier, more aimless progress as they just milled around us, still sometimes in tight and synchronised groupings of three or four, but increasingly as lone individuals. Their concerted breathing was now a continuous geyser-like roar, St. Pancras station in the days of steam, and this constant effusion of rank spray had by now so permeated the air above them, air that hung in an unmoving noxious cloud, that I felt that the sea had been turned upside down and inside out and here we were, now absorbed body and soul into the very heart of some fishy kingdom.

The light was still fading by almost imperceptible degrees. *Mingming* hung motionless save for a slight rolling and the whales' circlings wound down too until most were lying there on the surface, their heads and bodies half submerged and tails hung downwards. From time to time one would stand on its fluke, as it were, its head now vertical, and regard us with a tiny, ridge-rimmed eye. How I wish I could have accessed those neural networks and got some hint of what they made of *Mingming*. It was by now beyond argument that she exercised some strange and compelling attraction. The herd had now been with us for six hours. This was more than mere passing curiosity. The whales were now stretching out and resting right alongside, relaxed and calm. They did not want to leave. It was profoundly touching; we had become bedfellows.

Adrift in a sea of sleeping whales I too drooped to somnolence. Heavy-lidded, exhausted, my eyes wandered in and out of focus. I wanted to stay there in the hatchway and observe every last detail of the whales' behaviour until they finally left, but it was no good; tiredness got the better of me. Reluctantly I stretched out below and slept. It was a fitful slumber, pierced by the puffs and snorts of our companions. From time to time I woke and sneaked a look outside. The black forms still lay there, ebony logs shifting gently to the swell. But each time I looked there were fewer. They were moving away, to dive deep and hunt the squid they feed on. By morning they were gone.

15

For half a day we lay nailed to a silver-grey backdrop, fixed immutably, stuck. No wind, no movement, no progress. I cared somewhat less about our frozen state than I would have done twenty-four hours earlier. My head was still whirling with the images and sounds of the pilot whales. The whole episode had been astounding, but more than that, it had made my voyage worthwhile. Whatever happened from here on, I would go home happy. I had witnessed and been immersed in a most extraordinary encounter - unexpected, unimaginable, irreplaceable. A fragment of ocean life had been revealed in all its alien and impenetrable beauty; but it went beyond mere revelation. For a few seconds our lives, mine, that is, as a fumbling seeker-out of the nature of the sea, and theirs, as supremely evolved masters of their environment, had overlapped into a faint and tenuous companionship. Our voyage had taken us beyond the furthest limits of the conventional and the humdrum, and into the heart of wildness itself. I could ask for nothing more.

That was all very well, but in this calm there was work to be done. I made a rare sortie from the hatch and readjusted the lines from the self-steering to the tiller, which had stretched badly after such hard use. I modified my repairs to the broken battens, to discourage the splints from tangling with the topping lifts. I reworked the leads to the tiller lines to improve their performance. I worked through the list of all the marlin-spike chores I had delayed until just such a day.

Our noon position showed we had made good just ten nautical miles over the last twenty-four hours. I could have swum as far. It was in the wrong direction too; we had drifted to the south-west. Once more I pored over the chart, measuring and calculating, trying to revive my optimism, but knowing at heart that our goal of reaching north-east Iceland was slipping away. In two days' time we would have to turn south. Only an exceptionally favourable change in the weather would give us any hope of crossing the Arctic Circle.

The wind, when it came, gave me false hope. It started off just north of east, allowing us, for the first time in days, to head due north. Due north! That was more like it; but it was a lousy, gutless, indecisive simulacrum of a breeze, a rotten sham or, as I wrote in my log, a useless, fitful, lily-livered wind that was sort of getting us there in a half-hearted, reluctant way. My lack of faith was soon vindicated; by evening we were being forced further and further west as the wind backed once more towards the north. At six the following morning, fed up after a night of bucking to windward towards the most unsavoury part of the Icelandic coastline, I accepted the inevitable; we would not make it to the north-east fjords. With just a day left of our outward time allowance and an inconsistent headwind, our most northerly goals were beyond reach. No Arctic Circle, no Seyðisfjördur. Never mind. They were only aspirations; I could still shape a good voyage from here on. My real frustration was to be so close to the coast of Iceland with little prospect of actually seeing it. The plan that had been forming in the back of my mind for a few days now seemed the best option; I would run off to the west and see if we could fetch up at the Vestmann Islands. This group of small islands lay about a hundred miles away, just off the south-west coast. They included the island of Surtsey that had erupted out of the sea during volcanic activity only three decades previously. Just as enticing were the Myrdalsjökull and the Eyjafjallajökull, two mighty glaciers on the mainland coast a few miles to the north. With a fair wind we could be there within a day and a half. If we could get even a half-decent look I could then turn south feeling satisfied.

I eased the sheet and ran due west. For a while we revelled in the conditions. What a change it was to have the wind free and be racing along at a good pace. With a steady barometer and a settled sky that was even allowing a milky sun to peer through from time to time, I allowed myself the occasional moment of optimism; a quick run west, some clearer weather, close views of a sun-drenched glacier or two, a look at the world's most recently-formed island – it could be a worthy climax to the outward leg of the voyage.

Hope springs ever eternal but the winds spring often contrary. By six that evening we lay rolling and groaning in a heavy swell as the breeze eased and eased. Two Manx shearwaters, the first we had seen on this voyage, hurried their way past with a well-oiled sleekness that suddenly made our fulmar attendants look a shade cumbersome. The ship's log took on two distinct themes; on the one hand long and detailed conjecture as to whether Iceland really existed; on the other a series of desperate appeals, to skipper and crew, for the exercise of patience.

By one the next morning, Friday the thirteenth of July and within a few hours of completing our third week at sea, I had dropped the mainsail and lashed it firmly down; the banging and slatting as the heavy north-east swells rolled us one way and then the other had become unbearable. For four hours we suffered: no wind, no comfort, no sleep. Time was nearly up. We had lain within an easy day's sail of Iceland seemingly for ever. It was no good; we would soon be going home empty-handed. Unless…perhaps one last wind shift…

At about five that morning, under a covering of cloud that was just slightly higher and less oppressive than usual, a little breeze got up and my hopes were dashed. It was from the north-west. We were being headed once more as the wind followed us round. Ah well. I raised the main and got us sailing as close-hauled as was practicable in the light air with a patched-up rig. We moved off, making good a hesitant course a little south of west. I sat in the hatchway, despondent. It was no good; the time had come to turn south. I couldn't yet bring myself to alter course. Maybe the breeze would revert to north-east, giving us a last reprieve. We had achieved a lot, but I felt unfulfilled, dissatisfied. The previous year I had turned around in mid-ocean, a decision I would always regret. That still weighed heavily upon me. I baulked at the thought of having to do it again, with not a jot to show for it.

For several hours I sat and stared at sea and sky, wrangling with myself. I had no option but to turn south; I could not turn south. I stared at sea and sky and after a while realised that there was something odd about the clouds low on the northern horizon. A tiny bright patch that I had dismissed as a momentary trick of the light still persisted, now with hints of shadow too dark to match the surrounding clouds. I pulled out my binoculars and looked more closely. Land! It was scarcely credible, but there was no doubt about it. Directly to the north, just a degree or two above the horizon, lay a great whaleback of snow or ice, sometimes glinting as a distant sun patch moved across, and intersected by shoulders of black rock. I rushed below and pulled out my detailed chart of Iceland. Yes! There it was, the Oraefajokull, at seven thousand feet Iceland's highest glacier. It lay sixty miles to the north of us, just a few miles inland. A chance lifting and break in the clouds had revealed it, even at that distance. Iceland exists! I've seen it with my very own eyes! For an hour or so I studied the glacier with binoculars. The shifting cloud sometimes showed more crags to each side; sometimes it shrank almost out of sight. The highest point was always shrouded. I tried to film it, unsuccessfully; it was simply too far to show up. Camera still-shots worked, though, ultimately producing atmospheric blow-ups. My mood was transformed. It was a small thing, in many ways, to have such a pathetically limited sight of Iceland, but it anchored and defined the northern limit of our trajectory. It gave a modicum of sense to our turning point. We had at least sailed to within viewing distance of the Icelandic coastal hinterland. I had seen a glacier from the deck of *Mingming;* it was an improvement on fog, mist, and an endless glowering sky. I had had the thrill of an unexpected landfall. It was enough, just. It was also exquisitely timed, just one hour short of my twenty-one day deadline. Whilst not totally rid of the last week's frustrations and the disappointment of falling just short of my goal, I felt that the balance had nevertheless been redressed a little. I could turn south with a little more equanimity.

By midday the wind had backed further to the west and my mind was made up. I brought the helm up and eased *Mingming* off on to a southerly heading. Our next target lay just over three hundred miles due south. Rockall. Home of that lonely phallus and one of the stormiest sea areas of the British Isles. The name alone is enough to send a frisson of alert expectation, if not a flood of cold sweat, down any sailor's spine. It was curious and somehow comforting to be approaching it from the north. We would pass it on our way home. That robbed it of much of its prospective terror – it was already well within our compass, after all. I was by no means complacent, though. We would once more be heading straight into the tracks of the North Atlantic depressions. I did not expect a smooth ride. That was just as well.

16

With the wind now abaft the beam, a wind that was strengthening every hour and bringing with it huge clouds of well-delineated charcoal grey that gave a welcome change from the featureless wash in which we had been immersed for so long, *Mingming* leapt south with a will. The first vessel that we had met since our near miss with the Faroese fishing boat, a pristine cruise ship this time, all futuristic curves and sveldt streamlining, purred effortlessly across our bows heading east. The wind got up, the rain came down, and I knew then that we had achieved as much as was possible; any hanging about further north would only have led to more dismay and disappointment.

Mingming raced south then, not quite greyhound-like, but with the easy lope of a middle-aged but still-frisky setter unleashed on a rolling moorland. By early morning she was running softly before a blustery half-gale that had veered back to the habitual north-east. Before long we were under just the sail bundle, the fully lowered mainsail, that is, squared off to starboard and always surprisingly effective as a downwind motivator and by midday we had already notched up eighty-five nautical miles since turning for home. These were the miles that had been denied to us the other way. Eighty-five miles would have got us to the north-east fjords, or to the Vestmann Islands. Eighty-five miles every twenty-four hours would have had us inside the Arctic Circle with time to spare. Hell! - with eighty-five miles a day under our belt we might have been nosing around Jan Mayen or Scoresby Sound or thinking of a westwards passage through the Denmark Strait! Access to such a daily mileage had been withheld from us since the east coast of Scotland. Now the miles were doled out liberally; we were to cover the three hundred miles to Rockall in just four days.

I won't give a blow by blow account of those four days. It was an easy and comfortable run south, sometimes under the sail bundle, sometimes with a panel or two of sail set as the wind varied from Force 6 to the occasional gale-force squall, always from somewhere round about the north-east. We were now on my 'sleep' tack, so resting was less gymnastic. As each day passed the seas built. Steep green combers bore down from astern and *Mingming* showed off her marvellous sea-keeping talents, rising in untroubled calm to every swell and white cap, stable, buoyant, unstressed. For days an angry sky raced across, bringing with it a turbulent cloudscape, a kaleidoscopic cocktail of black-browed line squalls edged with yellow haze, sudden flashes of blinding sunlight, quick downpours. Despite being hundreds of miles offshore we met puffins continually, in small groupings or in pairs or alone. Their desperate whirring flight as they strove to keep their fulsome undercarriages and extravagant nose-cones just a foot or two aloft the waves was comically unmistakeable. As we neared the shallower waters of the Rockall Bank Manx shearwaters joined us, and the occasional sooty shearwater, and terns, for some reason aggressive in their relations with our friendly fulmars. Pelagic bird-life is a source of endless fascination. What adaptation, to be able to live out a life with such ease in this windblown desert.

As we bore down on Rockall itself it was clear that we would have to give it a wide berth. It would be foolhardy in these heavy seas to venture in close to the shallow reef on which it sits. I preferred to keep well to seawards and to follow the five hundred metre depth contour south. At midday on Tuesday the seventeenth of July, our twenty-sixth day at sea, we passed fifty miles to the west of Rockall. The waves had by now built sufficiently to infuse the moment with an appropriate level of boisterousness. I felt a mild satisfaction; this was, after all, one of the defining co-ordinates of our little voyage, a sort of wing mark on a grand scale. Its successful rounding made up for some of the earlier disappointment.

The half-gale from the north-east blew on and on, and as we ran south to clear the Rockall Bank, still lashed by showers as the heavy cloud poured over, we started to meet stragglers from more temperate seas. A Spanish-style fishing boat appeared low on the western horizon; the odd clump of buoy barnacles floated by; a few jack sail-by-the-winds, the little sailing jellyfish that we had met by the millions the previous year, struggled past, obviously separated from the main fleet and at the limit of their navigational capacity.

The north-easterly held on for another two days, but with a clearing sky it grew more fitful. I raised a panel or two of the sail to keep us moving well. Our latitude put us due west of Londonderry and Newcastle; sub-arctic waters were now well astern. I altered course to the south-east, angling us towards the south-western tip of Ireland. I pulled out my charts for southern Ireland and the western approaches. It had been a stupendously fast passage south.

Something else had changed, and it took me a while to figure out what it was; our fulmars had gone. For the first time since the Norfolk coast we were advancing without their wheeling presence. What threshold had we crossed that had caused them to abandon us, instinctively? Was it the length of the day, or the sea temperature, or food supply, or...I don't know? Their departure was sudden and unexpected. From here on we would meet lone fulmars from time to time, but there was no question that we had moved out of some defining territorial limit. It was only once they were gone that I realised how much company and entertainment they had provided.

By the evening of the nineteenth of July, a Thursday and therefore within a whisker of a month at sea, we were struggling along in weather that was gyrating from total calm to violent squall, the sort of weather in which you never have the right sail set, which has you up and down all night engaged in endless short-lived adjustments, weather which can sorely test your evenness of temper. What's more, we had lost the luxury of eternal twilight. By midnight it was dark, depressingly so. This blackness signalled a return to normality; we were back to humdrum latitudes. Worse, we were once more within range of the shipping forecast. Had I felt so minded, I could have listened to The Archers. We were still, in fact, a hundred and thirty miles off the west coast of Ireland, but everything is relative, and I now felt more than relatively close to re-entry into the sphere of platitudinous living. The only prospect now was a descent into the dull and the predictable. I need not have been too concerned. Mother Nature still held one or two surprises up her capacious sleeve.

17

Early next morning I lay dozing on my narrow berth, trying to recuperate from a night of restless activity. The breeze had at last settled to a steady Force 4, still from the north-east, that had us loping along at a good pace in seas calmer than anything we had seen for a good week. A series of breathy explosions woke me and brought me to the hatch. They're back! Pilot whales were once more crowding alongside, with more and more piling in from astern. A great joy gripped me; I had never imagined that we would once again meet up with another vast herd of these creatures. They arrived so quickly and willingly and once more adopted *Mingming* so wholeheartedly that at first I assumed they were our old friends come to rejoin us. In terms of their numbers, and the manner of their arrival, homing in in small and separate pods of six or ten animals to form a massive densely-packed aggregation of whales, it was an exact copy of the visitation of ten days earlier. But the conditions in which we were now plunging along together could scarcely have been more different. With a fine wind on the quarter *Mingming* was in her element and making a good four or five knots. The whales could now range permanently alongside us, holding their position rather than looping round and round. With our increased speed they were now more enervated and athletic; I no longer felt that we were holding them back. We were now much more an equal part of the advancing horde rather than an ailing slowcoach in need of constant shepherding.

As the sun rose above the Irish hills somewhere to the east and occasionally pierced the banks of high cloud we were doused in a magnificent light, crystalline and hard-edged. The whales ranged out half a mile on the port beam were strongly back-lit, their backs and fins starkly black against a brilliant silver sea. Every droplet of their steamy breaths showed up as a tiny glinting diamond. Sometimes the puffs transmuted to shimmering rainbows for the few seconds before they dissipated, blown by the breeze to ragged shreds and then to nothing. The whales were showing themselves, literally, in a different light, and the effect was mesmerising. Those to starboard were bathed in a flood of sunshine that highlighted every detail of their complex markings and made their backs shine and sparkle as they surfaced. I could now see them below the surface and trace their rising and falling and their occasional criss-crossings underneath *Mingming's* hull.

We settled into our rhythm and for the next six hours raced along together. It was a much more muscular advance than the previous time, and exhilarating beyond measure as we were swept up in this great army of leaping flesh. We were now in the vanguard, at the head of a phalanx of at least two hundred whales that spread half a mile on either side. Our position and acceptance into these legionary ranks were unequivocal; we were at the head and at the centre. The whales had organised themselves in perfect symmetry beside and behind us. Once more I pondered on what might have caused this unlikely adoption of little *Mingming* into their formation. I could only guess. Perhaps it was a combination of her size, similar to that of a mature male, her black-painted bottom, her two bilge-keels that vaguely echoed their own fins, and her quiet progress, that set off some hints of recognition and easy acceptability. There was no doubt that *Mingming* exercised a strange attraction over the whales. We had now encountered large herds in two widely separated locations and under quite different physical conditions. Both times they had not only stayed with us for many hours, but had made us the focal point of their activity.

On we drove, hour after hour, companions of the road, fellow-travellers, caught up in our joint enterprise of making all speed to the south-east, our minds, for the moment, as one. As the whales surfaced I looked closely at their markings to see if I could recognise any specific individuals from our last encounter. Sometimes I saw similarities, but could not be sure. After a while I concluded that it was unlikely that this was the same group. We were nearly six hundred miles from the previous meeting point. I knew nothing of the territorial or migratory habits of the pilot whale, but the chances of a second crossing of paths so far away were infinitesimal. I later learned that despite the depredations of the Faroese annual whale hunt, pilot whale numbers in the north-east Atlantic are reckoned to be in excess of eight hundred thousand.

On we sped then, right throughout the morning, with *Mingming* at the head of her brawny entourage. Sometimes it seemed that we were the whales' adopted pilot and general as they fell in behind, following our every move. Sometimes we felt more like a prisoner-of-war, a prize trophy, as they crowded in on us, tightly, unrelentingly, blocking any route of escape. But mostly the mood was of simple communion and unbounded *joie de vivre*. We were all alive, and glad of it.

For a while I sat below and once more absorbed their unworldly melodies. Their chatter was, as before, endless. How I wished I could have penetrated the sense of it, but four billion years of evolutionary divergence lay between us, guaranteeing incomprehension. I sat below and watched them too, through *Mingming's* tiny portlights, entranced by the closeness and curvature of their dorsal profiles.

Midday came, and with it a change of mood. The herd began to separate out. Groups dropped off behind and soon, in an increasing wind, we were leaping along with just forty or fifty remaining whales. As before, their behaviour gradually changed. Perhaps they needed some rest after the last six hours of exertion, or perhaps it was the inverse – they needed to rest and breathe deeply prior to making their hunting dives; pilot whales can dive to six hundred metres, a prodigious depth, and stay down for as long as an hour. Whatever the reason, they once more entered a docile, sleepy phase, lying idly on the surface, and as we were making a good speed we left them behind, one by one, as they abandoned the race south and turned their minds to other things. One or two stood erect in the water and watched us go and before long we were alone again but for a few gannets, immature birds in their motley rig-outs of shaggy browns and oranges.

The whales were gone and the weather was once more changing; the north-easterly that had powered us southwards so effectively was reaching the end of its useful life. By the next morning we lay totally becalmed, rolling gently on the smoothest of seas. A large green and white fishing boat, the *Symphonie*, passed close by, heading north. For the first time in eight days I exited the hatch to go forward and un-gasket the light weather headsail. Despite the calm conditions I felt vulnerable on deck and was soon scuttling back into my little refuge like the lowliest of creepy-crawlies. I took a morning celestial sight followed up by a meridian altitude, whose resultant fix at least put us to the west of Ireland, and a very small shark, its rather floppy dorsal fin just showing above the glassy water, its tail fin weaving lazily from side to side, passed across our stern. Little breezes taunted us from the north-west or from the south-west or from nowhere at all. For a while it blew gently from the south-east too and for the first time in a long time we were close-hauled and not progressing directly along our ideal track.

The midday shipping forecast of July the twenty-second, our thirty-first day at sea, announced the approach of a deep depression. Gales were expected in Sole, Fastnet and Shannon. We were now comfortably within the Shannon sea area. For nearly three weeks we had been spared any really stormy weather. As we neared home that was about to change. A rapid series of low pressure systems, five within a week, were about to cross the southern British Isles, bringing a second round of floods and storm damage. Plymouth now lay just three hundred and fifty miles or so ahead, but as we neared the south-west tip of Ireland and moved into the Celtic Sea, the dangers would escalate. Bad weather was the last thing I wanted here. I would have to tread a careful path to ensure a successful conclusion to our voyage.

18

The southern part of the sky was now a heavy mass of black and threatening cloud. This thinned and lightened overhead, while to the north harmless puffy clouds hung brilliant against a wash of deepest azure. We were positioned directly below the edge of the cloud bank that defined the approaching storm. It was easy to imagine the satellite view, the lollipop swirl advancing east. We lay just beneath its northern margin, caught fair and square beneath a schizophrenic sky. Our route took us south into the dark side. Once again I was presented with the problem of weather routeing. The depression was, according to the forecast, heading south-east. In theory, then, we could hold our course without too much danger.

I turned north though, giving up many of our recent hard-won miles. As had already been shown during the early days of this voyage, these depressions winging in from the Atlantic change track quickly and unpredictably. They also have a habit of deepening as they approach, whipping up from half-gale to full gale to severe gale. Even though it was clear that at that moment we were out of the danger zone, I was not willing to head on south. Only a relatively small change in the track of the storm would put us on a collision course with its centre, and worse, from the least-favoured north-east sector. It was hard to run back the way we had come, in a freshening south-easterly, but it kept us just at the edge of the weather system and allowed me to track the route of the storm myself. Sometimes we emerged into blinding sunlight as we ran out from under the cloud shadow. Once or twice darker clouds overtook us, sprinkling us with a few drops of rain. The wind was rising and slowly backing into the east, but the blue sky to the north was undiminished and as the afternoon wore on, spread reassuringly south along the western horizon. I allowed *Mingming* to follow the wind round until she was running west.

I was not in the least surprised at the next shipping forecast. The depression's centre was now expected in Plymouth rather than North FitzRoy. Force 9's were starting to creep into the lexicon. It was the usual story. We were sailing the wrong way, but it was the right thing to do; I was determined to weight conditions in our favour, however long it took.

I had no illusions that keeping clear of the cloud bank would save us from experiencing a good blow. Sure enough, by eight that evening we were heading west under minimal sail, driven on by a meaningful Force 7 out of the east. The backing wind had by this time thrown up a royal mess of a sea and within an hour or two it was worse. We plunged and rolled on under a clearing sky that now allowed a star or two to glimmer through. An extravagantly illuminated Spanish fishing boat mooched right in our path and forced a gybe in the heavy seas, a manoeuvre that by now held no fears for me, and that I had learned to manage without even disconnecting the self-steering lines. The gybe had us heading almost south, and although I had not planned to turn south until the next morning, the disappearing cloud mass gave me confidence to carry on. By midnight we were lying under the sail bundle in a full gale, thrown around by the most uncomfortable seas we had so far met this voyage, and overseen by a million limpid stars and the numbing blackness of space without end.

The cold blast from the east slowly blew itself out. The severe gales of the depression's centre worked their way east with commendable attention to detail, sparing no-one: Plymouth, Portland, Wight, Dover, Thames, Humber; all were given their due care and attention. By the next night we were becalmed and rolling so heavily that I lashed the sail bundle hard down to the coach roof to escape the stress and irritation of its constant slatting and banging. A second consecutive dawn brought skies of a cold and breathtaking blue, a postpartum flood of unalloyed brilliance. It couldn't last and it didn't. Within a few hours an ugly agglomeration of rain cloud, mean-looking and business-like, rolled in from the south-west and the fun started. This time there could be no escape.

For three days, in seas that grew increasingly turbulent as the heavy winds veered and backed and threw up great cross-swells, three days in which *Mingming* took as comprehensive a pummelling as she had ever known, three days of angry skies and swingeing squalls as 'complex lows', to use the weatherman's terminology, passed close to the south and then to the north and then again to the north of us and kept us pinned down into a narrow holding pattern, three days of back and forth, hove-to and fore-reaching, sometimes to the north-west or the west, sometimes to the south-east but never for long, for those three long and miserable days, now just a grey blur in my memory, I worked to keep *Mingming* in an optimum position, sixty to seventy miles off the south-west tip of Ireland, still fringing the depths of the Porcupine Sea Bight, still clinging on to sea room and deep water, still notionally safe should the gyrating but predominantly onshore wind ratchet itself up beyond a mere severe gale. I prepared my series drogue for deployment, should it come to that. I stowed the ship's papers and my cameras and a short note into a now-empty watertight food container, just in case. Mostly I just sat there and clung on, depressed, downcast, sick to death of the whole damn thing.

These were the storms that caused the second round of that summer's mayhem across the British Isles. We were caught squarely in their track. It seemed unfair that after well over thirty days at sea, and now so close to home, we had to ride this gauntlet of storm piled upon storm, but fairness has no place in the rhythms of nature, in the restless systems of circulating air, in the never-ending interplay of pressure and temperature that drive the engines of planetary weather. There was nothing to be done but to accept it and buckle down to day after day of grinding discomfort. My strategy was simple: I had to wait for the right conditions before turning south-east proper to pass south of Fastnet and across the yawning gape of the Celtic Sea.

For three days, then, we threaded our way back and forth through seas of a confused and cold grey lashed by bouts of merciless rain, fore-reaching ten or so miles one way, then ten or so miles back, our course a scribble of lines crossing and re-crossing as we held a tight position between the six hundred metre and one thousand metre depth contours. Sixty miles under our lee lay a battery of unwelcoming headlands: Mizen Head, Three Castle Head, Sheep's Head, Black Ball Head, Crow Head, Lamb's Head, Hog's Head, Bolus Head, Bray Head, Duncalla Head, Dunmore Head, Clogher Head, Ballydavid Head, these bluffs themselves fringed by a scattering of rocky outposts: The Bull, Scarrif Island, The Skelligs, Valentia Island, the Blaskets. Narrow and treacherous fingers of sea clawed their way inland to Bantry and to Kenmare and to Castlemaine and there, seventy miles or so due east of our meanderings, lay the mythic crag itself – the Fastnet Rock.

It was a coastline I wanted no part of.

On the morning of Thursday the twenty-sixth of July,

our thirty-fifth day at sea, the last of the depressions sped off to the north-east, leaving us to a monumentally confused sea and, at last, a wind veering to the west. It was still a big wind, half a gale of it, but with the skies clearing to a piercing blue it seemed the moment to give *Mingming* her head and strike out across the Celtic Sea. As if to underline this new phase in our journey a container ship, the first merchant vessel we had met since the east coast of England, passed by a couple of miles on the port beam, heading north-west. Our own course was reciprocal, and with just one panel up, all that was needed in this finest of quartering breezes, we romped homewards, driven on by the endless lines of swells, some still breaking heavily. The frustrations and claustrophobia of the previous few days now counted for nothing as I sat in the hatch, revelling in the wild seascape and our rolling, tumbling ride through it. We were now on soundings, turning the sea a brilliant turquoise green. The wave tops curled into tons of thundering white water that dissipated, once they had crashed down, into huge saucers of foamy suds and swirling turbulence. Every hill-like wave face was pitted with a million cat's-paws, every surface ripple delineated in startling clarity by the sharp morning light. Further off some residual aspect of the previous days of gales infused the air with a slightly hazy quality, softening the horizon, such as it was, and adding a subtle touch to the monstrous beauty of the day. *Mingming* raced on through it all, sedate as ever, and my heart sang. I could not have been happier.

19

On we raced, and at noon that day I realised a curious fact: we were now at the most southerly latitude of our voyage. We had not exactly come full circle, but those hard-won degrees of northing, twelve in all, seven hundred and twenty sea miles, dragged one by one out of storm and calm and headwind, were now all dissipated, lost to the baroque curlicues and twists and turns and back and forth of our restless wake. Once more the tone of our enterprise was in flux. The ghosts of the Norsemen were gone. The tingle of imminent adventure too. All that lay at our backs. As we sped on across the Celtic Sea, the Fastnet Rock now well astern, my dividers now stretching ahead to measure off the remaining miles to the Scillies and to Land's End (Land's Beginning, of course, for the returning mariner) and to the Lizard and to Plymouth Sound itself, all the imaginative possibilities fell away to be replaced by the one final and over-riding obsession, deathly dull, the great imperative: a safe landfall.

Driven on by the easing westerly under yet another sky of faultless blue and, later, a searingly bright moon marred by only the slightest distortion to its jovial rotundity, we posted a day's run of eighty miles, eighty miles that brought us to the English side of this last span of open water. That morning marked the end of our fifth week at sea. Five weeks! Thirty-five days already! In the failing breeze I exited the hatch for the first time in a while to un-gasket and set the light weather jib. Later, after an afternoon of futile ghosting, we passed a small shark whose lazy surface drift mirrored our own.

The wind picked up a little. We trundled gently on through another night of unblemished starlight and a now perfect moon. A brightly lit ship overtook us on the starboard beam, heading east. Everything looked set fair for the final approach, but the weatherman thought otherwise. Yet another low was sweeping in. By then we were on the cusp of a right royal gaggle of shipping areas: Sole, Plymouth, Fastnet, Lundy, each with its own variation on the approaching theme. Take your pick. The depression was expected to pass through Lundy, just to the north of us. A half-gale from the south-west was forecast. We would soon be passing to the south of the Scillies and heading for the Lizard. It was not the most enticing of prospects – another blow as we closed the land and a spaghetti junction of big-ship motorways.

Once more we found ourselves under a bipartite sky. To the north a mess of heavy rain cloud spoke for the Lundy low, while to the south the last vestiges of a Biscay high hung on, benignly blue. Before too long, though, the last stratum of clear sky had dropped below the southern horizon, leaving us to the thickening gloom and a sudden rash of merchant shipping that hared past us at uncomfortably close quarters. The *African* (or possibly *American) Sanderling*, the *Chiquita Deutschland* and the *Pioneer,* a rather natty little container ship, painted a sparkling blue and sporting its own array of cranes for doing the dockside work, all shared, for a brief rumbling moment, our little patch of ocean space, while further off a parade of more aloof vessels passed east and west. Two fishing boats fished. By noon we were twelve miles to the south of Bishop's Rock and within a few hours the dirty weather was upon us.

I am rarely scared at sea. Preparation, patience and an adequate level of self-confidence are usually enough to keep the bogeymen at bay. Sleep, if circumstances allow it, is a good antidote to fear. On this, our last full day and night at sea, I could not allow myself to sleep and I was scared. When the filthy half-gale came in from the south-west, as expected, it came with a thick bank of driving misty rain that obscured the whole world beyond a radius of about one hundred miserable yards. Three hundred feet of visibility was all that protected us from the advancing prows of the hundred-thousand-ton ships that ply east and west in unending lines, day and night, along the narrow corridor in which we were now sailing. Three hundred rain-filled feet was all that now lay between us and the somnolent eyes of watch keepers more attuned to radar screens and digital chart plotters than the nasty physical reality of the world beyond the purring warmth of their bridge-decks. At twenty knots a ship would eat up those three hundred feet in approximately nine seconds. The reality was simple: should a ship appear out of the murk on a collision course with *Mingming*, it was unlikely that we would be seen, and absolutely certain that neither vessel would have time to take effective evasive action. We were, in a frightening and almost literal way, a sitting duck. *Mingming* of course carries a radar reflector, but in the short and steep sea that was quickly building I did not delude myself that it would be of much use.

All I could do was to keep a constant watch. For the best part of twelve hours I sat in the hatchway and forced myself into an endless sequence of three hundred and sixty degree scanning. *Mingming's* spray hood gave little protection; the half-gale from astern drove the rain straight in. The after end of the spray hood can be closed off with a length of canvas that is rolled down and lashed, leaving me to rely on the little portlights in the hatch coamings for watch keeping. But this was unsatisfactory; I simply did not have good enough vision in these conditions. Every second would be vital, should a ship bear down on us. Wearing my yellow oilskin top for the first time since the Dogger Bank storm, I sat out in the weather, often with the spray hood folded down to give better vision forward, and peered round and round again and round again. Within a minute or two my spectacle lenses were fogged with spray and rain, setting up another task to be repeated over and over: their drying and cleaning with a tear of kitchen roll. I kept up my vigil, then, for hour after hour, and never spotted a single ship. This gave me no comfort. I knew they were there. They are always there.

By ten that night, a night as black and inhospitable as you could hope for, it was blowing a near-gale and we were down to just the sail bundle. A big and breaking sea, short and uncomfortable, added to the miserable cocktail. There was one consolation in all of this, though: we were making good progress. The Lizard was now astern, somewhere to the north-west. I could now gybe *Mingming* and head north-east, clawing gradually out of the shipping lanes to safer waters. At midnight a cross-sea caught us and gybed *Mingming* involuntarily, sending her south with all her settings locked in opposition. It took me a while to unpick the mess and get *Mingming* once more settled on her northerly board.

Storms come and storms go. Within a couple of hours the cloud-base lifted and there, on our port beam, was the Lizard light, reassuringly where it should have been, stolidly tapping out its sequence of light and dark, as constant and immutable as the sculpted rock on which it lay. My mood rose with the cloud. Now to leeward of the Lizard, with Plymouth Sound not far ahead and, if needed, the sheltered waters of the Fal just a short hop to the north of us, there was no reason we could not complete our voyage as planned. It was still blowing hard. *Mingming* was still taking the occasional hefty thump on the port quarter. I didn't care. The lines of big ships were now behind us. We had run the gauntlet and were still here, battling on through the fading night. Nothing could stop us now.

20

By breakfast time it was raining heavily again, but the wind had dropped completely and swung round to the north. We ghosted along in a smoothing sea and I caught up on sleep, euphoric catnaps interspersed with long perusals of the Cornish hills now spread grey and murkily across the northern horizon. A ship, its sides sporting the cryptic announcement BELUGA PROJECTS in monumental lettering, passed us, heading west. Two yachts, the first I had seen since the River Crouch, cut across our faint wake, bound for France. Four fishing boats clustered around an evidently fruitful patch. The rain continued. I raised the light weather jib, giving us enough momentum at least to produce a bubble or two at the bows. A little blue coaster, the *Irina Trader,* of Valletta, passed close on the starboard beam. I studied the officer of the watch with my binoculars. He returned the compliment. He and his glasses and his ship soon disappeared, but within thirty minutes they were back, or so I thought, until proximity revealed that this little blue coaster, so similar in size and configuration to the *Irina Trader*, was in fact the *Elspeth*. She in turn disappeared, and so too did the Cornish coast, lost behind a thickening veil of rain. We were back once more to nothing but sea and sky. Perhaps it was better that way.

On we drifted in a monochromatic dreamland, starved of colour and angle and edge, the featureless wash of the north, now so familiar and welcoming, transposed to this unnamed bay between the Lizard and the Start, a final reminder of our sub-Arctic days before it lifted for the last time, unveiling the contours of Cornwall and now Devon and caressing them with the soft sheen of an imminent sun. By noon I was astonished to find that we were only twenty-two miles from Rame Head, the conical guardian of Plymouth Sound. Some tidal eddy had evidently given us a timely push homewards.

It was late afternoon when the north-westerly change finally set in, rousing me out of my siesta and sending the last of the cloud scurrying off. A fresh leading wind and an unblemished sky! Eddystone light on the starboard beam! To the north the hills of Devon, all aglow under the westering sun, their curves and rifts and indents an echo of some great petrified seascape, nevertheless spoke solidly of the earth, of field and hedgerow and winding lane and, as we closed the coastline, bringing its broad wash into a focus of finer detail, of the less pretty too, for here now were the hard edges of sea-side conurbations, cubist montages of rectangles and squares and triangular gables and rooflines, tumbling and crowding from hilltop to water's edge, starkly at odds with the flow of the land, crudely superimposed, and reminding me that we would soon be back to the human press. A sliver of sea and a few hours were now all that kept us from the seething frenzy of life ashore.

It was a Sunday evening. The last of the weekenders had long gone as we passed under the lee of Rame Head, now black against the setting sun, and entered Plymouth Sound. There was no hurry. Ahead to port lay Cawsand Bay. We would fetch up there for the night and lie to anchor. We plugged gently on. There was no hurry. This was the moment to savour. Land was now close to, unthreatening, its rocky edge washed by the easy, sighing break of the faintest of swells. The slopes, heavily wooded, rose almost sheer out of the sea. I breathed the late evening odours that drifted off the shore, a heady mix of leaf-mould and summer grasses and somewhere in there the tang of wood smoke, all wrapped tight into a cool parcel and wafted our way by the dying north-westerly. It was the bitter-sweet moment of landfall, of voyage's end. The elation of an adventure safely accomplished was tempered by an undercurrent of regret. The purity and simplicity of life aboard *Mingming*, the reduction of existence to a primeval sparseness, the stripping away of all artifice and ambition in a bid to confront the raw nature of nature itself, would soon, for a while at least, be left behind.

I abandoned the warmth of the cabin and for the first time since leaving Burnham unhooked the tiller lines and started hand-steering. Penlee Point, the seaward extremity of Cawsand Bay, now lay a hundred metres to windward. Night had fallen, but a clear sky and the loom of a million lights from Plymouth and the Sound lit our way around the point and into our final beat to the head of the bay. We ghosted back and forth, sometimes accelerating to a mild puff, sometimes scarcely moving, bringing the lights of the town of Cawsand itself slowly closer. A little way off the shore I went forward and prepared the anchor, breaking its many lashings and unsealing the chain pipe. On we ghosted, now amongst the yachts moored and anchored a short way off the beach. It was nearly midnight. The stillness was palpable. I chose my spot and let go the anchor. Within a few minutes we were lying in total tranquillity, bathed by the shore-lights of the sleeping town. I cooked and ate a huge pan of food, then joined the landsfolk in their long and strangely stable slumber.

21

Habits die hard. I was still up and down during the night, still restless, still needing to look and check, look and check. Dawn came and I watched the little town wake up. Monday morning. My head was bursting with the imagery of our voyage, with whales and storms and endless tracts of empty sea, with wild islands and the glare of a distant glacier, with the sweetness of solitude, with the tingle and rush of proximate and ever-present danger. I stared at the façade of gaily-coloured houses along the waterfront as they came to life, normal workaday life ashore. Blinds and curtains and then front-doors and then car doors opened and the murmur of traffic revved itself up and voices broke the stillness of the bay and the daily round began. I watched, disconnected, unsure of my relation to it all.

At ten that morning, in the most fitful of north-westerlies that played cat and mouse under a clear sky, I got the anchor and headed out of the bay. My aim was to get us to the Cattewater at about low water at one, and into Queen Anne's Battery marina. It was as well I left plenty of time for this final short hop of five miles or so; the breeze came in gutless patches and our progress against the neap ebb was pitiful. We worked our way slowly past Drake Island and across the main shipping lane, happily empty of ferries and frigates, and up to the shoulder of Plymouth Hoe. I broke out my hand-held VHF radio from its waterproof container, loaded it with its batteries, and called up the marina. My voice, unused for nearly six weeks, had atrophied to a dry croak. After a long and awkward exchange, comprising questions about *Mingming's* size and our proposed length of stay from the marina and pleadings for a berth from myself, I was told that the marina could not take us. The Fastnet Race was finishing there in a few days' time. The marina was all booked up. We would have to go elsewhere. I tried Plymouth Yacht Haven, a little further up the Cattewater, on the opposite side. They had a berth available, and even better, it was on the outside pontoon. I could sail *Mingming* on to it.

Relieved, I headed up the Cattewater. It was still slack water. There was just enough of a zephyr from astern to push us through the lines of cruising yachts and sailing school dinghies moored just off the shore. I prepared a couple of lines and, having identified our spot on the pontoon, progressively lowered the mainsail as we ran gently in. With just a panel or two set I played the main halyard to control our speed as the wind puffed and died and puffed again. I could not have asked for an easier approach or for a calmer, more tranquil day. We crept up to the pontoon and I threw a line to a blond-haired guy of uncertain years who was standing there. Voyage over. Peace.

HEY GUYS!!! the line-taker on the pontoon suddenly yelled in a voice whose decibel count was probably verging on the illegal, *TAKE A LOOK AT THIS!!!* He had turned and was shouting towards a massive yacht tied up further along the pontoon.

Interesting boat, mate, he said to me, his Australian accent loud and clear, *what's that rig you've got there?*

It's a junk.

HEY GUYS!!! SHE'S A JUNK!!!

Message relayed, he turned back to me and spoke conversationally.

Looks like you're in from a good voyage. Where you been?

Iceland.

HEY GUYS!!! JUST IN FROM ICELAND!!! I was glad my mainsail was lowered; the blast from his mighty voice could well have blown out a panel or two. He turned back to me again.

How long you been at sea, mate?

Thirty-eight days.

HEY GUYS!!! YOU GET THAT? THIRTY-EIGHT DAYS AT SEA!!!

And so it went on. Every detail of our voyage was relayed immediately and with stentorian clarity to the 'guys'. These were half a dozen or so men and women lounging in the cockpit of a gargantuan expedition yacht, sixty or seventy feet long, new and shiny and bristling with every appointment and gizmo imaginable: *Mingming's* antithesis incarnate. They were the paying crew. My new-found publicity agent, who with brute Australian effectiveness had, I felt, broadcast our arrival and the raw outline of our adventure to Plymouth Yacht Haven, both shores of the Cattewater, the surrounding townships and the Devon coastline at least as far as Bigbury-on-Sea, was its skipper. No better man on earth, I thought, for getting a message to the fore deck in a Southern Ocean gale.

He drifted off and I was left to tidy up the ship and to enjoy that final moment of review and contemplation before stepping ashore. *Mingming* and I had now completed our second ocean voyage together, most of it under a patched-up rig. My confidence in the boat's ability had risen immeasurably; the ease with which she had handled the severest of weather had seen to that. I had learned new and unexpected techniques to keep her up to windward in gale conditions. The most recent modifications had brought

Mingming's ease of management and comfort to a new level. I had been on deck less than a dozen times in nearly a month and half at sea. Secure, dry and mostly warm in the haven of the cabin, relaxed under an unstressed and supremely flexible rig, I had moved that much nearer to the ideal I was striving for.

The winter ahead would be busy, nonetheless. I would have to rebuild the broken battens. The upper panels of the sail were in poor shape and would need many hours of work with needle and palm to make them sea-ready once again. I had already started sketching a design for a new mast-head fitting. I was unhappy with the angle of the upper main halyard block; towards the end of the voyage it had become increasingly difficult to set the last few feet of the full mainsail.

I pushed those thoughts away. Now was not the time. It was more appropriate, in these final minutes, to think back over our voyage and what had been accomplished. It had not been a total success. The Arctic Circle had eluded us. We had not managed to sail up an Icelandic fjord. That was disappointing, but not unduly so. I had little doubt that we would make another foray north before too long. The experience I had garnered would be invaluable. I would have a much better idea of how to go about it. More importantly, the attraction of those northern seas had now gone beyond a mere romantic notion. The reality had exceeded all expectation. The imaginary and the abstract had been translated into a deep-seated visceral knowledge, hot-blooded and physical. I had brushed the cool cheek of the north with a tentative would-be lover's kiss, but I knew now that I wanted more. Sooner or later I would take her to myself, unequivocally.

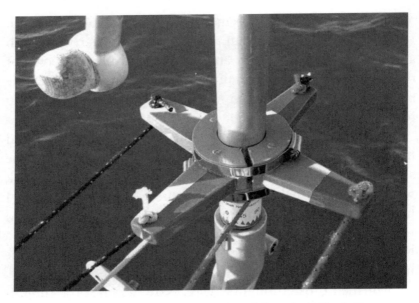

*My home-made remote control for the Windpilot
self-steering gear.*

*The new hatch coamings and folding spray hood viewed
from inside* Mingming.

Worsening weather off the Dogger Bank.

Mingming's *jury rig, mainly boat hooks and gaffer tape. We sailed well over two thousand miles under these patched up battens.*

'Before long they were crowding in right alongside...'

*'The whales had organised themselves in perfect symmetry
beside and behind us.'*

*'...their backs and fins starkly black
against a brilliant silver sea.'*

'Those to starboard were bathed in a flood of sunshine...'

PART TWO

HEADWINDS

As the day wore on the outlook worsened. An army of intimidating rain squalls, grotesque engines of war expanding blackly skywards, massed on the windward horizon. They were clearly up to no good, this lot, and they scared me a little. For once I reefed early, just in case, but in tune with the reigning schizophrenia of the moment it was not this lumbering bank of cloud that did for us, but the limpid evening sky that followed. At ten a squall came out of nowhere, a sudden blast which had us going from full sail to two panels in half a minute, an almost unheard of reduction in area for which I blessed the instant reefing ability of Mingming's rig, and which underlined the craziness of the weather. This was as nothing, though, to what followed.

1

The concept of the Jester Challenge was by now firmly established. In 2006 ten yachts, all of them thirty feet or less in length, most of them modest cruising craft, had left Plymouth for a single-handed 'race' to Newport, Rhode Island. The event, untroubled by the usual trappings of modern ocean racing - rules, for example, or committees, or entry fees, or inspections, or the demands of corporate sponsors, publicists, media executives and marketing consultants – and studiously unreceptive to anything that might hint at brouhaha, razzmatazz or song-and-dance, had been a quiet if unremarkable success. Two yachts had finished; eight, including *Mingming*, had retired gracefully. However there are no rules and therefore no time limits and therefore no reason why any starter cannot have another crack, which is exactly what the Australian Jester Challenger John Apps did. Frustrated in 2006 by a broken shroud that had reduced him to sailing on one tack only, a limiting though not terminal handicap, John set off again in 2007 aboard his UFO 27 *Glayva* and successfully reached Newport. In so doing John became the third finisher in an elapsed time of a mere four hundred and twenty days, twenty hours and fifty minutes. Nothing could better illustrate what the Jester Challenge is all about: unaided personal achievement, serious and seamanlike, but in an unbuttoned and somewhat batty context.

The elusive, slightly anarchic ethos of the Jester Challenge, with its antipathy towards any form of controlling authority and its consequent focus on total individual responsibility in the matter of sea-going, had touched a deep nerve somewhere within the yachting corpus. Despite the low profile and modest outcome of the first Jester Challenge, interest had soared and entries were pouring in for future events. The original idea had been for a transatlantic race every four years. However it was soon clear that four years was too long a gap to feed the spirit and enthusiasm that had quickly developed between Jester Challengers, existing and potential. Some sort of intermediate event was required. So the Jester Azores Challenge was born. This too would be every four years, intersecting the transatlantic races. As well as keeping everyone together and interested, the Jester Azores Challenge would be a good testing ground for skippers newer to ocean sailing. A one-way contest of about twelve hundred nautical miles, it was a much less daunting prospect than a full transatlantic voyage. Our cruise for 2008 had therefore already been determined; we would be sailing to the Azores and back. It was only the Jester Challenge that could get me heading south. My mind was still firmly focused on those northern wastes. I was already mulling over the where and when and how of our next voyage towards the Arctic. A plan was already taking shape, but it would have to wait.

Within a few days of her arrival at Plymouth, *Mingming* was hauled out and transported by road back to Burnham-on-Crouch. I had neither the time nor the inclination to make the long coastal passage. We had done it both ways the previous year but it now seemed a pointless exercise. *Mingming* had by now been honed for blue water sailing and that was all I really wanted to do.

For a month or two I dithered over what to do about *Mingming's* mainsail and battens. The two upper panels of the sail were in a sorry state. Yards of hasty hand stitching, frail and unravelling seams, gaping batten pockets, torn by the sharp ends of the fractured battens, all combined to form a picture of near total destruction. Three of the five battens were broken. It was not a pretty picture. For a while I considered scrapping the lot and buying a new sail and the latest thing in alloy articulating battens. It was a tempting prospect. I could chuck away the sail and old battens, save myself hours of tedious sewing and repairs, and take to the water the following year sporting a shiny and up-to-the-minute rig. Perhaps *Mingming* deserved it.

On an un-seasonally warm and sunny afternoon in late September I dragged everything out and spread it on the lawn. For half an hour or so I sat in a chair and surveyed the wreckage. I walked round the sail and examined all the tears and holes and damaged seams. I went over all my hand stitching and considered the state of the sail cloth, particularly at the leech. I looked hard at the broken battens and thought about how they could best be repaired. I reflected on whether I wanted to spend an amount not far off the original cost of *Mingming* on a new rig. More importantly, I reviewed and re-established what it was I was trying to achieve with *Mingming*. I reminded myself that the boundless satisfaction that sailing her gave me was derived from achieving the most with the least; that the guiding principle of simplicity in everything was bound up too with a philosophy of make do and mend; that, for me at any rate, *Mingming* symbolised an antithesis to crass and thoughtless over-consumption; that, in short, to lash out on expensive new gear, in preference to buckling down to a few hours of hard work and reviving the existing sail and battens, would be a kind of betrayal. By the end of the afternoon my mind was made up; I would rebuild the rig myself. I was sure I could get at least one more voyage out of it.

I immediately felt happier and set to work with a will. Once more I had plenty to occupy myself with during the long winter months. The fractured wooden cores of the upper battens were re-scarphed with spare timber from my store. The plastic piping in which these fitted was bought for about twenty pounds. I spent hours unstitching and re-sewing seams and earlier repairs to the sail. The torn batten pockets were re-stitched by hand. A long patch was cut from an old Bermudan jib found in the garage and Brenda, my long-suffering partner and dab hand as a seamstress, got to work with her sewing machine, applying it to the suspect leech. The resultant sail, as worn and patched as a pair of street urchin's trousers, would not have won prizes in any *concours d'élégance*, but what did I care? All that mattered was that it should be fit for the job in hand; the rest was mere frippery.

Meanwhile a new stainless steel masthead fitting, uncompromisingly robust, was being made and fitted. This enabled the main and jib halyard blocks to hang well clear of the mast, allowing the ropes to run cleanly in their sheeves. I had never fully trusted the original attachment points for the halyards, D-rings pop-riveted to the mast. The replacement arrangement, a masterpiece of adaptive naval architecture, whose final fitting was overseen by my marine engineer friend Simon Dunn, was an over-built and heart-warming belt-and-braces job, a far cry from the prissy flimsiness of modern yacht gear.

That winter did not pass without major expenditure, though. I decided to buy a road trailer for *Mingming*. This would enable me to trail her to whatever departure point was appropriate for the voyage in hand. No longer having to pay professional transporters, I would recoup the cost of the trailer within a year or two. It would also be much more convenient; co-ordinating the obtuse timetables of marinas and boatyards and hauliers for the lifting out, transporting and lifting off of *Mingming* had been something of a nightmare, and proof, if it were needed, that my usually placid temperament was still susceptible to the odd bout of rage.

The start of the Jester Azores Challenge was scheduled for 1400 hours on Saturday the thirty-first of May. At five in the morning of the Saturday two weeks before the start we hitched a stripped-out *Mingming* to the car and set off for Plymouth. The early departure time was partly designed to give me a bit of towing practice while the roads were still empty. Apart from a few anxious moments of huffing and puffing up the steep gradients past Exeter race-course the journey went surprisingly well, and by midday we were safely parked at Queen Anne's Battery marina. Two years previously it had taken me about a month to make the same distance by sea. This is not, of course, to decry coastal sailing; a Force 7 south-westerly off Portland Bill is still a more enticing prospect than nose-to-tail jams on the M5 motorway, and often more productive of forward progress.

My all-purpose sculls, fifteen feet long and doubling, or trebling, as jury spars, jury steering oars and, for a while, as provisional bowsprits, were now seconded to newer and even more exciting duties as sheer-legs for raising the mast. I hadn't tried this before and decided to proceed slowly. The marina had got me to slot *Mingming* into a row of expensive-looking powerboats. Any error of judgement leading to the mast going by the board, as it were, could well be costly; I was not at all convinced that my third party insurance extended to damage caused by boy-scout type shenanigans in marina boat parks. Saturday afternoon was spent erecting the sculls into a kind of A-frame, strengthened by cross-braces made from boat hooks, and well-anchored fore and aft. A block and tackle, hung at the top lashing of the A-frame about fourteen feet above the deck, would serve to haul the mast upright and against the frame. The mast would then have to be lifted manually, by means of a kind of bear-hug, and lowered through the partners to its step on the keel. Having had a long day I was not game to translate theory into practice there and then, and decided to sleep on it.

On Sunday morning I was at least partially refreshed after a night well-laced with mental rehearsals of the exercise, one or two of which ended with the spar eluding our control and crashing down through the pristine cabin-tops of the boats alongside. I need not have worried. The first piece of luck was the arrival of a very fit young couple at their racing yacht parked not far off. They willingly agreed to help us. Two extra pairs of hands gave me the confidence to get on with it. After one false start we quickly had the mast upright and reassuringly secure against the A-frame. A minute later the mast was in place and through-bolted to its step. Job done. More luck was to come. I had agreed with the marina management that *Mingming* would be launched sometime during the following week. The mast was hardly up when the yard foreman came along and asked me if I'd like them to put her in there and then. *Yes, please!* I would much rather return home knowing that *Mingming* was safely afloat. We would come back the following weekend with the sail bundle and all *Mingming's* sea-going gear.

By late Sunday afternoon *Mingming* was lying quietly at the visitors' pontoon, quite alone; the typically wet and rumbustious spring weather had discouraged even the hardiest sailors from a bout of early cruising. The tranquillity of the marina would not last. Jester Challengers, well over forty of them at the last count, were on their way to Plymouth. They were coming from all over: from the west coast and from the east coast, from Lancashire and from Wales, from Newcastle and from Yorkshire, from the

Channel Islands and from the Solent. But that was not the half of it. They were coming too from France and from Switzerland and from Belgium, from Sweden and from Russia. It was strange to think of all that effort and activity, spread so wide, underpinned by so many hopes and fears, all aimed at bringing so many yachts together at this one point where we now lay. Within ten days or so they would all be here; ordinary sailors in modest boats, fired by a collective will. It would be a privilege to be amongst them.

2

They came all right. From far and wide they came, until the visitors' pontoon was a heaving mass of wondrously diverse sea-going hardware, rafted alongside, four or five or six boats deep. Here were a thousand dreams and aspirations made real. Here was the voice of Everyman, raised loud and saying simply: *I can do it.* From far and wide they came, and none came further than Alexei Fedoruk, twenty-one days out from Saint Petersburg, non-stop, single-handed, his boat *Fason* self-built, painstakingly resurrected from the abandoned hulk of a wooden Dragon, every last part, down to the very screws and piston hanks, machined by his own hand. Compatriot Vitaly Elagin had sailed from Sweden and run the blockade of French fisherman at Cherbourg, dodging thrown bottles and potential rammings, to be there. Dominique Katan had trucked his yacht *Nea-Kameni* from Marseilles to northern France, then sailed the last leg. The weather was still not kind, with fierce north-easterly gales, but still they came, boats sleek, boats fat, boats, in the main, of a certain age, boats sporting every kind of self-steering contrivance, boats the apple of every skipper's eye, boats lovingly prepared, boats shown off with pride, still they came, at all hours, a stream of boats jamming the marina to capacity. Each new arrival set off a stir of interrogation and conjecture, attracted its little crowd of assessors. *So-and-so's here!* For two years the skippers and their craft had been little more than names on a list. Now they were filling space rather than computer screens. Hands were shaken, backs slapped. Flesh was put on a thousand e-mail exchanges. Most of the old Jester Challengers from 2006 were back. How could they not be? But this was now of a different scale as the boats kept coming. And what boats! Here was *Golden Dragon,* Graham Jewitt's junk-rigged Kingfisher 20, sporting her livery of the brightest and most uncompromising yellow and a startingly remodelled superstructure. Here once again was Bill Churchouse's Westerly 22 *Belgean,* as tubbily robust as one would expect a shipwright's floating home to be. Here too was the Royal Navy (Rtd.): Tony Head's Twister *Triple Venture,* back for another crack after a comprehensive electrical failure in 2006, and the Westerly Griffon *Pippin,* skippered by ex-naval captain John Gozzard and looking appropriately ship-shape. *And what on earth is this? Extraordinary!* Here was Peter Taylor's 5.5 Metre *Ballerina,* as slim and sprightly as her name implied, an aristocrat amongst the commonest of folk, plucked from her sheltered life on a Swiss lake, given a provisional lid and, of all things, a swing rig, and now ready for some real sailing. They all came, then, a hotchpotch of shapes and styles, with a catamaran and a trimaran, transatlantic veteran Nick Barham's *Tahiti Belle,* thrown in for good measure.

The diversity of the yachts, an edifying contrast to the identikit industrial clonage of the typical ocean racing fleet, was matched by that of their skippers. Here was the whole of society in miniature, from banker to bricklayer or, if you prefer, from bricklayer to banker, from twenty-something to pensioner, from the cash-strapped to the more-than-comfortably-off. Cut-glass accents interwove with meandering regional diphthongs and nobody gave a damn. There were no delusions here. The sea does not judge a man by his wallet or his provenance or his clubbability. There were more fundamental qualities at stake now, and everybody knew it.

They came, the skippers, not in a spirit of competition, but with the strongest sense of cooperation. They were not here to out-do each other; a mindless obsession with 'winning' held no sway here. The common goal was the success of the greatest number of participants. Success meant, firstly, arriving in the Azores in good order or, should circumstances militate against that, making port, wherever appropriate, in a seamanlike manner. As the boats crowded together in the lead-up to the off, so too did the skippers, freely exchanging advice and information, helping each other with last-minute fittings and repairs, giving spare items to those that needed them, joking, joshing, creating friendships, united by a simple idea.

There were the occasional moments of formality. Under a leaden sky and a steady downpour the skippers huddled on the deck of *Black Velvet*, Ewen Southby-Tailyour's gaff cutter, for the pre-race briefing. It was mercifully and, given the aversion of the participants to rule-makers and committee-wallahs, unsurprisingly brief, allowing us to pass quickly on to the more character-building business of helping Ewen dispose of the industrial quantities of real black velvet shipped aboard for the event. The formal dinner at the Royal Western Yacht Club ended in tears, tears of riotous laughter as yachting journalist and cartoonist Jake Kavanagh gave a masterly display of stand-up comedy based on his time as a Thames lock-keeper.

At last, just a day before the start, *Jester* herself arrived, by road. There could be no Jester Challenge without her. Blondie Hasler's original *Jester* had of course been lost at sea, mortally damaged when returning from a transatlantic race with skipper Mike Richey. Mike had subsequently made countless Atlantic crossings in the new *Jester*, the last at the age of eighty. This iconic yacht, still as revolutionary in its concept as the day it was launched, still growing in stature as a symbol of a certain kind of ocean sailing based on simple and uncompromising self-sufficiency, was now in the competent hands of Trevor Leek. She is the embodiment of all the Jester Challenge stands for. Her arrival gave the fleet its true heart, its soul, its completeness.

Mike Richey came too. Now into his nineties, as alert and solicitous as ever, held in awe by every Jester Challenge skipper, Mike provides the human link with almost half a century of single-handed transatlantic sailing and the proof of the rejuvenatory powers of a life spent at sea. His quiet presence on the pontoon, a shake of his hand, a nod of approval, were enough to make the skippers aware, perhaps for the first time, that they were indeed part of a continuum, that they were taking up a baton that had come perilously close to loss and abandonment. *Jester* and her ilk, small and simple yachts, had been excluded from the race they had pioneered; under Mike's kindly eye the Jester Challenge skippers were breathing new life into old values.

At midday on Saturday the thirty-first of May the fleet began to unravel the lines that held it together, dismantling the floating village. The mood was still jocular, good-natured, supportive, but somewhere in there was a new element, a hint of something darker, more introspective. For many of the skippers, perhaps the majority, this was the start of their first ocean voyage. It is no small thing, to cast off mooring ropes and head seawards, properly seawards, for the first time. It matters not a jot that thousands have done it before, thousands will follow. There is only a limited comfort to be had from a surrounding fleet. This is an intensely personal moment, an end and a beginning. The ties that bind are, as it were, cut. Behind now lies all that is warm and familiar, ahead lies...what? The soothing fluids of life ashore are soon to be replaced by a cold and implacable sea. The known, the regular, the habitual, all the building blocks and rituals that impose a veneer of order and meaning, are now cast aside. All that remains is a disorderly uncertainty. The givens are gone. Somewhere deep down in every skipper's psyche lies the unanswered, gnawing question: *Can I cope?* Small wonder, then, that the smiles and waves were interspersed with brief moments of distracted seriousness.

The weather was lousy: overcast, showery, virtually no wind. Denis Gorman aboard his Virgo Voyager *Auld Meg* had promised to tow *Mingming* out. The start was to be across a line stretching one mile west of the western breakwater. In the calm conditions we motored right to the mouth of Cawsand Bay before casting off the tow. A few minutes later *Black Velvet* arrived and anchored, now the outer marker for the starting line. The fitful southerly zephyr meant that we would have a windward start and soon forty or so yachts were jilling around on the line, stealing each other's air, scarcely moving, and the little island of Terceira, our goal twelve hundred long miles away, may as well have been on the moon. The spectator boat cruised around the fleet and there to entertain them aboard his Tomahawk 25 *Culica* was George Jepps, rotund and comprehensively bearded, wearing a jester's hat, bells and all, and piercing the early afternoon quiet with manic laughter and a display of yodelling.

The gun went and slowly, for the most part agonisingly slowly, the fleet beat its way seawards past Rame Head. The light displacement speedsters, Dominique Katan's Mistral 25 *Nea-Kameni,* Roger Fitzgerald's Dehler 29 *Ella Trout III,* for instance, pulled smoothly away, but most of us, the shrimps and minnows, common-or-garden cruising yachts, nothing special, worked our way out to sea at a more considered pace. It could have been worse, though, for before long a little breeze got up from the north-west and with the light weather jib set, the sheets eased, the self-steering now engaged and myself comfortably settled in below, with everything, that is to say, adjusted back to proper sea-going mode, *Mingming* ghosted away from the line of hazy hills astern.

It was a magical evening, diffused with an orange glow from a sun hung low and lazily behind a veil of mist. Under orange sails we drifted past the Eddystone Light, its tower too tinted with orange tones. An orange sea heaved gently beneath us. We were still not alone. Seven or eight yachts were ranged around, close and far, some to seaward, some towards the land, their sails in soft and grainy focus, all movement imperceptible. For a while the world stopped and we hung there, waiting for a wind, waiting for adventure, suspended. Night fell and with it came breeze and movement and, at last, the rush and bubble of water under the fore-foot and the sure knowledge that we were on our way.

3

On our way. For the third time in two years we crept away from land and I began to see, just a shade more clearly, what needs and motives underpinned these little voyages. To define simplicity is a complex enough business, to justify it is a great deal harder, but now, as the fleet around us dissolved below the horizons and we were left once more to our own little acreage of ocean and an unimpeded sky, I finally grasped an elusive thought. This tiny yacht, as basic and unencumbered as I knew how to make it, stripped as bare as I dared, remoulded by the work of my own hands, its economy rated in pence, as it were, rather than in pounds, was not just an exercise in uncompromising practicality; it was the halting expression of a world-view. Time was when a man could take himself off into the deepest woods and build himself a hut from self-hewn logs. In his ten by ten palace he could contemplate the folly of human aspiration and its ensuing servitude. He could reflect that the necessaries of life are few and that the man who has those and nothing more also has true freedom. *Mingming* was, as much as anything else, my frugal little hut, the ocean my wilderness.

It was only the coming back that made me realise how much I had missed it. For ten months I had suppressed a deep yearning. As the land fell away behind so too did the manacles of worldly obligation. Ahead lay a month or two of unalloyed freedom, the true freedom of simple self-sufficiency. I was beholden to nothing and to nobody. My timetables and rhythms were set by wave and wind. What joy, to be liberated from the dictatorship of the desk diary! This is not to say that I did not have work to do, and important work at that. The job of surviving ranks the highest. It is a noble occupation, and its greatest perk, aside from the reward of continued existence, is that it is unpaid. For two months I would no longer be selling whatever skills I may have acquired over the years. Life was no longer a pecuniary bargain, an oppressive trading floor in human commodity. I could now work, rather than labour. I could, for instance, devote much of my energy into doing nothing. To do nothing is an art not easily learned; like all subtle and worthwhile accomplishments it requires effort and practice. I now had too the time and freedom to look. I could look at the sky. Even better, I could look at the sea. There are few more profitable pastimes. I could think too, not the dull and linear thoughts of workaday, land-bound existence, but serendipitous, corner-of-the-eye thoughts that come from not really thinking, or from not thinking too hard, or from the liberation of the mind from strictly required processes. If I wanted relief from the exactions of doing nothing, if pure and undirected thinking became too burdensome, then I could take a break and write something down: a word perhaps, even a whole sentence.

This little boat, then, scarcely more than a few cubic feet of living space and taking up therefore as little of the known universe as is possible for a man's needs, this boat perched precariously at the interface between the deep ocean and limitless space is not, as might be supposed, some sort of temporary prison cell to be endured. Not at all. *Mingming* is the agent of my liberation. I am never more free than when enclosed in her modest capsule.

Taking this fruitful line of rumination a little further, it also occurred to me, while once again bidding farewell to the Lizard, that the limits of my liberty were in direct proportion to the simplicity of my yacht. Our man in his crude hut congratulates himself that he is free from the expense and upkeep of the trappings of fancy architecture; a man can soon enslave his life to the maintenance of Doric columns and heated swimming pools. Complexity breeds its own tyranny. It is no different afloat. Sitting so low in the water, as it were, *Mingming* and I had nowhere to fall. There was therefore nothing to worry about, nothing, that is, beyond regulating *Mingming's* sail to the wind of the moment, keeping us to our course, and maintaining a regular enough round of bodily intake and evacuation to ensure that the weird assemblage of cells known as myself kept some sort of a hold on life. Beyond that, all was untrammelled leisure or, to put it differently, undiluted freedom. *Mingming's* relative slowness, a function of her short waterline length and unhurried rig, further worked in my favour. A chap sailing a fast yacht is expected to get wherever he is going quickly. He is therefore prey to his own expectations and worse still, to everybody else's. He can scarcely be expected to take much pleasure from a few days of total calm or a punishing headwind. He needs to be getting on! He is unlikely to be receptive to the beauties of a mirrored ocean. Perish the thought that he should hang over the side and celebrate his immobility by peering long and hard into the glutinous depths; he is more likely to be fussing with a limp spinnaker. And of course the sailor who arrives well ahead of the pack has only succeeded in surrendering his freedom, if he ever really had it, in double-quick time. I have never fully understood the sailor's preoccupation with achieving the fastest possible passages; it seems to imply a desire to spend as little time at sea as possible. It is a reduction of sea-going to a technical exercise, which is fine as far as it goes, but it is also a kind of negation, a country walk undertaken on a Hell's Angel motorbike.

In light airs, then, mainly from the north, and the occasional calm, we worked our way out towards the Little Sole Bank and the pelagic depths. It was a slow start, but I was unconcerned. The voyage would take as long as it was going to take. I would of course always sail *Mingming* as well as I could, but with a proper respect for her limitations. I was by now, after two long voyages, more adept at sensing when she was in harmony and balance with sea and wind, more skilled at recognising what small adjustments would encourage that state of grace whereby she seemed to float, not in water, but on a cushion of air. I was not after speed at any price; I did not necessarily want to sail quickly, but to sail well. Sometimes there is a conjunction between the two, giving the best of both worlds, but from time to time the fastest sailing introduces an overtone of ugliness, a false note that I found increasingly unbearable. It was my growing conviction that the more attentive I was to these nuances of tuning, keeping *Mingming* progressing in well-tempered concord, the better she would look after me.

4

As we cleared the land and struck out into the Western Approaches the north-westerly raised itself a few notches and *Mingming* showed that she is not necessarily a slowcoach. Fully laden with two months' water and provisions she still clocked up a day's run of ninety-five nautical miles followed by another of ninety-two, two days of fine sailing that took us off soundings and into the Atlantic proper. The heavily repaired sail and battens were evidently working well. I had quickly settled to my sea-going rhythm with its endless round of watch and nap. It was as if we had taken up effortlessly from where we had left off ten months earlier. The old habits and rituals re-established themselves within a few hours. We were sailing a similar course to that of two years previously, but it was a different *Mingming* with a different skipper. Two winters' worth of additions and modifications had transformed *Mingming*'s manageability and comfort. Two thousand more hours of sea-time together had honed my skills at handling her. Six thousand more miles of ocean now lay in our unobtrusive wake. My confidence in our joint abilities was now rock solid.

In one sense I was frustrated to be sailing south; my head still brimmed with images of the sub-Arctic. That was where I really wanted to be heading. Nevertheless the Jester Challenge had its claims on me too; it was, after all, the catalyst that had got me back to sea. I had, as well, an uneasy ghost to exorcise - my abandonment of the first event. A successful completion of this second Jester Challenge would go some way to making up for that lapse.

The usual strategy when sailing to the Azores from northern Europe is, for the first half of the crossing, to keep a little to the south and east of the rhumb line. The hope is that by heading rather more south across the mouth of the Bay of Biscay, one will be favoured by the summer northerlies that so often blow here, thereby reducing the chance of constant headwinds from the south-west. Things are rarely so simple and sure enough by Wednesday the fourth of June, our fifth day at sea, we were bucking along close-hauled under one panel in a half-gale from that noxious quarter. With this first proper blow came a mess of cross-seas and a good dose of chilliness, but this after all was Biscay, whose two syllables, as short and contrapuntal as the seas they describe, evoke a library-load of heavy weather legend. In truth it was a half-hearted affair that fell far short of what might reasonably be expected hereabouts. For a day or so it kept us pinned down as we fore-reached grumpily south in a colourless world relieved only by the passing of a bright red tanker, the *BW Fjord*, that heaved by close on the starboard beam heading north-east and therefore rolling happily downwind, everything in its favour, everything as warm and as trim and as hunky and as dory as a few hundred thousand tons of steel and internal combustion engines and fabulous mechanical appointments can make it, while we, little *Mingming* and I, doubtless unobserved despite our proximity, no more than a trivial patch of discoloration in a turbulent seascape, not David to this crimson Goliath, but more like a faintly irritating mote in David's streaming eye, wound our way painfully south.

For another night we bashed on and suddenly, not out of the blue but out of the frigid pallor of an Atlantic dawn, there it was. A northerly! Not just any old northerly but a wonderful, fresh, Force 5 northerly that scattered all cloud to the far horizons and left the scene clear for a flood of unadulterated sunshine. What a transformation! Now it was *Mingming* and I who were the happy ones. With two panels set we raced downwind, skirts up in a field of blue, skipping and gambolling, pushed on by the gentle hills rolling underfoot, delirious at this sudden change of fortune. For the first time I felt that we were truly on our way. *Mingming* sped on easily, perfectly balanced and contained, her motion untroubled by any sort of snap or roll, her bow wave singing and gurgling. This latter was not just music to my ears; it was the food of my life, my ambrosian nourishment, my great reviver. I tried to count the years since that gentle burbling had first bewitched me. Fifty-three? Fifty-four? A long, long time, in any event, but not yet long enough to dull the thrill. Under its spell my cynical old shell dissolved and I was once more ten years old, a trillion cells of freshness and expectation and innocent wonder, heart now swelling at the latent possibilities of it all.

We were evidently at some shipping nexus. All day long a carnival of garish ships paraded by, sometimes far off, sometimes crowding in on us, once catching us in a tense pincer movement as a south-going vessel, untypically non-descript, even of name - the *Kommersk* or something similar - forced us into the path of the north-bound new-fangled shoe-box, the *Grande Benelux,* with her breezy yellow and white livery and the legend GRIMALDI LINES announcing her corporate provenance in letters at least a mile high on her slab sides. I suppose that there are Grimaldis other than those toy princes and princesses in their cutey-pie little palace at Monaco, but something about this ship's crude ostentation seemed appropriate. At ten that night the last of the fleet, the *Richard Maersk* of Kobnhavn, more tastefully done in light blue, crossed close across our bows and quickly disappeared, leaving us at last to an empty ocean and our own devices.

The Biscay northerly blew on, easing bit by bit, so that by the next morning I had raised full sail and set the light weather jib. In her element, *Mingming* sped easily on through a smoothing sea, the hiss and bubble of her bow wave undiminished, and notched up another day's run of ninety nautical miles. The sky's perfection was marred by nothing more than four or five brilliant white clouds, each one a tiny and apologetic streak of fluff, light and diaphanous, insubstantial as the air itself. We were by now within two hundred miles of the Spanish coast and there was indeed something Iberian about this shimmering skyscape, something redolent of baked earth and siesta. This was reflected at sea level too, where seemingly nothing moved save *Mingming.* All wildlife was gone, or nearly so. Two years previously we had sailed through great fleets of jack-sail-by-the-winds, millions of them that set the sea sparkling from rim to rim. Hereabouts too the sea had harboured endless lines of buoy barnacles in their symbiotic clumps; salps had drifted by in numbers beyond imagining. We had grown used to our entourages of fulmars and dolphins and whales, to the regular passage of darting petrels. By contrast, during that whole day, I saw no more than two jack-sail-by-the-winds, one rather scruffy immature gannet, and a few mackerel, no doubt fleeing something bigger and more toothy, skittering by at and just above the surface. These evasions looked ineffective, as the mackerels' brief flight was dead straight, returning them to the water and waiting mouths on a predictable trajectory. The evolutionary stroke of genius of the true *exocaetidae*, the real flying fish, was to develop the ability to make a sharp turn once in flight, thereby putting their would-be devourers well off the scent, as it were. As yet it seems they have not yet quite mastered the trick of evading the decks and, by extension, the frying pans, of passing cruising yachts.

The northerly faltered for a while, leaving us totally becalmed as the next day dawned. I had a kind of fright, the sort brought on by optical illusion combined with rabid imagination. Coming on watch in the half-light I saw with alarm that a small vessel the size of a fishing boat was sitting silent on the sea, just a few hundred yards off, unmoving, unlit, and clearly up to no good. Her dark and threatening immobility was more than puzzling; it scared the hell out of me. Pirates! They are not unknown even in these waters. Cruising yachts make rich pickings, what with all that fancy navigation gear and satellite telephones and passports and wads of nice crisp foreign currency and so on. Well, if they were thinking of boarding *Mingming* to strip her bare and start a new life on the Costas then they might be a teeny bit disappointed. You won't get far in life on the proceeds of a plastic sextant and two LED torches sold off at the local bar. There's not a big international market for well-used parallel rules. The euros I had on board might just buy a round of paella and San Miguels for the lads.

She lay there, this pirate ship, her desperate crew no doubt sizing *Mingming* up and deciding their plan of attack. I tried to shrink us into the ocean, to become invisible, but it's hard to do on a flat sea with the sun about to rise. Any moment I expected the ship to move in for the kill. What would I do? Overpower the crew in unarmed combat? Barter for my life and free passage with a tattered North Atlantic Chart and a half-full squeezy jar of Marmite? Maybe I could join them. I had a bright red handkerchief somewhere on board; with that and a gold earring I could become a swashbuckler myself.

Still she lay there, this pirate ship, toying with us, until the rising sun and better visibility and a certain improvement in my own visual and evaluative faculties showed that our aggressor was not a small ship lying close, but a very large ship a very long way away, going about its lawful business in complete ignorance of our distant presence on the same patch of ocean. Mightily relieved that I was not, after all, going to have to knock a few heads together, I thought instead about breakfast.

5

By midday we had been at sea for a week and the first, more southerly, phase of our voyage was coming to an end. We were by now just a hundred miles to the north-west of Cape Finisterre. It was time to launch ourselves more firmly to the west-south-west and head straight for the Azores. So far my plan had worked better than I had dared hope. Aided by predominantly northerly winds we had sailed over five hundred miles in the first week. The island of Terceira lay eight hundred miles ahead. We were well on track to complete the voyage within three weeks. I had never felt so comfortable and relaxed aboard *Mingming*. Despite so many sea miles together she could still surprise me with her sea-kindliness and downwind ease. We had enjoyed days of superb sailing, unstressed and harmonious, fluent and unhurried, totally uplifting. I was starting to feel that the hundreds of hours of preparation, together with the several thousand hours of sea time shared with *Mingming*, were now reaping their reward. We were an old couple grown comfortable with each other, no longer needing words or explicitness, accepting of limitations, skilled at maintaining the peace, solicitous of the sore points, rubbing along nicely. For the moment all was starry-eyed sweetness under a lucid sky.

This state of grace was reinforced by a sudden flurry of pelagic wildlife. Several pods of common and striped dolphins put on a gymnastic display at close quarters.

A dolphin leaping from the sea fills hearts with joy and laughter.

(It's somewhat less amusing for the fish he's chasing after.)

Less athletic were the Henslow's swimming crabs now skittering around the surface, hopelessly out of their depth.

Henslow's crab lives out his life atop twelve thousand feet of water.

He'd like to move to Gerrard's Cross, but wonders if he ought'er.

Overnight the wind freshened and backed to the north-east, gusting to Force 7. Cloud and light rain arrived. Our sparkly conditions had evaporated but we had a following wind, a soldier's wind, a farmer's wind, an old maid's wind, a wind to invite home and lavish with fine cuts and rare vintages. Nothing would be too good for such a wind. I could have happily erected a statue in honour of this fine upstanding wind. On it blew, almost from astern, and *Mingming* raced happily along, away from the old continent, now properly Atlantic-bound, little old *Mingming*, pushing thirty years of age, bringer of joy to an ancient heart.

The rain did not last for long and by midday I was back at my post in the open hatchway, observing the watery world and our progress through it. A huge breathy *hhrrmph*!, a sort of adenoidal avuncular snort of a tone and volume I had never before heard, from somewhere close behind, startled me from my contemplations. *What the hell was that?* I turned quickly and just caught the final moments of a rounded whale spout several metres high, now dissipating in the breeze just a few yards off the port quarter. A swirling slick on the sea surface showed where whatever it was had surfaced and dived. A few seconds later another throaty *hhrrmph*! and its accompanying spout erupted thirty or so yards on the starboard beam and there it was – a long whaleback rolling forward with lazy ease. I could scarcely believe what I saw. This massive tonnage of arching flesh was not black or blue or grey or any shade or tint that one expects from a good-sized whale. It was not even a white whale come to stamp some Melvillesque portent on our little voyage. No, here was something stranger still. This was a *yellow* whale. I had never heard of a *yellow* whale. *Yellow?* Surely not. But there it was, a great curved spine of *yellow* flesh, not a regular wash of colour and certainly not a *yellow* that might grace a good lemon or a healthy canary. No, this was an uneven, mottled *yellow* more at the tan end of the spectrum, a subdued sandy *yellow*, a tasteful earthy *yellow*, but damn my eyes whatever sort of *yellow* it was was adorning the back of a whale and excuse me whales are simply *not yellow*. But this one undoubtedly was, even its little fin as it rolled forward and once more disappeared. I dived too, into the cabin for my video camera. I had to get this on film. I would never be believed otherwise. I was back in the hatchway within a few seconds, ready to roll. Just in time. Whatever it was, and here I admit that intimations of an imminent zoological triumph were already filtering into my excited head, was heading our way, just a few feet below the surface. A shapely torpedo, pale at the head, then *yellow*, then darker brown, and at least as long as *Mingming*, was angling in on the starboard side. It came parallel with us just a few yards away and for one or two heady seconds I thought it was going to surface right there, right under my very nose. My febrile imagination was already racing ahead. A new species of whale! Discovered now, in the twenty-first century! I was already starting to feel distinctly Victorian and parson-like, white-whiskered, and thinking of the knotty monographs I would produce on my new find. The brain can work pretty damn quickly where personal success, fame and unbounded celebrity are at stake and within a fraction of a second I had the thing nicely described, classified, categorised, taxonomised and, yes, beautifully named. *Balaenus mingmingus taylorii* rolled off the tongue rather well, I thought. All I needed now was the evidence. No luck. I lost sight of it. A minute or so later it spouted again, about eighty yards away. That was the last I saw of it.

Stunned by the speed and oddness of this whole visitation it was a while before I went below again to consult my little whale book. Having just discovered a new species of whale I knew it wouldn't be in there. It was. That wretched French know-all Baron Cuvier had got there first. There it was, laid out in all its *yellow* and white and tan glory: Cuvier's beaked whale, the senior member of an obscure branch of the cetacean family, the beaked whales, that hitherto I had not known existed. Apparently it is fairly rare but sighted from time to time in Biscay. It already had its Latin moniker, a most unsatisfactory one in my unbiased view: *ziphius cavirostris,* a third-rate-Greek-actorish kind of name if ever there was.

Reading about them I was rather taken with the beaked whales. Their beaks are of course not the kind of thing you might find on a pelican, say, or even a house sparrow, but rather a dolphin-style set of protruding jaws. They are rather on the dainty side for whales, aristocratic and dandyish with their striking colouring and exotic names: Gervais' beaked whale, Sowerby's beaked whale and so on.

I was grateful for this encounter with such an unlikely leviathan, but it nonetheless left me dissatisfied. It was the big fellows I was after. Despite thousands of miles of voyaging I had yet to meet the true giants of the ocean, the blue and fin whales. That's what I wanted: mountains of uncompromising blubber, whales like nuclear submarines, real living monsters, good and black and terrifying.

I would just have to wait. In the meantime there were other compensations. The bank of low cloud that had weighed on us for a while moved away, leaving us once more to our downwind idyll in a world of fairytale blue. That afternoon the first Cory's shearwater of our voyage wheeled in, an outrider from the Atlantic islands. We had crossed some unmarked boundary. The wind veered further to the east and on we sped in glorious abandon.

6

Is there anything better than to plunge on and on and on with a following breeze, to girdle the world with such ease, shamelessly riding the elements? We surged forward on a building sea with just one panel of sail set, a tiny acreage, as it were, but enough to drive us across ninety miles of ocean in a day, and then ninety-eight miles; two days under the ethereal azure; two days that saw us out into the real ocean at last. With a strong and constant wind from north-east or thereabouts a mighty sea was now rolling along, whisking us on and on, a Rockall sea, this one, an old and bountiful friend of a sea.

It still seemed somehow silly, or unreal, or absurdly cheeky, to be thus revelling in this grandiose oceanscape. For all her reworking *Mingming* was nevertheless no more than a mere slip of a girl, light of bone and dainty of line. Conceived for undemanding work in waters in-shore and estuarine, she should by rights have been overwhelmed by the hungry combers ravaging her from astern. Not a bit of it. She shrugged them off with an easy balletic grace, light and airborne, an innocent beauty unfazed by the advancing packs of leering beasts. It still puzzled me, this self-possession. Despite a lifetime's advocacy of minimal ocean cruising, I could still be caught off-guard by the reality of a tiny boat sailing effortlessly in massive seas. It still seemed too good to be true. It was still shot through with a thread of counterintuition. It still seemed so unlikely. Yet there it was, as plain and undeniable as the midday sun that flooded the cabin; this twenty feet or so of curvaceous hull, spare and fine-ended, totally unremarkable, was as good a sea-boat as a man could wish for.

It may be thought too that I was for ever hankering after a more palatial interior, that the tight confinement of my tiny capsule was a trial to be endured rather than enjoyed. The opposite is the case. In the first place time and use always alter my conception of the space within which I live. The longer I spend at sea the more it seems to expand. The living area, that is to say the distance between the companionway and the forward watertight bulkhead, is little more than seven and a half feet long. At its widest it is less than six and a half feet, but six and a half feet well-laced with intervening lockers and interior joinery, and which in any case narrow to three feet or so at the forward end. It is a short and extremely narrow volume, squeezed down by the low coach roof and side decks, squeezed up by the tight turn of the bilge. Yet as time goes on, far from confining and pressing in on me, it seduces me with its increasing spaciousness. I often lie with my head propped on a pillow at the aft end of my bunk and admire the sweeping vista forward, right along the length of my well-swaddled body, on further along my legs to my distant feet, shrinking in the perspective, and then on further over acres of open bunk-top until finally stopping short at the edge of the world, here unequivocally delineated by the shelving fixed transversely to the forward bulkhead. As each day passes the sight-lines along the interior of the boat, whether enjoyed from forward or from aft, grow longer and more satisfying. No doubt a kind of applied relativity is at work, a compensatory recalibration of the scale of my world. Perhaps it is a crude survival mechanism, ensuring that a creeping claustrophobia does not send me bonkers.

Once, on one of the halcyon days of easy downwind sailing, I decided to exit the hatch and film *Mingming's* progress from as far aft as I could get on deck. Since the installation of my wind-vane adjuster, trips to the distant fastnesses of the after rail were a thing of the past. I had forgotten just how far it was. With the video recorder in one hand I worked my way aft, running the gauntlet of tiller lines and self-steering lines and all the other paraphernalia of single-handed ship management, awkwardly transferring my harness clips with the other hand. I finally reached the pushpit and turned round to settle in and film for a while. There before me, port and starboard, ran a breathtaking sweep of side decks that ran on past the distant mast and curved gently upwards to resolve themselves into a far-flung bow that dipped and rose, seemingly a mile ahead of our sedate position at the stern. *Mingming* felt enormous, not so much in girth, but in her new-found length of limb. She had stretched herself to a long and graceful greyhound of the sea. Hell, maybe we could try her for the America's Cup!

It was a stirring sight, *Mingming* transformed by some readjustment of perception from minnow to 12-metre, but after a few minutes I felt uneasy on deck. This was not my habitat. I longed already for the encircling comfort of my little cabin. I made my way forward and dropped down through the hatchway into my multi-purpose chamber. For here is the other great perk of minimal living: space is no longer subdivided unnecessarily and wastefully into a series of boxes with distinct functions. My room is whatever I want it to be at that moment. Three times a day it is a superb kitchen, with food, cooking utensils and a simple stove all within arm's reach. Food prepared, here is now a baronial dining room, with sea views thrown in too. A quick tidy up transforms it to a quiet study. Here I can now read and write and even, if the mood takes me, think. A slight rearrangement of materials now metamorphose the space to my chart room and navigational station. Work over, I can relax and sprawl in my sitting room, not having moved more than an inch or two, but rather having mentally redefined the spacial function. I don't doubt that the available area of the cabin sole, perhaps four feet long by fifteen inches wide, would provide the basis for an exemplary on-board dance floor, but the principal use for its flat surface is as an occasional stand for my little bucket. Viewed objectively there is nothing more absurd than the usual sea-going toilet of the modern production yacht. What expense and engineering, what a profligate use of space and materials, what a baroque concoction of pipes and valves and pumps and skin fittings, what a sop to over-developed human sensitivities, all for the purpose of transferring a small amount of matter a distance of about twelve inches, from here on the inside of the hull, to there on the outside of the hull. My little bucket is kept on a line in the cockpit, from where I can whisk it below when required. A dip overboard fills it with a few inches of water, after which it is settled in position at the base of the companionway. A few sheets of my all-purpose kitchen roll have already been quartered to handy-size squares. Having dropped all below-waist clothing to ankle level, I can now squat on the bucket, well braced port and starboard in the narrow space, totally secure in even the roughest of seas. My space is now a regal toilet and, if I may be permitted a moment of brutal honesty, a combination of regular diet and timing, along with the superior evacuative musculature of the oriental squat, as opposed to the vapid occidental sit, invariably produce a rapid and imperious stool, worthy of the great Kublai Khan himself. Once I have transferred the business overboard by simple physical rather than overblown mechanical means, my space now becomes a washroom, all abuzz with soap and razor and toothbrush. The versatility of my little cavern is still not exhausted, for here too, created with the quick unrolling of a blanket, is my bedroom. It is pantry too, and drawing room, and cellar and attic and conservatory. *Mingming* is the best of stately homes, and better still, for unlike any bricked and mortared pile, she can cross oceans too.

The azure turned to grey and the wind, bit by bit, fell. Our daily run was now eighty-five miles. After eleven days at sea we had our first breakage; the stainless steel stirrup that links the yard to the main halyard sheered. I had already applied a secondary rope lashing, just in case this happened, so, apart from a tangle with the topping lifts that gave me some trouble getting the sail down, no major harm was done. I fixed it with a heavier rope lashing, doubled with a more ferrous connection fashioned from a hose clip and shackle. The resultant repair, for all its rough-and-readiness, lasted the two thousand or so miles back to Plymouth without any further problem. This was my first real work of the voyage.

7

Across the Bay of Biscay the sky had been almost empty of birds. Used as we were to a constant presence of fulmars, backed up by auks and gannets and petrels, this emptiness had tinged our progress with shades of unaccustomed loneliness. I had grown more dependent than I realised on this companionship of the road. It was much more than mere entertainment and pleasurable observation. The flocks of pelagic species gave a kind of legitimacy to our own presence on the ocean. They showed that here too life had its everyday part, that it was not so odd, after all, to eke out this marginal existence so far from land. I always felt a kind of complicity with our friendlier, more inquisitive attendants.

The deserted air of Biscay irked me. I had no doubt that it had to do with habitats and available breeding grounds and food sources and so on, in other words that there were simple rational explanations for this absence of bird life. Be that as it may, the sea for a while felt more alien without a softening avian influence.

As we pulled further away from the Iberian peninsula things began to change. Every day brought bigger numbers of Cory's shearwaters into view. Similar in size to a fulmar, though more slender and less straight-winged, a soft chocolate brown above, white below, and graced with a gentle, intelligent eye, the Cory's shearwater is as ideal a fellow-traveller as one could hope for. Like fulmars they carry a spark of inquisitiveness. They will always soar in for a brief look-see, usually making several effortless passes around the boat, head tilted in interrogation. They are less direct and importunate than fulmars, rarely coming too close, except at night when bewitched by the stern light. In the main they keep the air, of which they have a complete and relaxed mastery. In open ocean they fly singly, or in loose associations of two or three, but always well-spaced, respectful of personal distance. Only a feeding frenzy of dolphins will bring them together into tighter groupings as they forage for scraps.

These shearwaters brought movement and interest and a kind of warmth to the seascape. At any one time there could be up to thirty or so within sight, weaving their equidistant patterns, a downwind warp cut with a crosswind weft as they swooped and veered.

That same afternoon a new and unexpected sighting confirmed that bird-wise things were picking up. The prettiest and most unmistakeable petrel of them all, Bulwer's Petrel, flew across our stern. A large black petrel, something of a cross between a sooty shearwater and a black tern, dainty, slender-winged and long-tailed, the Bulwer's Petrel breeds on the Azores. Like its smaller cousins it will not be deterred from its chosen path. It has no interest whatsoever in passing yachts, however bizarrely rigged. From then on I usually saw two or three every day. Their straight and dogged flight lines cut with trigonometrical accuracy across the random baroque curlicues traced by the shearwaters; their sultry coal-black elegance and aristocratic aloofness left me feeling clumsy and depressingly common.

The weather was changing. Our fine wind from the north-east was dying a fitful death. Sometimes it gave out completely, leaving us wandering erratically downwind, plagued by constant gybes. Then it would find the strength for a few more gasps, raising hopes, hopes that would soon and once again be dashed. All night we played this wearing on-off game, and all the following morning too. Our daily run was down to sixty miles.

With the wind such as it was still from dead astern, the self-steering gear just could not cope. Our gentle forward movement subtracted from the light zephyr gave an apparent wind of little more than zero, not enough to activate the wind vane. Sick of our uncontrolled meandering I decided to hand steer. Here was the moment to try out the final modification made over the previous winter. I believe that every well-found yacht should have an internal steering position. Few do. However well protected a cockpit may be with dodgers and spray hoods, however well cocooned a helmsman may be in layers of high technology clothing, the fact remains that long periods of external steering, particularly in extreme conditions, are stressful and debilitating. *Mingming's* guiding principle was that she could be sailed from below at all times. I therefore had to take into account the possible failure of her self-steering gear. Many years ago I had been forced, by a combination of circumstances that had destroyed both my self-steering and my internal steering arrangement, to hand steer a tiny yacht, on deck, for nearly a month. It was an experience I never wanted to repeat.

Over the winter I had therefore constructed a system for steering from inside, based on the ancient principle of the whipstaff. Like all the best ideas it was laughably simple. Lines from the tiller were lead through blocks, then inside through the after portlight, then through another set of blocks fixed to the coach roof, and attached via jam cleats to the top of a vertical stick – the whipstaff. I had made the whipstaff itself from an old broom handle, rendered suitably nautical with a few coats of varnish and a Turk's head decorative knot. The base of the whipstaff pivoted on a wooden plate I had made for the purpose out of scrap pine, and which sat on the cabin floor. The end result was that if I pushed the stick to port, the tiller moved to port; if I pushed it to starboard, the tiller moved to starboard. For a sailor used to a tiller everything was therefore perfectly intuitive. I had two internal compasses to steer by.

The joy derived of improvisation is in inverse proportion to its cost and in direct proportion to its usefulness. My little whipstaff was therefore a joyful thing. All afternoon I played with it and grew more self-congratulatory by the minute. It exceeded all my expectations. I tried it every possible way. I lay on my bunk and lazily manipulated it. I sat up comfortably, legs stretched out on my berth, and steered with my fingertips. I sat in the hatchway, the whipstaff between my knees, steering and keeping watch in total ease. I found that I could leave it to its own devices for short periods, freeing me to make an entry in the log or grab a handful of trail mix. It was immensely comforting to know that in the worst case I could thus control the ship's direction from below. I could now face a self-steering failure with somewhat more equanimity. It was another important building block in the edifice of stress-free manageability that I was slowly constructing. Since leaving Plymouth twelve days ago I had not yet had to wear oilskins. I had only ever gone on deck through choice, never through necessity. I was warm, dry, well-rested and relaxed. *Mingming* was now not far from the ideal ocean cruiser I was striving to create.

8

At fourteen minutes past four on that same afternoon the world, or at any rate my conception of it, changed for ever. A light but consistent wind had come up from the east, allowing me to put *Mingming* back on to self-steering. I had settled into my seat in the hatchway and resumed a lazy watch as we ran gently on in a smoothing sea. Few things could keep me from this constant observation. It was an article of faith. It was, after all, why I was there; to see what I could see; to learn what I could learn. I had no expectation of some sudden and immediate enlightenment, but I was nevertheless sure that to watch the ever-changing sea and sky, hour after hour, day after day, would somehow make me a little wiser. It would, at the very least, scour away the comforting illusions of that other life on land, and expose a raw and awful essence.

At fourteen minutes past four the sea erupted and my heart nearly stopped. The great whales had arrived. Nothing, not a life-time of reading, not a hundred imaginings, not a thousand pictures, had prepared me for this moment. A pod of five or six fin whales crossed our bows and the scale of the world changed. The ocean shrank. The seas to the very horizon contracted. Everything I knew about the natural world was immediately and unequivocally redefined. The relativities of size were recalibrated for ever. I had thought I knew what the word 'big' meant, but here, for the first time, was 'big' made flesh. Here they were, mountains of uncompromising blubber, whales like nuclear submarines, real living monsters, good and black and terrifying. That is what I had dreamed of, but my dreams were pathetically limp and lack-lustre and one-dimensional things compared to the reality. Nothing I had ever seen was so beautiful; nothing I had ever seen was so sad; nothing I had ever seen spoke so eloquently of the age of the world. The great hills of flesh broke the surface and moisture welled in my eyes. Here was the world as it once was. Here was the world as perhaps one would like it to be. These creatures had ranged the oceans for countless millions of years. The world was theirs; they were the history of the world. I felt like a crude interloper. The trappings of humanity, a sort of intelligence allied to a crippling self-awareness, were mean and tawdry baubles compared to the whales' unhurried majesty.

The blow of the fin whale is an exhalation of industrial proportions. It sends a stream of vapour a good twenty feet into the air. The accompanying roar has a factory-made quality too and on that calm afternoon could be heard for miles. It was hard to conceive how mere flesh and blood, for all its gargantuan dimensions, could generate such power. I tried to picture the innards of these sixty-foot leviathans, but the images were all of pipe-work and valves, steam hammers and pressure hoses, pistons and furnaces and forges. I saw armies of knotty-muscled gnomes hammering at red-hot anvils to Wagnerian accompaniment, oily grease-monkeys climbing into throbbing corners to add a touch more lubrication, sweating engineers checking valves and tightening nuts with out-size spanners. Red lights flashed and sirens whooped as the pressure built ready for the great release. Needles hovered near red. Then a great voice echoed through the chambers: *Let her go, lads!* Levers were thrown, valve wheels were spun, the labouring army crouched, hands over ears, and with a monumental, deafening *whoosh!* there, finally, she blows. *Thar she blows!*

The pod was more or less synchronised in its easy progress of surface and dive, so that the blows came in close-spaced groupings, forming short-lived copses of silvery young poplars that hung for a few seconds, their verticality all at odds with the dominant horizontal orientation of the oceanscape. Under this provisional forest each long black back rolled effortlessly forward, on and on, finally revealing the absurdly small and shapely fin, then disappeared. No flukes were raised.

For a minute or two the whales ranged around just ahead of us. I dropped the mainsail, the better to see them and to be sure that we did not sail over and away from them. Mostly they surfaced in profile, crisply black against the silver-grey sea, giant cut-outs that rotated forwards with a smooth mechanical sureness. This side view accentuated their astounding length. Just once one of the pod changed direction to surface in line with *Mingming*. I was now looking at it from aft, as it were. This gave, literally, a new dimension to its bulk. Although only a few feet of the whale showed above the surface, there was already eight to ten feet of beam showing, an intimation of its tremendous girth.

The pod was suddenly gone. Nothing in nature had ever touched me so profoundly. Circuits I scarcely knew existed had been activated and now buzzed red-hot in heart and brain. On a simple level, it was exciting enough to have come across a group of the world's second-largest living creatures. There was no question that their size alone, impressive in the abstract, was shocking in the flesh. It had made me quiver, not from fear, but from its sheer un-worldliness. It was like meeting something from another planet, but it was immediately clear that these animals were infinitely more at home than I or my species would ever be. Their relationship with the element in which they lived was untainted by ambiguity. Three billion years of leisurely adaptation had brought them to an easy harmony with the vast oceans they patrolled. The great baleen whales trouble no one or no thing, save the minute organisms, the krill, on which they feed.

A few last blows on the northern horizon showed the direction of the pod's stately progress. They were following a feeding route impressed into their circuitry through a hundred million lifetimes of repetition. The scene was from an age as Jurassic as it was nuclear. It was fitting that they had ignored us. What can man contribute to their lives, save slaughter and uncertainty?

(I still dream that one day I shall meet the largest and the noblest of them all, the blue whale. I dream that one day *Mingming* and I will be lying quietly, comprehensively becalmed, a thousand miles from land. All will be still. A blue whale will surface close by, firing off its thunderous spout, then lie gently alongside. We shall spend just a few minutes thus, little *Mingming* and, beside her, one hundred feet and one hundred and fifty tons of the most wondrous animal that ever lived. The whale will look at me with its wise lugubrious eye, all the history of a planet in that one moist sphere. I will look at the whale with the heat-seeking glare of humankind. I will talk to the whale. *Hello, blue whale,* I will say. What I would like then to say is - *Don't worry, friend. It will be all right.* That will not be possible. How could I lie to my new companion, adding deceit to the other transgressions? I will, if I am lucky, manage two hoarsely whispered words: *I'm sorry.*)

9

We had evidently entered a patch of well-stocked ocean. For two days the sea throbbed with life. More pods of fin whales passed at distance, their spouts and attendant roars unmistakable. Common dolphins played around our bows. A party of thirty or so striped dolphins, close-packed and intense, crossed our stern, leaping and cavorting, ignoring us completely. A leatherback turtle, startlingly pink and white in the late evening light, swam past on the port beam and there just beneath the surface, day and night, drifted unending thousands of small and chestnut-spotted jellyfish.

41°N 20°W. I made good note of the coordinates of this feeding ground. It would be interesting to see whether I encountered something similar on the return voyage, in either the same latitude or longitude. I was particularly interested in the whales, and whether they might be migrating north along this line of longitude. As it turned out the constant heavy weather of the return passage threw up huge and relentless seas that made meaningful whale observation almost impossible.

We finally lost our fine wind from astern as, still fitful, it veered to the south-east. With the breeze now on the port beam *Mingming* could carry her light weather jib, but in the constantly changing conditions our progress was nervy.

To carry a headsail on an un-stayed mast is a risky strategy. I have tried to minimise the risk as much as is possible. My two headsails, a very light nylon multi-purpose genoa and an old dinghy jib, are by any standards tiny, about thirty square feet and twenty square feet respectively. Set with their short luffs low, they exert more pressure on the bowsprit than the masthead. I never crank up the halyard too excessively. There is no doubt, however, that in a weight of wind or a squall they can induce an unhealthy amount of bend at the masthead. I have therefore made sure that I can lower them quickly from the hatch. Each sail has a downhaul threaded through rings sewn to its luff and leading back to the cockpit. I can bring the sail down to deck level, and more often than not contained within the pulpit netting, within a few seconds.

These sails are very small, but their effect on our speed is at times considerable. In particular they punch well above their weight when the wind is forward of the beam. In very light airs the nylon genoa can keep us ghosting along when we would otherwise have stopped. To windward in stronger winds I often keep the small jib set even when the mainsail has been well reefed. I can only guess that a slotting effect, improving the airflow over the leeward side of the mainsail, helps deliver more power to the rig. It is this undeniable extra drive that makes the risk and anxiety and the occasional need to go forward tolerable – just. Without the headsails I would never have reason to exit the hatch at sea. With the headsails I have to go forward from time to time to change them or to gasket or un-gasket them.

It is only the headsails that can induce indecision and worry. Reefing and un-reefing the mainsail is so quick and effortless that decisions can be made and happily rescinded with no harm done. The major decisions pertaining to the headsails, by contrast, involve stressful and potentially dangerous trips to the fore deck. A poor decision that may need immediate revising can result in a deal of misspent energy. There are awkward trade-offs to be made, too, between our speed and the well-being of the rig. In the main I err on the side of caution. Over-stressing the rig makes me tense too and destroys the easy harmony which I am always at pains to create aboard. In principle I would love to ditch the headsails and enjoy the ease and simplicity of the single mainsail, but they are too useful to abandon.

My reluctance to venture onto the fore deck might strike the reader as somewhat precious. Isn't this what ocean sailors are supposed to do? Are not manly heroics on a bucking bow, wrestling with armfuls of untameable headsail while up to the waist in water, what it is all about? What sort of a sailor wants to skulk below in tranquil warmth?

Apart from the obvious defence that the more I am below the less I am at risk of accident, injury, stress or hypothermia, I can offer up one other excuse for my dislike of going forward; on a small junk-rigged yacht it is in fact quite difficult to get there. On a balanced lugsail the boom does not of course stop at the mast. It carries on forward, in *Mingming's* case by several feet. However even when we are sailing close-hauled the boom is never fully amidships. At the most it is brought in to sit over the quarter. The section of the boom forward of the mast is therefore angled across the narrow side-deck. As we ease off the wind the boom comes squarer across the passage forward. It is no more than about thirty inches off the deck. To go right forward I have to worm myself through a small aperture bounded by the lifelines on one side, the coach roof on the other side and the boom above. The downhaul leading to the mast base from the forward end of the boom further complicates the obstacle course. If I am fully togged out in layers of clothing plus oilskins and harness it is an exceedingly tight and awkward squeeze. I have to crawl on my knees. Things catch. My harness lines get in a tangle. I can get hot and bothered and have even been known to swear. It is not fun.

Eventually I always make it through. Am I then rewarded for my trouble with a wide and rolling acreage of pristine deck? Not a bit of it. *Mingming's* fore deck is tiny. It has all the features of a fore deck: a bow roller, a chain-pipe, a mooring cleat and anchor chocks bearing a well-lashed anchor. What the fore deck does not have is deck, or very much of it. It is an isosceles triangle about four feet across the base and with sides also about four feet long. This creates a total area of about eight square feet and, once the anchor and cleat and chain-pipe and the narrowing V forward have been factored in, and not forgetting too the sail bag used to stow the headsails in heavy weather, and the space taken up by my two sculls that lie along each side, a working area of half that. There is just about room to squat or kneel.

The barriers to the bow section of *Mingming* effectively divide her deck area into two quite separate principalities, each with its own system of governance and its own national characteristics. To cross from one to the other is something akin to breaching a kind of Berlin Wall. On the one side, the after side, that is, we have a calm democracy. Life progresses in a self-assured and relaxed manner, on an even keel, as it were. All the levers of state are close to hand. Crises are few, rebellion and dissent unknown. At its best, life aft of the mast aspires to a utopian perfection.

Crawl through to that other place known as the fore deck and in short measure you'll get a taste of anarchy. Nothing is predictable. The world is in constant flux, thrown from crest to trough, buffeted from all sides, an unending switchback. This is a state for thugs and opportunists. All labour is hurried, inclined towards the slapdash. Just get on with it fast and hang the consequences. Soonest done, soonest we're out of here.

How I loathed the prospect of struggling through to that wild little territory! And yet, just occasionally, the effort was repaid with more than the reward of keeping *Mingming* sailing well and looking shipshape. Once in a while I would make it through to the fore deck on a good day. On such a day there was no better place to be. Disorder showed its positive face. The pitching to the waves was a delight; the twist and turn and splash were thrilling. Here the music of the bow wave was at its strongest. Here our rush through the water was at its most impressive. Here was a changed perspective on life as I looked aft along the lines of my plunging ship. Danger was now a tonic; a good ducking a pleasure. How much more fun it was to be up here and living on the edge, rather than mouldering in that sedate and predictable world aft! I need to get out more often, dammit!

It never lasted for long, this euphoria of the fore deck. The sea demands pragmatism, not idle reverie. Playing the living figurehead was all very well, but crossing oceans requires a dour and boring persistence, a willingness to accept a twenty-four hour round of simple tasks repeated stubbornly day after day after day. I had to get back aft, back to my routines, back to clerking and scrivening, back to cooking and cleaning. I had teeth to brush and nails to clip.

I had to attend too to the weather. Bit by bit it was changing. I could smell something in the air. So far we had had a charmed run, held up only once by an adverse blow in Biscay. We had been at sea for just under two weeks and were already within three hundred miles of Terceira. Terceira. The Third Island. It would be my first Azores island. It was now less than a hand's span away on my chart. With a fair wind we could be there in three days, but something told me this would be unlikely. The wind was slowly hauling round to the south-west. Terciera now lay pretty much to the south-west. It was not reasonable to expect a passage to the Azores without some prolonged weather from the south-west. This was, after all, the dominant wind. I feared the worst and my worst fears were fulfilled.

10

Our change of fortune was heralded by a night of heavy rain and a south-westerly gale, a malicious lump of weather that set the tone for the final leg of our voyage. With just one panel set we fore-reached slowly westwards, although by the time leeway and drift were factored in our course made good was somewhat north of west.

At first light, round about four in the morning, I saw that the whole self-steering gear had somehow canted forward from its vertical position, leaving the tiller lines slack. How this had happened was a mystery. The self-steering mechanism is fixed with a half inch bolt to sturdy brackets on the stern. I could only guess that the bolt had somehow loosened. The sea was by now much too lumpy for me to go aft and try to fix the problem. In fact when conditions finally allowed me to examine the bolt, later that day, I found that it was still extremely tight; it was impossible for me to push the gear back into position. I could only guess that something must have hit the pendulum-blade in the water, rotating the gear on its axis. Even this was odd, as the blade itself is not fixed too tightly for exactly this reason; it is supposed to pivot if hit, sparing the rest of the gear. Nothing made any sense, but there it was. I found that even at this new and un-recommended angle the self-steering gear in fact functioned reasonably well. I was unwilling to loosen the retaining bolt and risk having the heavy gear swinging about before I could reset it in position, damaging itself, or myself, or *Mingming*, or all three of us, and so I left it as it was.

The gale soon blew itself out, allowing me to raise four panels of the mainsail and settle *Mingming* in to her first real spell of windward sailing for the voyage. The cloud cleared away too and once more I sensed some change in the feel of the world; the powdery Wedgwood blue of the sky had taken on a firmer texture; I almost felt I could reach out and stroke it. The sea was a darker, richer indigo, but more than anything the sun now meant business, forcing me to consider a change of wardrobe. It was getting too hot for wearing thermals.

By noon we had been at sea for two weeks and recorded our worst day's run so far – thirty-eight nautical miles and little of that in the right direction. With the wind as it was this was unlikely to change. There were no longer any whales or dolphins to relieve the bleak outlook, only another lone turtle, this one a deep and fiery orange, and a lesser black-backed gull, unexpected out there, that inadvertently mocked us by heading off straight for Terceira. The first ship of many days passed half a mile ahead, heading south. Neither the westerly lay of port tack nor the southerly lay of starboard tack held any particular advantage for us and so I decided to sail for five hours on each board until the conditions changed, which, sooner or later, they must.

It is easy enough for the lone sailor to impute a sort of personality, benevolent or vindictive as the case may be, to the vagaries of the weather. The winds do, after all, dictate every aspect of a voyage's progression. They set the speed; they control, to a large extent, the direction in which one can sail; the sea state itself is nothing if not a reinterpretation of the air flows above it. The wind soon becomes an abiding obsession. It is not long before this obsession takes on all the worst characteristics of an unhealthy and one-sided relationship. The wind is of course supremely indifferent. The sailor's love of it, on those days when it is stroking his cheek with a fine and favourable caress, will always be unrequited. That beautiful wind can turn in a second to a mean and nasty crone. That wind can break a man's spirit, his heart too.

It was clear that we were now out of favour with the wind, but like all easy-come-easy-go lovers she had it in mind to fool around a little longer before letting us know what she really thought of us. Thus could a mean-spirited wind exert power over a helpless sailor and his little yacht. The wind hauled round towards the north-west. I put *Mingming* on starboard tack and under five panels of the mainsail and the small jib we raced along for a night and a morning, still close-hauled, but at least a little more on course for Terceira. If it were the compasses that had the final say, we would have been right on target, but the discrepancy between our magnetic heading and our actual course made good was huge, something of the order of thirty degrees. A number of factors were contributing to this difference. Now that we were sailing hard on the wind our leeway was at its most pronounced. As we moved west into the Atlantic the anomalies in the earth's magnetic field increased, pulling the compass needles further and further from true north. We were also coming under the influence of the Azores Current, a south-flowing stream that was to add its own contribution to life's difficulties over the next week.

By noon we had made good seventy miles, a creditable distance given the headwind. However the combination of wind and current was edging us further south than I would have liked. At the rate we were going we would be lying due east of Terceira, at about one hundred and eighty miles distance, within a day or so. I did not much fancy being set down-current of my target, with it still to windward as well, but for the moment I had no choice but to carry on as we were; to have gone about would have had us heading for Ireland or thereabouts.

The wind continued its games, blowing harder as the day wore on, and forcing me to drop the jib and, progressively, panels of the mainsail until by dawn we were down to two panels only, almost a storm configuration. The new day brought a mess of black and ugly rain squalls that by good fortune we avoided and the perfidious wind handed out its final favour by veering twenty-five degrees towards the north, twenty-five precious degrees that for the moment put us back on line for Terceira. Ever the hapless lover, I thought that there may be some consistency to this gift. A couple of twiddles of the divider on my chart had us in Terceira within two days after a passage of just eighteen days. I ran a little ahead of myself, already savouring the plate of salt cod and Portuguese potatoes that I would soon be tucking into. Just a couple of days were all that now lay between my parched throat and a glass of chilled white wine. We ought not to be too far behind the Jester Challenge fleet either. How I loved this fine wind from the north-north-west, this noble, up-standing breeze, benevolence personified! All afternoon it blew on, sending *Mingming* bounding along at four knots under jib and four panels. The squalls had moved off and under a brilliant sky we leaped on towards Terceira and the little harbour of Praia da Vitoria. Nearly there! I fancied I might already be able to smell land. Hell, I might even see a mountain peak tomorrow! A medium-sized ship, the *Alam Aman II,* of, I think, Port Kelang, crossed our bows just a third of a mile ahead, heading east, and I felt a warm complicity with her skipper and her mates and her engineers and cooks and stewards and deckhands; all of us borne on the ocean, getting where we were going, happy in our work, with never a care to crease our brows.

11

By six that evening the wind was dropping and by ten it had
gone. Abandoned, we rolled and heaved in the left-over swell
from the north-west. To be thus slighted was a bitter enough
blow, made worse in this instance by the pernicious quality
of the calm that followed. The absence of wind has as many
gradations to its character as does its presence. There are
good calms and bad calms, calms tolerable, calms intolerable.
Whilst a calm is rarely to be welcomed, it can from time to
time be enjoyed. A flat and glassy sea, moved only by the
faintest respiration from beneath, a total stillness, a seeming
suspension of the rush and motion of the world, all can exert
their charm. An unruffled surface opens a window to the
ocean depths, adding another infinitely downwards
dimension. I have spent many an hour staring thus into the
eye of the sea and been none the worse for it.

The calm which came that night, though, was a petty,
delinquent kind of calm, a window-breaking, car-scratching
kind of calm, the kind of calm that invokes fury rather than
resignation. There was nothing to enjoy about this calm, not
one single mitigating feature. The wind had gone, but the sea
seemed unaware and kept up its procession of steep-faced
waves that threw us from one side to the other as they
marched through, flinging the heavily-battened junk sail this
way and that, snapping the headsail back and forth in the
little pockets of air that came and went with each advancing

hillock, whacking the halyards against the mast. There is nothing calming about such a calm; it is a kind of torture, not simply of unrelieved and random motion, but of maddening sound. *Mingming* is at her noisiest in such a calm. The rig and rigging and innards of the boat smash one way and then the other and the racket that goes along with all of this can, by the third or fourth or fifth hour, drive you to distraction.

Think of any onomatopoeic words you like: *creak, hiss, bang, groan, whine, thud, ping, clang,* for example. Then make up a few more: *clipple, dink, sprug, kerlumph, pronk.* Elide them all together and you just may start to capture a faint hint of the kind of noise generated aboard a little junk-rigged yacht in a spiteful mid-ocean calm. Something like this:

creakhissbanggroanwhinethudpingclangclippledinksprug

Then, without hesitation, it begins again, in a slightly transformed order:

hissthudclipplecreakdinkgroankerlumphwhinepronkclang

Then the accents come in:

dinkgroanTHUDhisskerlumphCREAKwhinePING

Add some repetitions:

kerlumphDINKDINKpingthudpronkPRONKcreakthud

Then remember that this is often in two-part or three-part harmony, with endless lines of noise-based counterpoint running simultaneously:

$$\left\{ \begin{array}{l} \textit{clangthudDINKpingsprugsprugcreakCLIPPLEgroanhiss} \\ \textit{creakPINGPINGclipplehissGROANthudTHUDclang} \\ \textit{angbanggroanCLANGclangdinkclipplethudpronkCREAK} \end{array} \right\}$$

As I lay there, hour after hour, drowned in this cacophonous nightmare, I began to curse my musical training. Long years of practice had habituated me to finding the rhythm and pitch and melody in every unlikely series of sounds. Instead of shutting out this diabolic symphony and letting me sleep peacefully, my wretched brain was constantly at work trying to analyse and notate the whole damn lot. To make things worse there was an easily discernible form and order to the seemingly random sounds. Wave motion is intensely rhythmic and it was wave motion that was powering every noise. The eerie repetitions and restatements generated a horribly logical counterpoint. Each squeak and groan had not just its own pitch but its own maddeningly clear tonality. Little notatable tunes and phrases and fragments repeated themselves *ad nauseam.* Insane figures, stretti, little rondos, subjects, counter-subjects, developments and re-workings of a theme were hovering at the edge of recognition. Sonata form had nothing on the complexity of this infernal music. A thousand weird instrumentations suggested themselves. I could hear a D-major trumpet underpinned by bass clarinet. A barber's shop quartet growled along in close harmony. An army of percussionists kept up a tireless improvisation. The dominant clacking themes, the banging and thudding and knocking, were overlaid with kaleidoscopic washes that suggested the unlikeliest of sound pictures: the whistling of a hundred hung-over milkmen, the baby bawlings of a metropolitan maternity unit or, less distinct but most haunting of all, the death screams of some hellish abattoir. There was no limit to these wild juxtapositions. I tried to think of a composer who had attempted to capture this kind of incongruity. Ives perhaps, Webern or Berg in pointillist mode, but it was no good – this quasi-musical pandemonium surpassed human invention.

In these conditions I sometimes capitulate and lower the mainsail, lashing it down as firmly as I can to minimise any movement. The mainsail, with its boom and battens and yard swinging and banging around the mast, is the principal source of all this noise. The mast itself, locked between the partners and its step and passing just a foot or two from my head, serves as a tinny loudspeaker, relaying and amplifying the slightest whimper from above. Suppressing the mainsail can bring some relief, but it also means that we are no longer, in any sense, sailing. If a little breeze does come up it will pass us by, unutilised. To lower and lash the mainsail is to accept that for the moment we are going nowhere. Our motive power, however ineffective, is gone. This emasculation is almost as unbearable as the bedlam it is relieving.

For all that long night we rolled around and I kept the mainsail set. The occasional hint of a zephyr from here or there was enough to keep me from total surrender. I fussed around with the self-steering and our sail settings, sometimes succeeding in teasing out a minute or two of pathetic forward movement, triumphs quickly offset by another hour of noisy immobility. I lay down and tried to sleep but the symphonic racket tormented me with its brazen *dies irae.* I stuffed plugs in my ears and buried my head under the blanket but there was no escaping it. I got up and fussed some more. I ate an energy bar. I lay down and instead of sleeping found myself sketching out in my head a snatch of the ambient music. A little later I noted down an extract:

The full score would have twenty-six parts and last for about thirty-seven hours, without interval.

Eventually I dozed until my alarm woke me. A little wind had come in from the south-west, enough to get us moving nicely under the full mainsail and light weather jib. The sun pulled itself aloft and shone weakly through a haze of milky blue. Close-hauled on port tack *Mingming* assumed once more her usual range of sea sounds, the slaps and gurgles and gentle creakings of a ship happy in her work. We were back into our headwind, but any wind was better than none. We passed by a strange buoy with a tall pole and a radar reflector stuck on the top, seemingly immobile in four thousand metres of water. It was odd to have a reference point for our progress. We soon lost it astern and before long met the US navy. Coming along on a reciprocal course was what I took to be the oil supply ship for the US air base on Terceira, grey as an Atlantic dawn, her decks a mass of complicated derricks wielding massive hoses, the number 198 painted on her bows. She passed close by on the starboard side. She was one mighty fine-looking ship. I was tempted to call her up and wish the boys howdy and have a nice day.

12

My own day was not so nice. It deteriorated with mathematical precision. At noon, after a day's run of fifty-eight miles, and with the south-westerly now gusting well beyond Force 4, I was forced to go forward and replace the light weather genoa with the small jib. The pale sky had darkened to a grey murk. Within two hours I was once more crawling through to the fore deck, this time to gasket the jib which I had been forced to lower in the still-increasing wind. This was my third trip forward in twenty-four hours. I was unused to this sort of hard labour and wondered whether a spot of unionisation might ease the seaman's lot aboard *Mingming*. A little renegotiation of the terms and conditions might not go amiss. There had been hints of mutiny at the command to go forward and tie down the flogging lowered jib, but the skipper, in all his brass-bound authority, had prevailed. It had been a close-run contest of wills between the warmth- and bunk-loving fore-peak lawyer, a lazy, hair-splitting kind of fellow, unsuitable for life at sea, who argued that the jib would come to no harm as it was, the wind was bound to ease again soon anyway, and what was all the fuss about, and the implacable Ahab aft, who ran a tight ship and wanted everything royally ship shape and Bristol fashion and now, dammit! Ahab's better judgement is sometimes overruled, I am ashamed to admit, but not on this occasion and within a few hours I had cause to rejoice at this.

Having done away with the headsails I was soon forced to start reefing the main. Every hour or so another panel was dropped. The sky had darkened further and by mid-afternoon we were down to three panels, punching along into a south-westerly trying to be a half-gale but not quite succeeding. A fair old sea was getting up, inevitably, and we were by now well into our dogged heavy weather windward mode. This is a curious kind of progress occupying the no-man's-land somewhere between real sailing and out-and-out fore-reaching. Were I to ease *Mingming* another ten degrees off the wind she would pick up her skirts and hare off, but with several unappealing consequences; she would, for instance, now be taking the seas much more on the beam, and at higher speed, giving an increasingly stressful and uncomfortable ride and, what's more, in a less favourable direction. The well-established and perfectly legitimate arguments about maintaining boat speed rather than trying to point too high lose their force when sailing a very small boat in big seas. Meaningful windward progress is going to be limited, whatever one does. I have found that with *Mingming* there is an ideal spot that she can occupy relative to wind and sea, achieved with the self-steering set at about forty degrees to the apparent wind and the mainsail not too hard in. Every wind and sea state demands its own slight variation on this to achieve the optimum configuration. In a Force 7 this will usually keep her moving along at about two knots, an unexciting speed maybe, but with her bows still sufficiently into the approaching wave faces to avoid taking too many blows on the beam, or risking a knockdown by a breaking comber. This is not to say that the odd crest coming in at an obtuse angle does not from time to time give us a healthy reminder of the power of a large volume of water in motion, but for the most part we can jog along in relative comfort. It is something of a compromise strategy, but I have yet to find anything better.

By six in the evening, dinner time, we were well settled into this steady windward groove and now back to four panels of sail as the wind eased slightly. I cooked my usual one-pot meal of rice, tinned fish and vegetables, quickly done and using a minimal amount of cooking time and fuel. I had by then taken to using bigger cans of food to add to my rice or pasta or mashed potato. This created a heavy pan of nosh, a third of which I would eat immediately, my one bit of hot food each day. Another third or so would be consumed overnight and the rest for breakfast. I had lost the taste for my old standby of muesli and milk. Dinner was finished off with a long-life dessert of some kind, followed by a large slice of home-made fruit cake.

Well-satisfied, I stuck my head out of the hatch for a quick look around. A few yards off the starboard quarter a luxury catamaran, blindingly white, one of these profligate high and wide things that take up more sea room and air space than seems decent, was racing by, heading the other way with our nasty wind fair on its quarter. It too was well reefed down. I was shocked at how close it was. I was jolted too, after several weeks of observing the soft contours of wave and sky, by the unexpected hard-edged clarity of all its delineations. Three figures, two men and a woman, they too unnaturally sharp and three-dimensional, stood in the capacious cockpit, waving heartily. I waved back as casually as I could, as if I had known all along that they were there and had finally decided to acknowledge them, at the same time wondering guiltily whether they had changed course to pass close by, or whether we had just avoided a collision by a whisker. I will never know. In the meantime I was admiring three pairs of brilliantly laundered shorts and their accompanying tanned legs, a combination that suggested clean-living Teutonic healthiness and a desire, even in this miserable blow, to inject a holiday spirit into the proceedings.

They sped quickly off, leaving me to my grubby isolation and my enduring conviction that the crossing of oceans in small boats is anything but sparkly-toothed fun.

There could scarcely have been a greater contrast between the two passing yachts, and I wondered what the three waving sailors made of *Mingming*. A combination of circumstances had, I hoped, worked in our favour. It was just as well that I had looked out when I did. At least I was not asleep on the job, as it were. *Mingming* was sailing well and snugly, not over-pressed but still well-canvased for the conditions, a pocket yacht slogging gamely to windward in an Atlantic blow. I wished I could have seen her from their perspective. Not only was she nicely snugged down, her fore deck was a model of applied seamanship. How proud I was of those tightly gasketed headsails, with not a square inch of loose sail or a trailing rope's end to be seen! How pleased I was that earlier that afternoon I had leapt forward with not a second's thought or moment's hesitation and spent a happy five minutes putting everything in order! *Mingming* must have made a fine picture, I thought. It could so easily have been otherwise.

13

The weather was starting to confuse me; it was impossible to find any discernible pattern or logic in the constant shifts of wind strength and direction. I was used to the tight depressions of the north Atlantic, with their rain-laden south-westerlies followed by clearing skies and a north-westerly change as predictable as it was refreshing. All day we had sailed into a rain-laden south-westerly. By ten that night we had moved out from under the cloud bank but instead of a blustery north-westerly we soon met another belt of rain and a failing wind. We had now spent five days or so struggling along in anything from a flat calm to a full gale; the wind direction too was in constant flux, but within a narrow vector that never strayed too far from south-west. There was something unfamiliar too about the scale and density of each passing agglomeration of cloud. Perhaps it had to do with our distance from the any sizeable land mass, particularly to the west, and the effects of the bigger changes of temperature and surface geography that go with *terra firma*. There was less interference here, less to break down the atmospheric gyrations into smaller units. In these more southerly latitudes the weather patterns themselves operate on a bigger scale than further north, adapting, no doubt, to the increased circumference of the globe. There was certainly an outlandish sculpted grandeur to the cloud forms we were now meeting, but my attempts to divine what was coming next were increasingly wide of the mark.

By breakfast time we were once more becalmed, but I had still failed to grasp a very simple fact. The ship's log still rattled on about the imminence of a north-westerly change. It was a constant theme, a madman's *idée fixe*. So keenly did I long to be freed up from these stultifying headwinds and regular calms that I was ignoring the plain and palpable evidence above and around me. Here is a prime example of optimism triumphing over rational analysis, lifted verbatim from my log entry of 0830 hours on the morning of Wednesday the eighteenth of June:

Currently becalmed in yesterday's left-over slop and an up and down wind that I'm sure will become a true NWesterly soon, giving us a lead to Terceira.

In retrospect it beggars belief, but there we are. I have not the slightest idea on what reasoning that bold assertion of an imminent north-westerly was based. Eighteen days at sea had obviously addled my insufficient brain, turning already wishy-washy grey matter into yesterday's dish-water. Pragmatism had become idle prattle.

Fortunately I was soon distracted by other matters. The sea astern was suddenly alive with a feeding frenzy of hundreds of dolphins, leaping and thrashing and churning the surface. This in turn brought in a concentration of a dozen or so Cory's shearwaters, the biggest close grouping I had so far seen. They had abandoned their usual smooth gliding and now twisted and turned and hovered and swooped to pick scraps off the surface, milling close in raucous agitation, suddenly enervated by the prospect of a full gullet. Further down, unwitting lives expired, violently. This slice of life in the raw moved closer and closer. I ducked below to prepare my cameras; this might well be the photo-shoot of the voyage. I had for many days been trying to capture

Cory's shearwaters on film, but they were too fast and never quite close enough. This was my moment.

The dolphins and shearwaters were now just a few yards off *Mingming's* stern. There was no question that the sequence of a lifetime was coming up. An innocuous bang preceded the sudden swinging of the boom out square from the ship, where it waved around out of control. Yards of mainsheet trailed in the water. I could scarcely believe the timing. The pin of the shackle holding one of the mainsheet blocks to the pushpit had failed. The block itself was now fifteen feet aloft, pulled up as the mainsheet had overhauled itself. I had no choice but to sort out the mess immediately, lowering the sail, retrieving the block, finding and fitting a replacement shackle, raising the mainsail and getting us once more settled on course. In the middle of all this *Mingming* became the centrepiece of the furious activity above and below the surface. Dolphins milled around us, foaming the surface; Cory's shearwaters hovered almost overhead. I hoped that they would still be there once I could start filming but of course they weren't; the drama had moved off and I missed the whole performance.

As the day wore on I became increasingly tight-lipped. There was nothing to say. Our daily distance made good had totalled a miserable thirty-six miles. There was now a light breeze from west-south-west. Terceira lay squarely in the eye of this unhelpful wind. The south-flowing current was picking up. I calculated that each three miles of sailing would bring us one mile closer to our target. We still had about one hundred miles to cover. At our present rate of progress to windward that would take about four days.

I was not necessarily bothered about making a fast passage; that was an obsession I was happy to cede to other more industrialised ocean crossers. I had scarcely thought too about the other Jester Challengers and their likely progress.

The fleet of forty-two yachts was too big and too varied to track by imagination alone. My personal challenge was to make a good showing relative to the two other most closely matched yachts in the fleet, Bill Churchouse's Westerly 22 *Belgean*, and Graham Jewitt's Kingfisher 20 *Golden Dragon*, but even that was a low priority. All I really wanted was to complete a satisfying voyage with minimum fuss.

It was galling, nonetheless, to feel all the gains of the earlier part of the passage slipping away. Our momentum was gone. For two weeks we had been averaging well over eighty miles a day, but this average was now being trimmed brutally by the hour. I should have known better than to expect anything else; *Mingming* maintains a remarkably consistent average daily run of sixty-five or so miles for all her voyages.

Creeping in too were overtones of the previous year's frustrations off the south coast of Iceland. I knew all about being stuck a hundred miles or so offshore, a day's sail from my destination, and getting nowhere. At least this time I had plenty of time in hand. I was victualled too for the Azores and back, with a large reserve for emergencies, and so could keep the sea for as long as it took.

With this in mind I started to harden my resolve. I had been having it too easy. Two weeks of following winds had softened me up. I was becoming a fair weather sailor. It seemed unlikely that from here on we would have an easy run in to Praia da Vitoria but it was about time we had a dose of reality. We could quite conceivably have had a screaming south-westerly all the way from Rame Head. I had no cause for complaint.

We were evidently crossing a shipping route. At nine that evening a massive red container ship, so boxy and angular that its lack of aesthetic appeal risked becoming an ironic design statement in itself, crossed our bows heading east, and a short time later I had to take evasive action to keep us well clear of the track of the *Gulf Grace* of Nassau, also heading east. It was by now dark and I was pleased that her officer-of-the-watch had obviously spotted *Mingming's* navigation lights, for a searchlight was directed at us from the wing of the bridge. We were too far off for the light to illuminate us, giving us the best of both worlds: recognition without exposure.

All night we carried on in a gutless headwind, with the light weather headsail, released from its tight swaddling twenty four hours earlier, helping to keep us moving, though never in a direction that gave me much pleasure. The breeze was still swinging around in its narrow range, keeping me busy throughout the night trying to find the optimum board, and for a little while, the wind backing towards the south a little, we made some useful westing. By dawn the wind was getting up again and I was forced to drop the headsail quickly. This led to the usual arguments between skipper and crew as to whether it should be gasketed or not. After a bit of a tussle Old Ahab finally had his way, on the basis that there was a lot of nasty rain cloud about and things looked likely to get worse before better, but it was a truculent seaman who crawled forward to do the job, a cursing recalcitrant hanging-back kind of seaman, unhappy at this hard usage and wet work at the cold break of day, a so-called seaman who may as well have been a lubberly clodhopper for all the good he did, for he made a rushed and un-seamanlike job of it, being as he was too damned keen to get back below. He was soon to be found out, though. The sea does not tolerate carelessness.

14

The sea. By noon we had crossed one thousand two hundred and eighty-nine nautical miles of it, taking as our measure the sum total of our daily runs. These are the straight-line distances between our midday positions. How far we had actually sailed through the water, taking into account our constant snakings as *Mingming* strayed off course to be corrected sooner or later by the self-steering gear, and taking into account our wanderings up hill and down dale on the stormier days, and not forgetting the pernicious effect of a headwind, that might have us going from Plymouth to the Azores via Oporto or Newfoundland, or even both, I had no idea. Neither did I care; it was of no relevance. All that mattered was that we were now *here*, whereas yesterday and the day before we had been *there* and *there*. With two hand-held GPS units to back up my celestial navigation I was unlikely ever to be denied an accurate position fix.

Mingming is delightfully and deliberately unburdened by the indispensable instrumentation of the modern yacht. Not only do I therefore never know how far we have actually sailed, I also have no way of knowing precisely how fast we are going. I always, of course, have a rough idea, but this is usually no more than an educated guess based on the feel of the boat, the noise of the bow wave, the rate of passage of the bubbles alongside, the foaminess of our wake. *Mingming* is, almost, an instrument-free zone. This is how I prefer it. It is a kind of liberation. I am not subject to the tyranny of the computer read-out. My relationship with my environment is direct and uncomplicated. My own bodily sensors work away twenty-four hours a day. I have no choice but to observe and feel and make my own assessments and calculations. Constant practice can yield some surprises. My pre-noon estimate of our daily run, made not from any precise mathematical analysis, but from the sub-conscious absorption of all the facets of our progress over the previous twenty-four hours, is usual correct to within five miles. Similarly my pre-noon guess at our actual position is rarely very wide of the mark.

To be thus freed from too much reliance on electronic circuitry makes sea-going a more wholesome and satisfying undertaking. Success is based not on depth of pocket, nor on the reliability of mass-produced goods and their installation, nor on computer-handling ability, but on simple seamanlike observation and awareness. In the long run it is more instructive to spend hours watching sea and sky rather than an array of screens. The former is outward-looking, a real engagement with the real world; the latter, with its reinterpretation of life outside into a precise but narrowly selective set of cold data, tends towards a kind of denial. I was told not long ago of a cross-Channel passage during which the navigator never once came on deck. Worse, I read recently about a US merchant ship whose gyro-compasses had malfunctioned. She was supposed to be heading south. The skipper woke in his starboard-side bunk to find the morning sun streaming through the port-hole. He raced to the bridge to find out what was going on. The first mate assured him that they were steering south; the compass said so.

The less one needs in order to effect an ocean passage, the more confident one can be of achieving it. The eternal question of the minimal sailor is not *What do I need?* but *What can I do without?* I suspect that these days few sailors realise just how little they really need. Yachts come over-loaded as a matter of course. Chasing down the latest bit of kit is an article of faith. While most of the indispensable gadgets and gizmos may be fun to use, and while they may well give a false sense of well-being to the under-confident sailor, and while they may give the impression that life afloat is essentially as comfortable and secure as life ashore, give or take some extra motion, they add little, in the final analysis, to the raw ability of a yacht to complete an ocean passage. In many ways they are counter-productive. They add weight; they take up space; they demand batteries and chargers and care and attention; they develop dependencies in the user and sooner or later they will break down.

The sea is an uncompromising and unforgiving environment. I prefer to prepare for that environment on the basis of simple, strong, uncomplicated equipment, and as little of that as possible. The rudimentary will always take preference over the sophisticated. Better the crude contraption that can easily be fixed than the high-tech wonder that once broken is irredeemable. In a boat whose gear is honed down to the raw and absolute necessities, and where those necessities themselves are kept as basic and robust as is possible, and where the guiding principle is that *less is more*, the capacity for unpleasant surprises or crippling dysfunctions is immeasurably reduced. True self-sufficiency, on the other hand, is greatly increased. My water bottle will never break down; nor will my bucket. I'll never suffer an engine failure. I'll never have water in the electrics. My batteries will never be flat. I'll never be stuck in a foreign port, waiting for an engineer or a spare part. I'll never lose the comforts I never had. I'll never miss the delights of gadgets I never knew. I'll never waste time and energy on baubles and peripherals.

Stringent limitation combined with make do and mend keep my costs to a minimum but multiply a thousand-fold all my little sea-going pleasures. I meet the sea in hand to hand combat, as it were, at its own level. I look it straight in the eye. There is no virtual warfare, no engagement via remote control. To grapple thus with the ocean, without artifice, simply, directly, is the means better to know it. Sometimes I like it a little more; sometimes I loathe it; but rubbing along with it day after day after day, skin to skin, in a close and unrelenting clasp, soon teaches its moods and foibles, strips it bare of mystique and myth, and engenders, in time, a kind of edgy companionship.

This quest for a simple form of voyaging, as basic and unmediated as possible, unstressed and harmonious, can easily be misinterpreted as some sort of daft third-age mysticism, tree-hugging gone to sea. Nothing could be more wrong; this is in fact ruthless risk management afloat, the exportation offshore of the fundamental skills of my land-bound occupation. I have tried to combine a lifetime of sailing experience with the hard-won skills of a risk manager to cut through the accretion of commercial interest and largely unchallenged received wisdoms that so cloud and distort the modern approach to ocean sailing. There are fundamentally only three requirements for a boat to cross an ocean: it must remain afloat; it must have some form of motive power; it must be able to be steered. This is the basic hierarchy of needs, and in that order. These are the core risks. They should preoccupy a sailor for a good eighty per cent of his preparation and of his time at sea. The other twenty per cent, all the other aspects to do with communications and so-called safety and speed and comfort and so on, are at most secondary or tertiary and at worst totally irrelevant.

To sail an unsinkable yacht, simply but robustly outfitted,

with constant and close regard to its well-being, making every effort to minimise stresses to hull and rig and rudder, nursing it patiently, striving always for its optimum, least aggressive, configuration to wind and sea, and with a total and uncompromising personal responsibility in the matter of survival, is anything but unhinged. It may seem somewhat old-fashioned, sadly deprived of the mast-toppling, keel-breaking, sail-delaminating, hull-splitting, instant-podcast thrills of today's commercially-induced ocean romps, but it carries its own incontrovertible logic. The quiet and the rational may well be *passé*, but they work.

15

Sixty miles was all that now lay between us and Praia da Vitoria. Perhaps it should have felt as if our voyage was nearly over, but the increasingly vindictive weather soon scotched any optimism on that score. I could make neither head nor tail of its hard cop soft cop contradictions. The sun could scarcely pierce an atmosphere now heavy with a wan, anaemic haze, yet this was our hottest day so far. It was humid too, chokingly so, but with the day's turgid limpness offset by a furious, gusting wind, still, mostly, from dead ahead. It was hard to reconcile the one with the other. A small fishing boat crossed our bows half a mile ahead, the first intimation of the proximity of land, and an hour later a very modestly proportioned container ship, the *Polarstream* of Monrovia, blue-hulled and more than likely engaged in the island trade, overtook us close on the starboard beam.

As the day wore on the outlook worsened. An army of intimidating rain squalls, grotesque engines of war expanding blackly skywards, massed on the windward horizon. They were clearly up to no good, this lot, and they scared me a little. For once I reefed early, just in case, but in tune with the reigning schizophrenia of the moment it was not this lumbering bank of cloud that did for us, but the limpid evening sky that followed. At ten a squall came out of nowhere, a sudden blast which had us going from full sail to two panels in half a minute, an almost unheard of reduction in area for which I blessed the instant reefing ability of *Mingming's* rig, and which underlined the craziness of the weather. This was as nothing, though, to what followed. By one in the morning we were enjoying a prancing merry-go-round ride of squalls and calms, thunder, lightning and bouts of monsoon-like rain. It was one of those nights: endless adjustment, incessant fiddling, unlimited frustration. The wind veered and backed and veered and backed again, encouraging us from one tack to the other, only to push us further away from our target and demand another going about, increasingly difficult and wearing and time-consuming as the waves built up, and soon to be replaced by the expedient of gybing round, the sure sign of a hostile and impassable sea.

Despite the inconstancy of the wind it had, by dawn, roused up something of an alpine seascape, a swirling mess of peaks and escarpments, white-flecked cols and ridges, folds and crevasses and arêtes, deep valleys and plunging couloirs. On another day I might well have revelled in this magnificent confusion, but there was nothing to celebrate here; it was all heading our way and for once poor old *Mingming* was hard put to maintain her usual poise. Avalanches of white water tumbled off the summits, catching us from time to time with a hissing thud. We threaded a hesitant route through the hills and passes, without hope of any real progress, just keeping sailing, on and on. There was nothing else to do.

The sky itself became a fractured but grander mirror image of the scene below. Here too were towering ranges stretched horizon to horizon, each chain separated by a wide lake of pale azure. Every passing cordillera grew taller and whiter, more hewn, more monumental. The mountains here were hugely square and slab-sided and precipitous, colossal Notre Dames with ballooning spires and turrets that scraped the limits of the sky. I had never seen such air-borne shapes, such indiscriminate voluptuousness of form. It was a stirring reminder of what architecture could be, or might have been, but the scale and grandeur of it all did not deflect me from my deluded obsession with the imminence of a north-westerly change. Every new cloud-top that pushed above the horizon was scanned eagerly. Every outline and grouping and formation was analysed hopefully for some sign of relief from this murderous headwind. I saw what I wanted to see. I had never before cast eye on more perfect north-westerly clouds! Look at those fellows up there! Did anything ever hold more promise of a north-westerly shift? And see how that great mass over there is breaking up! Another hour and we'll have a perfect leading wind!

This wind, though, a dour and unreceptive fellow, held in the south-west and blew ever harder. At nine-thirty that morning, from the crest of a higher wave, I spotted a blue-grey smudge of land low on the port beam: Terceira, just where it should have been, thirty miles distant, as fair and square into the teeth of the advancing waves and wind as it was possible for any landfall to be. Land was there, then, but land in the most unlikely of its manifestations. This was not a slab of continent; not even some outlying aberration. This was not an Unst or an Iona. Drain away the sea and *Mingming* would be flying at ten or twelve thousand feet towards a fairy-tale pinnacle. These sea-mounts of the mid-Atlantic, forced skywards as the crusty tectonic plates rub and grind, force, from time to time, their topmost peaks out into the air itself. We were sailing over a sunken Himalaya, beneath Eiger-faced clouds. The slopes and summits of the sea were puny by comparison, a niggardly pastiche of the outsize forms above and below, but they were enough to keep *Mingming* in constant struggle as we forced our way grimly wind-wards.

Nothing I tried was going to bring us any closer to our target. A massive eddy of the Gulf Stream swirls round the eastern end of the Azores, aiding and abetting the westerly air flow. I could never bring it on our lee bow and extract some offsetting gain from it; whichever tack we sailed on we were forced away from Terceira. Starboard tack took us past the southern tip of the island; port tack led well to the north. Now fore-reaching, sometimes under three panels, sometimes under two as the great cloud masses unleashed another rain squall, we went back and forth, buffeted by the ugly slop, and mocked by the dim outline of the island as, once in a while, it rose above the angry crests.

Frustration introduced another sinuous delusion into my analysis of the weather. A secondary conviction grew stronger by the hour. The wind, I thought, despite the obvious and glorious north-west intent of the sky, may not yet be inclined to veer but surely, surely, it was very soon going to *ease*. Yes, that was it! Never mind a veering wind, let's have an *easing* wind! With an *easing* wind, anything was possible. Think of it: a smooth sea, a full set of sail. We'd eat up these few remaining miles in no time!

Every little lull in the persistent blast now fed my new-found node of optimism. Yes, that wind is coming off now, I thought, every twenty minutes or so. We're over the worst. Now we can make some real progress!

It blew harder, still shifting around and encouraging a mess of cross-seas, steep and breaking and maleficent. The discomfort below increased. I had been at sea for twenty days and so was inured to the incessant motion, but the rhythm of the sea had here become sharp-edged and graceless. There was nothing to be enjoyed. By noon we were within twenty-seven miles of Terceira, but that proximity was itself a torment. I was sick of the noise, too. There was little here that could translate to even the most outlandish hint of melody. Orpheus was long gone. Here was nothing but a percussive and random mish-mash of slaps and bangs and crashes overlaid with the whining vibration of sheets and halyards. There was no sense or form to any of it; it just kept on and on, anarchic and infuriating, maddeningly persistent.

The belts of cloud kept up their regular passage too. Every cathedral in the world passed overhead, magnified a thousand-fold: Cologne, Rheims, Chartres, St Paul's, cheek by jowl with outsized Kremlins and towering pagodas and merged seamlessly with wilder Gaudian inventions, all extravagant curves and demented buttresses. Up they stretched, a fine sight in the approach, but cruelly rain-laden as they crossed, the rain whipped on by unstable gusts that gyrated twenty degrees in a few seconds. At deck level the downpours fused with the spray and constant submersions as wave-tops broke on us and climbed aboard, running aft and filling *Mingming's* tiny cockpit. A little water found its way below, but mercifully nothing that could not be swabbed up with a few sheets of kitchen roll.

Between noon and four in the afternoon we had sailed seven miles south, but advanced our cause towards Praia da Vitoria by less than half of this. In reality we were no closer. On this tack we would miss the island; the other board would take us back along the same track. We could come closer to Terceira, certainly, but with no meaningful improvement in our position. Unless the conditions changed we were condemned to an eternal patrol, back and forth. Would Azorean maidens stand on wind-swept cliffs and bewail the hopeless passing of this tiny Flying Dutchman? I thought about the other Jester Challengers, no doubt all arrived and sunning themselves on a sheltered dockside, glass in hand, content with the world, and wondering what was keeping us. Had I voice enough I could have yelled into the breeze that we were nearly there. The island rose and dipped to windward, sometimes veiled behind the showers, sometimes clean-lined and tantalising. I ground my teeth and tried to ignore it, but it had been the focus of my thoughts for the best part of a month and was not so easily dislodged. Ghosts of the recent past danced through my head, wailing and leering; the Faroes, similarly held at bay by an offshore wind; Iceland, glimpsed by the merest chance and then abandoned. It was not impossible for this wind to keep up for weeks. What if it did? Would I relinquish Terceira and head for a more attainable island? Would I throw in the towel and run back north, scudding comfortably before it?

At six that evening the wind shifted twenty-five degrees in one almighty gust and stayed there. It may as well not have bothered. We could now almost lay the south-east tip of the island, but would still miss it. In any event I did not want to press on too far that way and risk being set further and further south by the strengthening current. The other board took us away from the island, to the north-east. It was hopeless. Worse still, the wind shift had encouraged the build-up of an even more spiteful cross-sea. There was now no hint of sense or order to the passage of the wave-tops. Poor *Mingming* was flung one way and then the other, and all the while Terceira lay there on the western horizon, unmoved, unmoving, as unfeeling and as leaden as the lump of rock it was.

Throughout the afternoon, wind and wave had been working away at the untying of lubberly lashings. It is almost incomprehensible how air and water can work so well together to unravel imperfect rope-work. It is the mindless persistence that does it. They slog away at it for hour after hour, pushing and pulling and loosening and unthreading. After a hundred tries the lazy overhand turn is finally pushed off the cleat. Now, at last, the elements have a loose end to play with. Now the fun can really begin! Whirl and swirl this end a thousand times and eventually all will combine to pass it off the other arm of the cleat. Now we're getting somewhere! Another three or four, or eight or ten or however many hours of whisking this lengthening pendant up and down and back and forth will release it from all those figures of eight on the cleat. Oh joy! Now we can get to work on the sail as well! As the lashing slackens, its end now liberated and flicking around in the breeze, a good weight of water, expertly directed, can loosen a fold of sail. The wind now takes up the challenge, forcing an incessant snap and billow of this fold until a handkerchief of area becomes a pillow case that shrugs off its lashing and now you're in real trouble because the whole sail is about to break loose. Its flogging will destroy itself and drive you crazy in the process.

In this instance it took wind and wave thirty-six hours to complete their task to perfection. At eight-fifteen that evening, as we bucked and plunged through an implacable sea, my light weather jib was finally released from every last inch of its restraining bonds, and set free to dance and caper in the liberating airs. With what joy and abandon it celebrated its new-found freedom, twirling and flicking and cracking, bent on its own destruction and a flamboyant exit from this world.

Old Ahab was not pleased. He already had enough on his plate, what with an island taunting him just over the lip of the sea and not a hope in hell of getting there, what with the grinding discomfort and the maddening noise. This was not the time to be lumbered too with a potato-eared plough-boy of a crew, a ham-fisted cabbage-grower of a so-called sailor, incapable of the simplest task of the lowliest of seamen. I won't repeat the whole of the dressing-down he gave to his useless shipmate. In short, Old Ahab waxed lyrical on the shortcomings of his unhappy fore deck hand, employing language of a rare and finely-turned invention, and laid out the hapless cowherd's punishment in no uncertain terms. The poor lad was to get forward, and now. Old Ahab did not give a damn how rough and dangerous it was out there. He couldn't care less how cold and wet it might be. He was not the least bit interested in how long it might take. The boy was to retrieve and lash and swaddle that headsail so well that even a hurricane would not dislodge it. He was to mummify the wretched thing so comprehensively that it would pass muster in the Egyptian section of the British Museum. He was to rectify the fruits of his own lackadaisical incompetence and learn a hard lesson in the process.

16

Chastened, I prepared myself to go forward and sort out the disgraceful mess. I dug out my proper wet weather gear from its stowage point on what had been the port quarter berth and was now my bosun's locker and wet store. It was the first time in the whole voyage that I had needed it. I took off my homely bootees and pulled on the thick yellow over-trousers, high-waisted and bibbed and braced, fisherman style. They stank of old sea water and rubbery chemicals. I struggled into the heavy jacket, drew up the industrial zip that closed it, and secured the zip's protective flap with press studs. I pulled on my sea-boots and carefully arranged the elasticated inner bottoms of the trousers over them; I was going to be in for a wet ride and wanted to minimise the chances of water finding its way into my normal clothing. After the usual fiddling with its webbing straps, which always seem to twist and rotate themselves into an insoluble puzzle when stowed, I managed to get my harness on. I made sure that its two lines with their spring clips were untwisted and ready to go. It took a while, all this contorted dressing in the tight confines of the cabin, but there was now nothing left to do but to pull myself out into the real world and begin my ghastly penance.

I opened the hatch and folded the spray hood forwards. The entrance to my warm retreat below was now gaping and unprotected. I clipped one of the harness lines to the strong point fixed to the after end of the coach roof and squeezed myself up and out and over into the tiny cockpit, using the hatch coamings and the windward grab rail for handholds to stop me being pitched summarily overboard. I quickly closed the hatch and secured it.

After days spent happily within the protective cocoon of *Mingming's* little hull, soothed by an amniotic warmth and lulled by daily repetition and ritual into a sense of humdrum normality, it was a shock to be once more on deck. With all the comforts and constructions ripped away there was nothing to contemplate but the dour face of an indifferent world, and the absurdity of our passage through it. *What the hell am I doing here?*

Old Ahab was at my ear, though, and there was no time to study the anarchic, tumbling seascape, no time to let the relentless breeze scour my cheek, no time for farmerly philosophising. The jib was still intent on a furious self-destruction. Working my clips from one strong point to the next I crawled along the windward deck. It was only a few feet, but may as well have been a mile. I forced my way through the usual obstacles around the mast and settled on my knees on the fore deck, making sure I was attached by both lifelines. Up here at the bow every contour of each passing wave was faithfully reproduced, hurling us cloud-wards to momentary apogees, pitching us down into watery nadirs, flinging us to port and then to starboard. Patiently I did my work. Deeply ashamed of the poor job I had made of the previous gasketing, I had no intention now of hurrying. I freed up the long line used to lash down the jib and started again. Never has a sail been so rigorously contained. Every turn around it was pulled bar taut. The turns themselves were just a few inches apart. I passed the line through the clew ring and took an extra turn. I cleated the end of the line with half a dozen locking turns. Thirty square feet of nylon were treated as if they were the main course of the *Thermopylae*. I trussed that sail with a grim will, all the while cavorting up crest and down trough in a welter of driving spray and the occasional plunge into solid water.

With the job done I allowed myself a moment or two to observe what lay around and ahead. There on the starboard bow sat Terceira, now more substantial and raised higher by proximity and my increased height of eye. The bulk of its mountain mass rose towards the northern end of the island, tapering away to the south. The island's eastern face was spread wide before us, with Praia da Vitoria somewhere at its centre, now less than twenty miles away but still firmly in the eye of the wind. The light was fading and it was clear that yet another nasty night was imminent. I had by now given up all hope of a north-westerly change. I had abandoned any expectation of an easing of the furious conditions. All was now dull acceptance; we would sit out here for as long as it took.

I crawled back aft and dropped gratefully down into my haven. The dressing ritual was reversed: off with harness, off with boots, off with jacket, off with trousers. Everything was stowed away and with a few squares of kitchen roll I dried off all the drips on my bunk and on the cabin sole. I rubbed my face and hands with a towel. Slowly I re-established the orderly composure of life below. I ate an energy bar. I drank a mug of water laced with lime juice. I switched on the navigation lights. I wrote up my log. I set the alarms and slept for a few minutes.

The island had taunted me for a whole span of daylight, but as darkness fell a new element of torment crept into our uneasy relationship. By day Terceira had been no more than a natural feature, an impersonal mountain peak set low on the horizon. Now it blazed with man-made light. I had not in any way expected this. From north to south stretched a virtually unbroken pattern of well-lit towns and villages, sprinkling the coastal hinterland with a million pinpricks of yellow. The industrial lighting of the port and harbour of Praia da Vitoria, garishly bright and unselfconscious, dominated this light show. With another miserable night in prospect, it was doubly depressing to see all those illuminations. They spoke of warm living rooms and soft beds, of crowded bars and restaurants, of chatter and of laughter.

For a short while the wind toyed with us again, veering and bringing us almost on course for Praia da Vitoria itself, but it was unlikely to last and it didn't. Before long we were once more being forced past the southern tip of the island. At one in the morning I tacked to head back offshore. With my bunk now on the leeward side I could at least rest a little better. Slowly we moved away from land, pushed round from our north-westerly compass course almost to the north-east by the breaking seas and strong southerly set. It was hopeless. The lights of Praia da Vitoria dipped below the horizon, but their loom still indicated where we were supposed to be heading. I clenched my jaw and tried to ignore them.

For five hours we lurched along, fore-reaching painfully through the black and noisy night. I slept a little and fought to retain some resolve. We might still be out here for a long time to come. The headwinds had been blowing for eight days now. They could carry on just as long again.

The change came so quickly and unexpectedly that at first I had trouble absorbing it. At six that morning, in ragged seas under a doom-laden sky, I gybed *Mingming* back onto her landwards tack. There was nothing else to do; I could not head north-east for ever. Within a few seconds, without hint or preamble, the wind swung right round from south-west to north. It did not even have the decency to pause for a second or two at north-west and thus deliver a smidgeon of credibility to my weather forecasting efforts. The self-steering gear of course followed the wind shift round and there we were, comfortably laying the northern tip of the island.

How can I describe that moment? How can I convey what it meant, or how it felt, to be so summarily released from the grip of that headwind? I had by then given up all hope of a reprieve. I had steeled myself for the worst. I had pushed aside all idiotic dreams of north-westerly changes or easing winds. I had thrown overboard the last dregs of optimism and left them well astern.

Now, in a second, life had changed. Everything was once more possible. How I loved that northerly wind! What a magnificent sky was bringing it! Why had I thought those waves to be nasty and threatening? I raised a couple of panels of sail to harness fully that fabulous breeze and off we sped, comfortably landwards.

Still wary, though, of the south-going current and of leeway and of the possibility that the wind might yet revert to its old habits, I kept us well up to windward. I would close the coast as far as possible to the north before bearing off for Praia da Vitoria. I did ease *Mingming* off just a shade, nonetheless, to get her moving well. It was too tempting not to. Ah, how good it felt, to have the wind even slightly free! The joy of it! The release! On we bounded and the coast of Terceira now loomed rapidly ahead, growing and clarifying itself by the second. Pale patches resolved into patterns of individual houses; rough contours turned to trees and woods; a prominent terracotta streak low on the coast refocused itself into the cliffs of the Punta da Ma Merenda, just to the north of our target; and bit by bit, still deliciously under our lee, the breakwaters and lighthouse of Praia da Vitoria harbour presented themselves out of the bland mass of construction that was the town itself.

For weeks I had reflected on our moment of arrival and the conditions that we might meet as we made our landfall. For the engineless sailor this is critical; the last mile or two are the most dangerous. Everything now combined in our favour. The northerly shift had taken the vicious edge off the wind, a softening that soon allowed me to set all but the last panel of sail. As we neared the land and its protection from the south-west swell, the seas too relented, smoothing rapidly, and before long we were racing, haring, leaping along and all, at last, was again well with the world.

I sat in the hatchway, binoculars in hand, and revelled in our approach. I had been right to keep to windward. The current was pushing us south, but it was by now clear that the wind was well set and that there was no risk of us being carried past the harbour entrance. I eased us off just a degree or two more and now *Mingming* was flying. From time to time shafts of morning sunlight ranged along the coastline, bringing every last detail into high relief. The lower slopes, more populated than I would ever have imagined, gleamed with their covering of close-spaced white houses. Behind, the land rose in long tiered whalebacks, pushing skywards into the cloud that enveloped the highest peaks.

Four hours of glorious sailing was all it took to bring us close. We were now just a mile or so off the high cliffs of the Punta da Ma Merenda, topped with its fort-like building. I had long since picked out the red and white striped lighthouse that marked the southern end of the harbour entrance. A small ship arrived and anchored well to the south of us. I pulled myself on deck and took over the steering. Now we could run off a little, straight for the half-mile gap between the breakwaters. With the wind on her quarter *Mingming* picked herself up and careered along, foaming and bubbling, joyously. I played the mainsheet, dinghy-style, for once glad of this physical connection with our progress. It seemed fitting that for this last short leg I should take over as helmsman and reassert our union. The entrance was now just a hundred yards away. There was the cardinal marker to leave to starboard. A big catamaran, loaded with waving passengers, no doubt on a Saturday day trip, motored out to leeward of us. We skimmed between the breakwaters. I checked my watch; this was, after all, the finishing line of the Jester Azores Challenge. Ten forty-six. I let off a long blast of my foghorn, brought on deck for the purpose. I had no expectation that it would be heard, this raucous alarum to the high heavens, but I fired it off anyway. It made me feel better.

17

The harbour at Praia da Vitoria is excellent. Sheltered behind the two breakwaters is a stretch of water half a mile wide and, on its north-south axis, about a mile long. Tucked away in the north-west corner is the municipally-owned marina. To the east of this is a fine anchorage giving onto a sandy beach. At the southern end of the harbour lie the fishing port and commercial wharf. The town itself, with its beaches of dusky volcanic sand, its waterfront parks and restaurants and bars, its palm trees and its white buildings detailed in startlingly unrestrained colours, runs down the west side of the harbour.

We shot between the breakwaters into this spacious and tranquil lake, its surface brushed by the brisk breeze from the north. Smooth water, with not even the faintest swell to disturb it. I hardened in the sheet, ready for the short beat up the harbour to the anchorage. Six or seven cruising yachts already lay there. Leaving *Mingming* to sail herself I went forward to un-lash the anchor and to cut away the tape sealing the chain-pipe. I need not have bothered. As we neared the anchorage a dinghy, powered by an outboard motor and well-laden with passengers, appeared from behind the marina wall, heading in our direction. At first I assumed it was from one of the anchored yachts and carried on sailing. The dinghy, though, kept on straight for us, and as it neared I could see arms waving and gesticulating. I let go the mainsheet and we lay gently there, waiting. Here in the dinghy, signalling for me to lower the mainsail, was Trevor Leek of *Jester,* here was George Jepps of *Culica,* here was Denis Gorman of *Auld Meg,* as fine a cross-section of Jester Challengers as one could hope to meet, come out to greet us and to tow us into the marina. In the stern of the dinghy, operating the motor, sat a young local in a smart white polo shirt and blue shorts. A short line was made fast to the bow of the dinghy, which then set off at speed, in reverse, with *Mingming* following close behind. In this strange configuration, nose-to-nose, we waltzed our way into the marina, where we were deposited, with a few crashes and bangs, into a berth. Within a few seconds a crowd appeared on the pontoon, laughing and joking and shouting congratulations and taking photographs. And what a crowd! Here now were John Gozzard of *Pippin* and Tony Head of *Triple Venture,* who handed me a juicy orange, and Nick Bridges of *Dolphin* and Stan Snape of *Moonbow* and Dominique Katan of *Nea-Kameni.* Here now were Graham Jewitt of *Golden Dragon* and Tim McCloy of *China Blue.* Richard Cutsforth of *Sprinter* was there, and so too were John Margarson of *Lucy* and Roger Fitzgerald of *Ella Trout.* Here they all were, packed close together on the narrow pontoon, noisy and excited, united by the long and lonely ocean passage each one had just completed, cemented in a brotherhood of the sea, happy to excess to see another of their number arrive and join them. I stood by *Mingming's* mast and grinned stupidly, overcome by this babble of voices, by this sudden rush of humanity, by the warmth and camaraderie of this bunch of unassuming, extraordinary sailors. A hundred questions were flung my way but my answers were hoarse and monosyllabic. All I could do was grin, stupidly. I felt light-headed, levitational. The blood in my veins coursed hotly. A more formal photograph was called for. Trevor Leek of *Jester* stepped aboard and we posed in a handshake as the shutters clicked. The laughter and joshing continued. Little by little I got a sense of what had gone on. First in was the Frenchman Dominique Katan, in *Nea-kameni*, in about eleven days. This was not unexpected but I was delighted for him. Out of the forty-two starters, *Mingming* was twenty-fifth to arrive. Not bad. There had been the inevitable retirements. Several yachts were still at sea. We had arrived just three days after *Jester* herself. Not bad. Of our close contenders, *Golden Dragon* had arrived two days previously and *Belgean* was still at sea. I was happy with this. *Mingming* had done well.

Now there were calls to come ashore! Come and have a beer! Come and have a cup of tea! It was all too much. My head was reeling with so much stimulation. Denis Gorman, sensing my hesitation, put a simple question: *Roger, what would you most like right now?* I answered from the heart, not quite, at the time, seeing the irony in my reply: *I'd just like to spend a couple of minutes on my own.*

It may seem crazy. I had just spent twenty-one days, less two hours, on my own. I was not yet ready, though, to go ashore, to abandon *Mingming*. I needed a little time before launching into the usual social exchanges. That morning's turnaround in our fortunes had been so complete and unexpected that I could scarcely believe that we were there. The transition from the agonies of the previous few days to this heady moment of welcome had been too rapid. I just wanted to lay down below for half an hour or so, to enjoy the stillness and savour the feeling of a voyage well executed. I wanted to tidy the deck and put everything in order. I wanted to sit quietly in the hatchway and observe this new island world. I needed a little time to let the frustrations and anxieties of the last week drain away.

The Jester Challengers drifted off and I spent a happy hour coming slowly back to earth. It was now after midday.

Aromas were wafting over from the restaurants nearby, reviving dreams about salt cod and Portuguese potatoes. It was time to dig out some money and take a run ashore.

Postscript

We left Praia da Vitoria just two and a half days later, bound once more for Plymouth. It was a magical stay on a charming island; charming, that is, if you ignored the constant low passes of the US Air Force jets based there. The locals could not have been more welcoming; the municipality even laid on a bus, air-conditioned and sumptuously leathered, to give us a tour. They organised a reception in the foyer of the local theatre, but it was on a public holiday, and no-one turned up to receive us. As ever, it was young Duarte who stepped into the breach. Duarte it was who, in his capacity of marina employee and boat handler, had reversed the dinghy from mid-harbour into a marina berth, with *Mingming* in tow. Duarte it was who, now transformed to state bureaucrat, had taken me through the clearance procedures in the marina office. Duarte the language teacher it was who had taught me the correct way to pronounce Terceira – *Toorsay-eera.* Duarte it was who had effortlessly become our tour guide and given us an impressively professional commentary throughout our coach ride. And so, inevitably, when the *Presidente,* as the mayor is called, failed to show up at his own reception, Duarte it was who gave a fluent and gracious speech of welcome in perfect English, and accepted the Jester pennant on the mayor's behalf. I have high hopes for Duarte. One day he will surely be *Presidente.*

On the first night we all went out to dinner to celebrate

Mingming's arrival. I was still heavy with salt cod and Portuguese potatoes, but managed to squeeze in a plateful of fine local octopus. On the second night we all went out to dinner to celebrate my birthday, and the arrival of Bill Churchouse in *Belgean*. *Mingming* had scraped in just twelve hours ahead of him. By now heavy with two lunches of salt cod and Portuguese potatoes, interspersed with a plateful of fine local octopus, I found room for another plateful of fine local octopus.

On the third evening, following our coach tour and reception, *Mingming* and I sailed out of the marina at six in the evening and headed homewards. For a day or two the wind puffed uselessly out of the north-east, and then the fun started. The westerlies came and they came with a vengeance. Day after day it blew Force 6 or more, on and on without let-up, day after day after day, building an ugly sea, to be sure, but a sea that was slightly aft of the beam and therefore almost a following sea, a home-going sea, a sea which dealt out its fair share of awkwardness and discomfort but which was essentially working for us rather than against us and which I could therefore not, in any way, regret. We were lashed by squalls under black skies and lashed by squalls out of the piercing blue. I saw a few whale spouts but any meaningful observation was impossible in those massive swells. For a day the weather relented as we crossed onto soundings at the Little Sole Bank. A pod of four or five pilot whales joined us for a few minutes, but *Mingming* could not bewitch them as she had their northern cousins. A hundred miles out from the Lizard a vicious south-westerly gale swept past but we ran happily on before it and clocked up one hundred and ten miles in the day, *Mingming's* best run to date. At dusk on a quiet summer's evening, in an uncanny re-run of the previous year, we dropped anchor in Cawsand Bay in Plymouth Sound, just sixteen days and two hours out from Praia da Vitoria.

It had been a wild, breathless run.

The next morning I took *Mingming* into Queen Anne's Battery Marina and within a couple of hours she was once more ashore. It would be ten months before we would sail together again. I could hardly wait. My mind was long since made up. We would once more be heading to the far north.

Mingming's *new stainless steel masthead fitting*

Jordan Series Drogue cone attached to its warp. Mingming's
drogue has eighty-six cones.

Mingming *moored at Queen Anne's Battery Marina, between (l.) Alexei Fedoruk's converted Dragon* Fason, *and (r.) Graham Jewitt's Kingfisher 20* Golden Dragon.

Leaving Plymouth Sound, with Jester *herself, and skipper Trevor Leek, astern.*

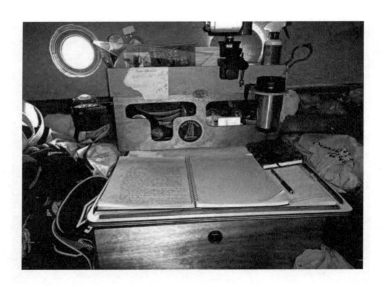

Mingming's *combined chart table, writing desk and dining table. It swings round to give access to her single burner alcohol stove.*

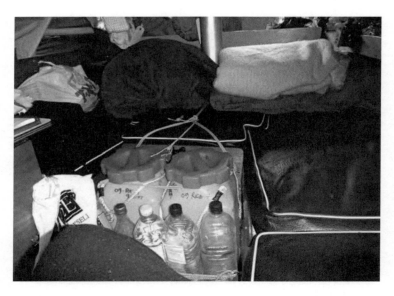

Mingming's *interior, looking forward. The labelled containers hold a set number of main meals.*

Mingming *and I just a few minutes after arriving at Praia da Vitoria. (Courtesy of Tony Head.)*

Farewell to the Azores.

PART THREE

ICE

Ah, but wasn't it great! What a wonderful and uplifting thing it was, to sail through this frozen waste in the tiniest of sailboats!

1

A single thought nourished me throughout the long winter months. It was an unrealistic image, hopelessly romantic, dangerously seductive. Under a sky of brilliant blue *Mingming* drifted through fields of ice. The floes and bergs, slabbed and corniced into unworldly, fantastical shapes, glinted and sparkled. It was an enchanted scene, suspended and silent save for the faintest creak and groan of frozen ice-block on frozen ice-block. It was a scene of the ends of the earth, of the last imaginary place, a scene of the most delicious desolation. The more the picture took form and shape and colour the more I longed for it. To sail *Mingming* in ice! Now that would be something! It need not be for long. Half a day, even half an hour, would do. What better apotheosis for an aged Corribee and her declining skipper? It would define the unlikeliness of our partnership. Hell, you don't sail little plastic yachts into the pack, single-handed. So then, let's get on and do it.

I pulled out my northern charts and pondered, measuring distances with spread fingers. Several things quickly became clear. Given that I still had only six weeks or so available for a voyage, it would make sense this time to start from further north. Were we to leave from northern Scotland, then two locations, place names that had resounded in my head, unattainably, for a lifetime, suddenly became viable objectives.

The first was Jan Mayen. Few people have heard of this

extraordinary island; even fewer know where it is. It is the only land lying, roughly speaking, between the Shetlands and the North Pole. It is just thirty miles long, on a narrow south-west to north-east axis, the last majestic outcrop of the mid-Atlantic ridge and therefore a distant cousin to the Azorean peaks. It can learn nothing from these in the matter of dramatic topography. At its northern end the volcano Mount Beerenberg rises sheer out of the Arctic waters to a height of seven thousand feet. Until recently Jan Mayen marked the eastern boundary of the winter pack ice; it was, in effect, frozen in. Climate change has forced the winter ice to recede about eighty miles to the west. As a lifelong reader of the books of the extraordinary navigator and mountaineer Bill Tilman I had for years known of Jan Mayen. It was here that Tilman had lost his beloved pilot cutter *Mischief*. Perhaps we too could sail in the same distant waters as the great man, and with a happier outcome.

At the height of summer we would not find ice at Jan Mayen, but it was not too far away. My finger traced west towards the Greenland coast, just three hundred miles distant. My heart jumped a little as two words appeared: Scoresby Sound. There was something almost terrifying in the contemplation of these thirteen seemingly innocuous letters. Here was the world's largest fjord, pretty much permanently icebound, named for its discoverer, the younger of those great Arctic explorers, Martin Scoresby and his eponymous son. This is not a place to be taken lightly. The water temperature hovers around zero degrees. Even in July and August it is difficult and dangerous to approach. Calving bergs and leftover winter pack are carried down from further north by the East Greenland Current. The fields of ice swirl in kaleidoscopic unpredictability. Even the wary can quickly be surrounded and entrapped. This is a place that demands reinforced steel prows, thunderous engines, masthead lookouts, refreshed crews and a good dose of luck. *Mingming* scarcely qualified. Nevertheless, the temptation was too great; to sail due west from Jan Mayen would give me a good chance of the kind of brief encounter I was looking for. It was unlikely that at that latitude, about 71°N, I would be able to make any contact with the Greenland coast, but that was bye the bye. It was the ice I was after.

My eye ranged further around the charts and another flurry of measurement confirmed my suspicion; a third objective, as outrageous for little *Mingming* as Jan Mayen and the Greenland ice, was, given a reasonably fast passage, quite feasible. From the vicinity of Scoresby Sound we could shape a course homewards by first sailing south through the Denmark Strait, the two hundred mile wide stretch of water between Iceland and Greenland. This would give an altogether more satisfyingly circular configuration to our voyage. It would add a lot of distance, but would take us close to the most interesting region of Iceland, the north-west fjords. It would bring the whole of Iceland within our compass. Given that two years previously we had struggled even to graze her southern coast, that was an attractive thought; I was determined to lay to rest our failure to reach north-east Iceland and the Arctic Circle. The loose shape of our prospective voyage was now clear in my head; north to Jan Mayen, west towards Scoresby Sound, south through the Denmark Strait and then, all being well, home.

The play of my imagination had run its course. Now it was time for the hard work of uncompromising preparation. It was not practical to make *Mingming* any stronger, but I could still make her a lot warmer. A constant chill, overlaid with a permanently damp and dripping coach roof, had been a feature of our previous northern voyage. I had often lain shivering at night. My knees had kept up a dull ache. I was now intending to sail well over five hundred miles further north, and west too into the East Greenland Current. The low water and air temperatures were a serious consideration. I decided to line the whole of the hull and coach roof with insulating foam and carpet. This would help keep the cold out, the warmth in, and would minimise any condensation. A little research uncovered an ideal material for the job. Plastazote is a strong and inert nitrogen-blown foam, with excellent insulation and flotation qualities. It is often used in buoyancy aids and can be bought in different thicknesses and densities. My plan was to line the hull with an inch thick layer, with carpet on the inside of this; for the coach roof I would use half inch foam and carpet.

I can describe my intentions in a single sentence, but the execution took nine months of cramped and dirty work. I had to strip out all of *Mingming's* stores and equipment. I had to remove all of her existing hull lining, a vinyl-type material backed by thin foam that after nearly thirty years was rotten and flaking. The remains of this foam had to be scraped off and the hull interior sanded back to take the fresh glue. However much I tried to keep the job clean, I was working constantly in a mess of detritus and dust. As I worked my way around the hull the new lining foam had to be cut and shaped to a hundred awkward patterns. Each one was then used as the template for the carpet that would cover it; I had bought a couple of rolls of off-cut for a few quid.

The fitting was hard, but the gluing itself tested my patience to the limit. Normal contact glue, which is quick and efficient, is also highly flammable, even potentially explosive in confined spaces, and so unsuitable for the job. I had to use a water-based alternative. Once applied to the two surfaces to be joined it has to be left for the water to evaporate before being offered up. Inside a cold hull, with no air circulation, this could take hours and hours. I accelerated the process using a hair dryer and so spent most of the winter wafting it back and forth over acres of damp glue. Every piece of foam to be fitted required four surfaces to be prepared for gluing: the hull itself, both sides of the foam and the backing of the carpet. Every surface had to be thoroughly dried out once I had brushed on the glue. The music of that winter was the whir and whoosh of my little hair dryer as I swung it back and forth, over and round, up and down, on and on, for hour after hour, interminably. The one consolation was that it kept me warm.

The hull lining gradually advanced, lending a cosier feel to *Mingming's* interior. I realised that I was constructing an exemplary padded cell; it seemed somehow appropriate. Outside, in the real world, I had one other major task for the winter: the construction of a pair of sweeps. I already had provision to scull *Mingming*; to propel her, that is, by means of a long oar used over the stern in a figure-of-eight movement. This was fine for moving her around marinas and docks. I was not convinced, however, that sculling would be particularly efficient in the open sea. My fifteen foot sculls would be difficult to manhandle, too, in anything of a seaway. I needed an alternative method of moving *Mingming* along, should it be necessary.

I was well aware that for this voyage I might well have to row in open sea. I was intending to take an engineless yacht into ice. To be becalmed amongst floes and bergs which, pushed around by deeper currents, move to their own unfathomable logic, is doubly dangerous; they can shoulder you along wherever they fancy. Bill Tilman's next pilot cutter, *Sea Breeze,* was lost in this way. Becalmed off Angmassalik on the East Greenland coast, with a defunct engine and no sweeps, she had been pushed onto a rocky outcrop and sunk. Tilman and his crew were lucky to have been able to scramble onto a nearby ledge and even more fortunate to have been spotted the next day by a local fisherman. I decided to equip *Mingming* with two ten foot sweeps. They might also be useful for fending off any over-friendly ice.

I was about to buy some Douglas fir and build a pair of sweeps when luck intervened. Late one wintry Saturday afternoon I was up in Woodbridge, Suffolk, prior to giving a yacht club talk. With half an hour to kill I wandered around the town's endlessly fascinating waterfront area. I meandered along to Andy Seedhouse's dinghy park and his Aladdin's cave of a second-hand chandlery and there they were. Tucked away up against a wall, mixed in with a load of assorted junk too long or too awkward to fit inside, were not two but three old but beautiful sweeps. None of them matched, but it wouldn't take much work to fashion two into an identical pair. They were slightly longer than I wanted. Well, it would be easy enough to shorten them a little.

Within a week, and with the invaluable help of Paul Webster, skipper of the smack *The Quiz* and my host at the Woodbridge Cruising Club, I had the two sweeps I had selected back at my workshop in Burnham, laid out side by side on trestles, and ready for resuscitation. With a snub plane I took a few shavings off each loom to expose the raw wood beneath. Yes! Here was dense and honey-coloured ash, as good as the day it was hewn. I measured the diameter of each loom. Both were two and a half inches across, an identical match and as solid as they come. One blade was longer and wider than the other, but not for long; half an hour with saw and plane had them neatly twinned. They had been stood up in damp earth for so long that the grip ends of both looms were starting to rot. I sawed an inch off each, bringing the ends back to sound timber. I trimmed the blades to create two sweeps exactly ten feet long.

The sweeps were to be used fisherman-style, leaned on with the operator facing forward. I had already fixed heavy mahogany blocks, run through with stainless steel thole pins, to each side of the cockpit coaming. I soon had the sweeps nicely leathered and fixed to the thole pins with thick rope grommets. The sweeps would lay there permanently along the after side decks, ready to be run out for immediate service.

Every winter entailed resuscitatory work on *Mingming's* mainsail; it was by now a mass of patches and hand stitching. The junk rig, fully-battened and soft, is forgiving on a sail but, as far as the two top panels were concerned, I decided that enough was enough. These panels are my storm canvas. I had already shown that they could keep *Mingming* to windward in Force 9 conditions. I did not doubt that plenty of heavy weather was in prospect for this voyage; we would twice have to run the gauntlet of the Atlantic lows as we headed to and from the Arctic. I carried the sail over the road to Mike Williams at Wilkinsons Sails, and asked him to replace the two top panels.

Once more a winter's work had made a step change in *Mingming's* fitness for purpose. Her new sweeps, painted in *Mingming's* trademark Atlantic grey, had her deck bristling with apparatus like some miniature engine of war. Below, her new lining had transformed her potentially icy interior into a warm and welcoming space. During the coming months at sea I would many times curl up in foetal tightness and relish the comfort of my sea-going womb. With new storm panels, the first replacement to *Mingming's* mainsail in twenty-nine years, we were now ready for anything the north Atlantic may care to throw at us. My excitement was growing. After ten months ashore it was time, once more, to get going.

2

On the southern shore of the Moray Firth lies what was once an archetypal Scottish fishing village. Heavy single-storey houses of sombre grey stone, so squat that they seem to be burrowing into the hillside as a defence against the northerly gales, line the street that wends down to the harbour. The architecture here is a study in the solid and the immutable. The sea has no certainty; let our homes at least feel earth-bound, permanent, safe.

The fishing has now all but gone. The sheds and commercial buildings around the dock lie mostly empty. A few small creel boats still work their pots, but the real fishing craft, seventy-footers that ranged the seas from Rockall to Muckle Flugga with crews of five or six or seven, are all sold or scrapped. Old photographs show a harbour packed with identical wooden double-enders, smartly painted and numbered, their decks a mess of heavy spars and ropes and gear. There is a beauty in the repetition, in the sense of faith in these craft, in the communality of the enterprise.

A decade or so ago the Commissioners of Whitehills Harbour faced up to the inevitable: the fishing was dead. Survival meant adaptation; the harbour would henceforth be given over to 'recreational' use. Pontoon berths were installed to provide homes for the shiny yachts of oil industry executives. A long visitors' pontoon was introduced into the outer harbour to cater for the passing trade of cruising yachtsmen. Such is the tale the length and breadth of the Scottish coastline. A few of the bigger harbours have been retained for what is left of the deep-sea fishing heritage; the rest are tentatively joining the smart new world of the marina, the security code and the electronic point of sale.

Whitehills Harbour has just forty permanent berths. Its scale matched that of *Mingming*. It seemed that it may be an ideal location to start and finish our voyage. Once out of the harbour there is a clear run north past the Orkneys and Shetlands. Should I have difficult conditions when making our return landfall the wide mouth of the Moray Firth gives room and enough to heave to and wait for the right moment to come in. In the depths of that winter I contacted the harbourmaster, David Findlay, himself a former deep-sea fishing skipper, outlining my plans and what I would need. His reply was so positive and friendly that my mind was immediately made up: our voyage would start and, if all went well, finish at Whitehills.

I arrived with *Mingming* in tow one overcast evening in late June after a fifteen hour drive from Burnham-on-Crouch. A light smear of rain was attempting to fall. It was low tide, turning the inner and outer harbours into deep square pits. I was impressed by the unnecessary thickness of the harbour's concrete wall, until a friendly yachtsman gave me the code for the harbour's showers and kitchen. Photographs lined the walls, several showing massive seas breaking over the harbour, drowning the berthed yachts virtually to the masthead in a mix of driving spray and solid water. I remembered the Almanac's warning that the harbour entrance is dangerous in strong onshore winds. Quite.

I parked in front of the harbourmaster's office and slept on board. The next morning, without ado, I was introduced to the friendliness of Whitehills. Here was genuine interest and a willingness to help. David Findlay was recovering from an operation. In his stead was another ex-fishing skipper, Jim Abel. Jim's deep-set eyes and lined face, his quiet authority, had evolved from a lifetime of hard and dangerous work. He told me of his time off the Western Isles, of his techniques for handling his ship in the worst of storms. He explained the difficulties of getting a seventy-foot boat into port when the sea was up. Whitehills has the narrowest of entrances, bound on one side by rocks, on the other by the harbour wall. At the end of this narrow corridor a skipper must make a ninety degree turn to port through a gap not much wider than the boat itself. To bring a ship in, laden with fish, through the surf and surge, was no mean feat of seamanship. From time to time skippers would be forced to do it in the worst of weather. Other ports were safer, but they bristled with inspectors. A catch could be landed at home with fewer questions asked. Here was the classic conflict of interest between a faceless bureaucracy, and the immediate needs of men who must feed their children and pay their mortgages.

I moved *Mingming* down to the dockside, ready for craning in. A spotless dark green Land Rover drew up alongside. A face, lightly bearded and wound about with cigarette smoke, poked from the driver's side and asked in the soft local lilt: *Roger Taylor, I presume?* I nodded in assent. *I'm Jimmy. I'm in charge of ordering your crane. When would you like it for?* I was puzzled. *Are you one of the Commissioners, Jimmy? Aye, and I like to help out.*

It summed up Whitehills. Jimmy Forbes had a farm a couple of miles along the coast. For all my time at Whitehills, both before and after the voyage, he was a constant helpful presence. Within an hour of meeting him a mobile crane had arrived from Macduff Shipyards. With Jim and Jimmy and various bystanders helping out we soon had *Mingming* afloat and tied up in her berth.

It was a few more days before we could leave. *Mingming's*

trailer was to be kept at Whitehills, but I had to drive my vehicle back south and return by train and bus. On Thursday the twenty-fifth of June, well-laden with fresh last-minute stores - green apples, a hand of unripe bananas and a couple of loaves of long-life bread - I caught a train from Euston and headed north. My plan had been to leave some time over the following weekend, but as I studied the newspaper weather charts I realised that a perfect weather window was already there for the taking. High pressure with a steady easterly airflow was settling in. I did not dare waste it. High water was at three o'clock the next morning. By the time I had reached Aberdeen my mind was made up: we would leave that night.

There remained the problem of getting *Mingming* out of Whitehills Harbour. During the daytime one of the creel boats could pull me out, but at two or three in morning I would have to shift for myself. I was reconciled to a long row out at slack water. At least the new sweeps would get a good blooding. I need not have worried. Chatting with some of the local yachtsmen once back at Whitehills, I discovered that one was leaving too that night, to go to the opening celebrations of the new marina at Wick, further up the coast. He was intending to depart at two o'clock. He would be happy to take a line and pull us out. Perfect. Ten months of planning and hard work had brought us to this one point where everything had gelled so fortuitously that I felt we were in line for a good and rewarding voyage. Good and rewarding it indeed turned out to be, but it was long and tough too, and left no room, not one tiny sliver of daylight, between those twin and opposing peaks of success and disaster.

3

It took us a while to get going. Once we were well clear of the harbour entrance I had signalled to Keith Alderton, skipper of *Traigh Mhor*, to cast off the tow-line. We had shouted final wishes of good luck and as I hauled up *Mingming's* mainsail *Traigh Mhor's* stern light had shrunk into the gloom ahead. A fortuitous little patch of wind on the starboard quarter had quickly given us a mile or so of offing, enough for comfort on this ebb tide, and then moved on. We now lay there, pulsing gently to the softest of swells. Despite the haze and the threat of fog banks, the Scottish half-night was evaporating rapidly, dulling the uneven scatterings of coastal lights and giving outline then shade and then form to the easy undulations of the Speyside hills astern. Strange geometric textures resolved into the close-packed rooflines of Banff and Macduff. To the west bolder headlands solidified, blackly. As the pre-dawn light intensified a row of gangly white giants, their arms twirling in synchronised semaphore, sprang up on the skyline above Whitehills. They had wind to drive them, these turbines up on the hills, but we had nothing, not a breath. I didn't care. We were once more at sea. *Mingming* was alive again. The tide was pushing us slowly offshore, narrowing the band of low hills to the south, hills now glowing in patches on their topmost eastern flanks as a weak sun imposed itself through the early morning haze. We drifted away and I swelled once more with the happiness of freedom and imminent adventure. I stared long and hard at the receding landscape, imprinting it on my memory and wondering when and if I would see it again.

The wind came slowly at first, a zephyr from east-north-east. I hardened in the mainsail and *Mingming* set off north. The self-steering gear was not yet connected. The tiller was unlashed. In a perfect and uncanny balance *Mingming*, every inch the well-mannered yacht, sailed herself while I, busying myself below, was struck by how quickly we were settling once more to our sea-going partnership. It was our fourth consecutive year of voyaging. Those thousands of ocean miles were now counting for something. The routines were second nature; the learning curve was flattening. I felt totally at ease.

By noon we were just twelve miles offshore when the expected breeze came in. *That's more like it!* With a glorious Force 4 from just ahead of the beam I finally hooked up the self-steering and *Mingming* bounded forward, creaming the waters of the Moray Firth under her forefoot. The bubbling set my heart soaring. *Now we're on our way!* The midday sun had burned off any remaining mist. The ocean sparkled. We were not alone; parties of common guillemots and black guillemots and razorbills and puffins zipped here and there, interspersed with more sedate groupings of kittiwakes and wheeling fulmars. The occasional gannet or two lumbered by. How good it felt to be back once more in this other world. From time to time a ship plied north or south and by late afternoon, with land just a distant smudge, we had our first close encounter as a small container ship, the *Selfoss*, bearing the enigmatic legend GIMSKIP in bold lettering on her sides, passed astern, heading for Wick or perhaps the Pentland Firth. Ahead, a blue and white fishing boat mooched back and forth.

Meanwhile I was facing a dilemma. I had to make a

decision, and soon. I had a problem. It was all to do with Jimmy's steak and sausages. Jimmy had presented them to me the evening before: a gift of home-grown Aberdeen Angus steak and six stubby sausages, fresh out of his freezer, as fine a pack of meat as a departing sailor could wish for. It was an offering I could not refuse. Perhaps I should have done, but I did not have it in me to meet generosity with churlishness. Jimmy had been so kind. He was rightly proud of the meat he produced. How could I tell him I did not really want it? I had accepted Jimmy's steak and sausages and now they lay in *Mingming's* cool bilge locker, thawing nicely, soon to be perfect for cooking, their presence gnawing away at me. What was I going to do?

I had not eaten meat for the best part of thirty years. There was no particular dogma attached to this. Through circumstance I had stopped eating meat, felt better for it, and without much conscious thought had become, more or less, a vegetarian. Fish still figured, from time to time, in my diet, but meat had been off the menu for decades.

Therein lay my dilemma. I had accepted Jimmy's steak and sausages; I had to eat them. I was a vegetarian; I could not eat them. I was hoist on my own cowardly petard. To sling Jimmy's steak and sausages overboard would be a gross betrayal of kindness; to eat Jimmy's steak and sausages would be to undermine some vaguely principled notions.

I thought long and hard about Jimmy's steak and sausages and grew hungry with the effort. It was getting on for dinner time. The prospect of a fresh Aberdeen Angus steak sizzling in my frying pan turned from mildly repulsive to succulently enticing. Perhaps it was all that fresh sea air. Perhaps it was two long days with little sleep. The more I considered the dilemma of Jimmy's steak and sausages, the more strongly I could smell delicious meaty odours wafting through the cabin. I could hear the happy spit and splutter of flesh searing in hot fat. By now I was ravenous. My genetic imprint took over. Buried in there was the carnivorousness of the caveman. It was no good. With a sudden rush I lit the stove and threw the steak, now fully thawed and oozing blood, into the frying pan. Within a minute or two it was spitting and spluttering and sending delicious meaty odours through the cabin. My saliva was flowing full tilt. I could almost have grabbed the steak from the pan and gnashed at the half-raw and bloody fibre there and then. With admirable restraint I cooked it thoroughly, concerned about making myself ill with this new dietary input, and ate it straight from the pan, cutting small slices and chewing them over and over, grinding the meat down to a soft and digestible pulp. God it was good! As I munched the steak I soon rationalised away the betrayal of my vague vegetarian principles. *I had to do it,* I thought, licking my fingers. *It's for Jimmy's sake*, I added, cutting another slice. *It's only just this once*, I told myself, coming up with a particularly tender and nicely browned morsel. *Waste not want not*, I intoned, rejoicing that it was such a good-sized steak.

We sailed on into the long northern evening in a breeze now well set and freshening. Around midnight I took over the steering with tiller lines to negotiate our way past a fishing boat shooting its nets. I could hear the clank and rattle of its gear and see two crewmen working on the after deck under bright floodlights. *Mingming* sped quietly by, tiny and unseen.

4

I was consumed by a single thought: *Head north*. For the moment little else mattered. It was northing I wanted, as much and as quickly as possible. The Arctic Circle wound its hypothetical girdle around the earth about five hundred miles away; Jan Mayen lay another three hundred miles or so further on. These were not huge distances, even for little *Mingming*, but with the constant threat of strong northerly winds I needed to be uncompromising in my intent. My aim was to lay down the straightest course possible, un-tempted by thoughts of the Faroes to our north-west or the coast of Norway to the east. A meandering course two years previously had eventually cost us more degrees of northerly latitude than I would have liked. I was not going to make the same mistake again. This time every inch sailed due north would be an inch well sailed; the rest would count for nothing.

By five thirty that morning we were already forty miles due east of the Pentland Firth and once more leaving the mainland astern. A chill wind was blowing, but it was a fair wind out of a faultless sky, encouraging *Mingming* forward at a healthy four knots. An oil rig service ship like a massive flat-bed truck overtook us to starboard. The first Arctic skua of the voyage sidled by astern, to be followed soon after by our first stormy petrel; confirmation, if it were needed, that we were now properly at sea.

I sat in the hatchway and watched the world, happy in my

work. At eleven I went below and with scarcely a qualm set Jimmy's sausages a-sizzling in the frying pan. I watched in fascination as the fat oozed out, half drowning the stubby fingers in a bubbling sea that popped and crackled like distant fireworks. I carefully turned each sausage to brown it thickly and evenly. Ancient memory reminded me to spear each one a few times with a fork, but still the meat forced its way out of each sausage end. There was something vaguely indecent about these growing protrusions of raw meat, but they soon browned too, and within a few minutes six perfect and princely bangers, magnificently odorous, disgustingly appetising, hopelessly irresistible, were ready. I ate a couple there and then, searingly hot straight from the pan, and left the rest to cool for later.

Tearing myself away from this scene of abject gluttony I checked the horizon and there, fine on the starboard bow, as yet little more than a darker insinuation along the rim of the sea, she was. Fair Isle! Last time we had passed this way, further to the east, a constant haze had obscured all land. Now, with conditions ideal for slipping through the Fair Isle Channel with only the slightest of jinks in our northerly trajectory and with, moreover, a less overcast set to the air, the islands and headlands that had previously been shrouded from view would all be revealed.

It took until ten in the evening for the scene to reach its culminating triangulation. All afternoon we worked our way past Fair Isle, sneaking by just a few miles to the west with the ebb tide beneath us. Softly lit by a slowly declining sun that set off every roll and dimple of her curvaceous form, she, for the island demanded, that day at least, the feminine pronoun, lived up to her name. The high grassy slopes, shimmering olive-blue, rolled down to cliffs devoid, for once, of any threat. The white-painted lighthouse and the buildings of the southern settlement slid slowly from view as we moved on north, pushing out into the Atlantic proper. As the evening wore on the points of the triangle settled themselves into an almost perfect symmetry: now well astern, on our starboard quarter, Fair Isle; ahead, on our starboard bow, Foula, the westernmost Shetland isle; intersecting the two, way off square on our starboard beam, Sumburgh Head, the southerly point of the Shetland mainland. My eyes ranged constantly round the three points. As the sun settled, each nodule of land glowed a different orange, its shade and intensity determined by distance and orientation and the sheerness or otherwise of cliff and hill. It was a singular, bewitching moment; I felt there and then that our voyage was already worth it.

The night was a short, twilight affair, but it was night nonetheless, until about two in the morning, when fire took hold of the clouds behind Foula, now almost abeam and a stark silhouette against a golden dawn. Way to seaward another flat-bed truck chugged north, its low square tray laced with fairy lights, but my attention was all the other way, on Foula, still a black cut-out, spiky and angular, its western end a dizzying drop from cloud to water. Foula; Fugloy; Fowl Eye; Bird Island. The linguistics of it dawned as suddenly and simply as the sun that now turned fire to inferno. It was a hellish scene of aching beauty; ebony cliffs backed by white-hot liquid gold.

The day proper soon came. By six that morning Foula was falling away to our south-east. It was time for a real sea-going chart; no need now for anything small-scale and coastal and parochial. With a flourish I pulled out the passage chart for the whole prospective voyage: Admiralty 4010 – 'Norwegian Sea and Adjacent Seas'. I had poured over this marvel for months, tracing lines with an optimistic fingertip, measuring and mulling. With this chart we could sail to Spitsbergen. We could head round the North Cape of Norway and make our way to the White Sea. With these few square feet of paper we could sail due west to Cape Farewell at the southern tip of Greenland. Jan Mayen lay only halfway up the grand expanse of sea laid out to the north. We could run on into the Greenland Sea. If the fancy took us we could make a little easterly detour into the Barents Sea. This was a chart alive with adventure and possibility. Angmassalik anyone? Murmansk? How about Bear Island? It was all here. I tingled with expectation and plotted a course to Jan Mayen. Three four six degrees true. Distance six hundred and eighty nautical miles.

A leading wind blew gently from east-north-east and we settled into the long haul north.

5

We crept away from Foula and the breeze stuttered a little, forcing me to go forward and un-gasket the light weather jib. My relationship with *Mingming's* two tiny headsails fell effortlessly once more into its love-hate mode. How many times had I sworn that I would never set the damn things again? How often had I promised myself that I would save them for the direst emergency only? I had left Whitehills intending to sail this whole voyage under mainsail alone, avoiding those nasty crawls forward and maintaining the purity of the junk configuration. The headsails were, after all, a kind of aberration unsuited, in engineering terms, to an un-stayed rig. They upset the subtle mechanics of mast and mainsail. I never felt at ease with a headsail flying; there was always a hint, in all but the lightest of airs, of impending disaster. I would watch the masthead anxiously, checking for signs of excessive bend, alert to the slightest intimation of an approaching squall.

The trouble was they worked. They could convert immobility to progress. Close-hauled they could give a noticeable turbo-charge to a stalled mainsail. With the wind a little freer they could add a knot or so to our speed. Hard as I tried, I just could not ignore them.

With the orange nylon genoa reluctantly set, then, we ghosted on over a strangely silent sea, stripped of the expected whirr and bustle of breeding auks and gannets. A few fulmars were settling in astern, though, forming an escort that would keep us company, albeit with constant changes of personnel, for the best part of three thousand miles. In the log I sketched an outline of Foula from the north-west. The sun burned hotter. By noon we were already a hundred and seventy-two miles from Whitehills and within a whisker of clear ocean. A tough-looking red fishing boat, LK 986, crossed our stern heading south-west, noisily. It gave us a few cheeky and un-seamanlike hoots of its siren, whether in derision, or out of companionship or boredom or high spirits was impossible to say, but I was glad to see the back of it; the raucous fellow had destroyed the composure of an early afternoon. Ahead lay the Clair oil rig and I altered course to the north-west to be sure of skirting it with a good margin; there was still enough tide and current hereabouts to do us mischief if the wind died completely. A couple of miles off our stern an out-sized cruise ship, luminously white and packed to the state-rooms, no doubt, with returning Arctic explorers, purred its way south-east. The afternoon wore on and a layer of dish-watery cloud took control of sky and horizon, bearing down heavily, trapping the day's warmth and turning the distant spire of the Clair rig into a misty and insubstantial phallus. Helped eventually by a more perky wind and the turn of the tide it took until ten that evening to work ourselves to the north of this last outpost of the industrialised world.

Now liberated, or so I thought, I settled on my narrow bunk for a celebratory nap. It did not last long. All sorts of motion and commotion soon penetrated my slumberous state, waking me with a start and forcing me to the hatch. We were careering along, way too fast and way too over-canvased, in a vicious rain squall that had leapt spitefully out of a placid sky. The light weather jib was, as it were, at the end of its tether, straining like billy-o and testing the strength of the masthead to its limits. The cabin boy fired off a self-righteous

Told you so or two, leaving old Ahab to handle and co-ordinate, using two hands and teeth, the three lines, sheet, halyard and downhaul, whose judicious interplay would bring the sail down snugly within the fore-deck netting. Well-doused and rudely awake I stood in the hatch and manipulated the jib with all the deftness of a coachman of an eight-in-hand, calming the bolting beast and reducing us to our usual stately trot. For good measure I also dropped a panel of the mainsail and, the squall having been the forerunner of a veering of the wind into the east, reset the self-steering.

We had not been quite alone throughout this little drama. The same oil rig delivery ship that I had seen the previous day was now crossing our bows, heading north-east. It was obviously doing the rounds, but I was puzzled; according to my chart there was no installation out that way. I slept fitfully through the shortest of nights, waking at one point to find we had mysteriously gybed and were heading south again. *No, no! Anywhere but south!* Annoyed at having lost some of our precious northing I quickly settled *Mingming* back on track.

Within an hour or two the third dawn of our voyage spread from the east, infusing the seascape with a startling clarity. Something about the air had changed. All hint of murk or haze was gone. The rim of the world circled us in a crisp unbroken line; I could almost see its curve and sphericality. I tried to comprehend this planetary scale and awful symmetry, to grasp the strange notion that we were adrift on the surface of a great ball and could sail on and on around it, afloat on an element-filled soup that itself lay on mud that lay on rock that itself floated on its own red-hot, unthinkable ocean; that there we all were, neatly layered and never falling apart; while the other way, skywards, there was no limit, absolutely no limit, nothing ever to stop us, a billion

billion possible gravitational traps excluded, should we have it in mind to abandon our horizontal trajectory and try, for a change, for the vertical.

These intergalactic musings were cut short by the appearance of a space-ship. It had evidently landed that night and was now implanting itself into the ocean a few miles on our starboard beam. It was a monstrous glinting construct that had lowered six massively-squared and close-spaced legs, cunningly cross-beamed and cross-braced, to the ocean floor now many hundreds of metres below. It was topped off with a dizzying array of unworldly flights-of-fancy: pipes and platforms and all manner of projection and protuberance. Cranes from outer space spiked the air at crazy angles. I had never seen anything so futuristic and misplaced. It was the missing oil rig, evidently still under construction and in seriously deep water.

We sailed on by and at seven that morning had our final encounter with the last outrider of the civilised world before, at last, breaking free; here was yet another cruise ship. It nosed its way over the western horizon, a shining blot on the seascape, and resolved into a gargantuan floating billboard, for its high sides were painted with a gaudy cyber-message: WWW.SMYRIL-LINE.COM. Happy in the knowledge that we, at least, were invisible to even the most hawk-eyed passenger watching from a Smyril Line breakfast bar, I turned my gaze to the northern horizon ahead. There we had a clear run towards an unblemished sky.

A little later we sailed within a foot or two of a fulmar. It sat there quietly, wings neatly folded, head drooped beneath the surface, dead in the water.

6

We had finally pierced the normal lines of sea-bound commerce and activity and were now, at long last, on our own. I spanned my hand around the chart and made a rough calculation. Ahead lay a million square miles of ocean. A million square miles! It fell easily enough under the eye, this vast wilderness; I could take it in with one rapid glance. It was almost inconceivable, though, at the scale of its yard by yard detail.

Over the next few days our progress faltered. The breeze still blew from the east but it grew more miserly in its mood, giving us less and less, withdrawing its bounty completely for long hours at a time. We often lay inert on the stillest of seas. Fulmars, sometimes several hundred of them, sat companionably with us, dozing or paddling inquisitively around *Mingming's* hull, from time to time breaking the peace with a short round of bickering. Once a great skua joined the floating escort, a dark addition accepted uneasily. A little pilot fish had adopted us, and occasionally flicked out from under our bilge to snatch a titbit from the surface with a swirl and a slap.

I had rarely seen a sea so smooth. The faintest hint of a reviving breeze soon had us gently on the move. Forward motion was indicated by almost imperceptible ripples from bow and quarter. I became expert at the assessment of these tiny undulations and, during brief spells of marginally more energetic air movement, of bubbles too. It was during this period that the seeds of a new theory of velocity, to be developed later in this voyage, were sown.

We eked out our northing, somehow never squeezing out less than forty miles per day, and usually around sixty, despite the general aura of inertia. As we moved towards the Arctic Circle the days grew hotter. I sweltered through afternoons that now hung on and on almost to midnight and I wished I had brought my wide-brimmed sun hat. Often I was forced to raise the folding hatch to keep the sun's rays from penetrating *Mingming's* cabin, whose new and remarkably effective insulation was, on this occasion, keeping unwanted heat in rather than cold out. It all seemed topsy-turvy and illogical and I worried that if it kept on like this there wasn't going to be much ice left further north.

One afternoon a whale blew softly and surfaced a hundred yards or so on our port beam. A second surfaced behind it, just as sedately; it was a pair of minke whales whose quiet understatement matched the somnolent mood.

The sea grew more glutinous by the day; we were drifting in a limitless vat of the finest hand-pressed olive oil. The reflected sun set the surface alight with a million dazzling ovoid patterns that split and grew and contracted and reformed in a fluid and unending dance that, if watched carefully for long enough, lost all connection with the real world of matter and became a kind of sensual abstraction, utterly absorbing, giddily mesmerising.

By noon on Wednesday the first of July we had been at sea for five and a half days and were now further north, by four nautical miles, than we had ever sailed. The Arctic Circle lay just two hundred miles away; about four hundred and seventy miles separated us from Jan Mayen. The decision to start our voyage from northern Scotland was already paying off handsomely. We had raced north effortlessly and were already entering what was for us unexplored territory. For the first time on this voyage I felt the heady elation of that moment of passage from the familiar to the unknown. On our last northern voyage it was the rounding of Unst and Muckle Flugga, aided by a similar south-easterly on the starboard quarter that was now driving us on into the Norwegian Sea, that had suddenly lifted my spirits and transformed the voyage from exercise to adventure. I had been surprised, this time, by how little I was affected in this way as we had cleared the Shetlands. Their proximity to our point of departure had no doubt dulled much of their exotic sheen; my focus, too, was so uncompromisingly fixed on the distant northerly targets that, despite the arresting beauty of Fair Isle and Foula, I had only, as it were, seen them at the edge of my vision, *en passant*. Now, at last, all the stimulatory ingredients – distance, solitude, uncertainty and danger – had combined to form their intoxicating brew.

As if on cue the weather began to change. A band of low and drizzly-looking cloud obscured the sun and bore down lower and lower, finally wrapping us up in a thick fog. The breeze that came with it, a respectable Force 3, pulled round into the south, a merciful wind for a north-bound sailor. I gybed *Mingming* onto port tack and for the first time on this voyage enjoyed the luxury of having my bunk on the downhill, comfortable side. The theme of comfort continued first thing the next morning, when I replaced my cotton sailing trousers with thermal long johns topped with woollen tracksuit bottoms. I pulled on a second pair of thick socks. I had been wearing a thermal long-sleeved vest for the whole voyage so far. The polo shirt and submarine sweater that covered it now became a permanent part of this sub-polar rig-out.

At seven that morning the wind hauled round to the north-west. At eight it started to ease. At eight-fifteen we were engulfed in heart-stopping mayhem.

7

It started innocuously enough, reached a rapid crescendo and was all over in just two or three minutes. At first there was nothing more than a fin, a single black tower, hydrodynamic, lethal, six feet high, scything the surface fifty yards astern. It moved at a speed I had never seen in any sea creature, nor thought possible. In a second or two it was gone, but not before the briefest impression of pied head markings had confirmed what I had immediately known; here, coming straight for us, was a very large, very male and very fast killer whale.

In those few seconds of that first sighting my mood leapt from morning torpor to tingling alertness and expectation. This was the encounter I had been longing for, and dreading, for many years. If there was anything living in the ocean that had both the capacity and possibly the will to attack *Mingming*, it was the killer whale. These huge predators, viciously toothed, hunt in ferocious well-organised pods. They batter away at larger whales, taking turns to drive their great solid heads into their out-sized cousins, weakening them into submission before tearing out and devouring their massive tongues. They launch themselves out of the water to take seals off ice floes or beaches. They have a well-developed and ruthless repertoire for getting at anything remotely edible.

I had often speculated on how they might react to *Mingming*. With her black-painted bottom and fin-like twin keels, would she be mistaken for a slow-moving sick whale? Might a group of killer whales be minded to give her a nudge or two out of curiosity? Pilot whales had slapped *Mingming's* hull with their tails, seemingly looking for a reaction. Even the mildest exploratory head-butt from a killer whale would shatter *Mingming's* fibreglass hull like eggshell. Even if they recognised that *Mingming* herself were inanimate and not worth the bother, might they sense the flesh within and try to prise it out? I had often wondered what I would do when the moment came, which, given the time I was spending at sea each year, it inevitably would. Would there be any way to repel an attack? Would a radio turned on full blast and held against the hull scare them off? Would I be able to bash them with an oar? What if I just yelled at them to bugger off?

A second killer whale surfaced to port and almost simultaneously there was one to starboard and within a few seconds they were everywhere, criss-crossing in seemingly random directions, some close, some a few hundred yards off. I was too rapt to feel fear. I had never seen such a combination of bulk and velocity. Here were creatures of five or six tons arcing between sea and sky at twenty knots. At each surfacing their powerful heads and fore-bodies shouldered aside the water, revealing, for the briefest of moments, the line and curve and somehow incongruous black and white mottling of their bodies. From time to time there was a hint of dull ochre somewhere in the colouring. It was easy to spot the smaller sickle-shaped fins of the females and the young.

The rhythm and patterning of the pod's progress was unlike anything I had seen before. There was none of the balletic grace and timing of close-packed pilot whales, none of the collective *joie de vivre* and leaping synchronisation of the smaller dolphins. Unlike the great whales, which seem to inhabit a different, slower time frame stripped of all hurry and urgency, the killer whales raced headlong, stealing a march on time, somehow always a fraction ahead of the clock by dint of their sheer speed and aggressive intent.

I had never witnessed such blatant self-confidence in the wild. These creatures feared nothing, and it showed. Within a few seconds they took command of the sea around us, dominating it, scouring it effortlessly in an electrifying display of brute power. There were, I think, about twenty of them. There was no discernible pattern to their interaction. They were well-spread. They surfaced singly. The pod arrived from the south and departed to the west. There was an overall direction of movement, then, but within that general heading they ranged around willy-nilly, slashing the surface in a furious series of random knife-cuts that left the sea boiling.

The sky erupted too. The enervation of the moment infected our normally placid fulmars. Hundreds were drawn in from their nearby territories, wheeling and hovering and swooping, topping off this column of sea- and sky-bound frenzy.

The great whales we had seen the previous year had imposed a new scale on the world, somehow turning the ocean into little more than a grand garden lake. These killer whales had a transformational power too, but it was at the level of intensity rather than scale. They suffused the sea and sky around them with a million-volt charge. Everything fizzed and shimmered and pulsated in a delicious terror. The pack sped along within this self-created aura, a great unseen miasma that somehow had every living molecule spinning and jostling at a madly heightened rate. I was as affected as anything else; I could have shrieked in joy for this moment. Here was something absolutely primeval, Jurassic, dog-eat-dog. Here were water-borne velociraptors, as fast and as uncompromising as their terrestrial counterparts. I could have shrieked, yes, but instead my murmured mantra, each time a pied tonnage cut the surface, was an awed *Oh my God.*

I watched and watched and quickly realised two things. Firstly *Mingming* was, to this foraging pack, an irrelevance. My little ship was of no account whatsoever. They were not interested; they couldn't care less. We may possibly have been examined surreptitiously from below, but no killer whale (I don't like to call them simply whales as technically they are a kind of dolphin) surfaced closer than about thirty yards. If they were at all curious they disguised it well. This lack of close approach was disappointing, but only mildly so, for the other realisation was that any thought of trying to dissuade a killer whale from its predetermined course of action was optimistic in the extreme. These were creatures that were going to do what they were going to do. The idea of swatting at them with a little oar was suddenly laughable. These fellows could destroy *Mingming* in a few seconds. A little distance between us was no bad thing.

Then they were gone. Within a few seconds the pod dissolved over the horizon, leaving us curiously bereft. The excitement drained off. The day lost its charge. Intensity faded. Normality returned. The sea was, for a moment, dull, empty, disappointing. I sat in the hatch and willed the pack to return. Already I wanted to taste again that raw animality, to know better that startling interface between the streamlined beauty of the killer and the finality of the killed. There was something to be learned here but it hovered just out of grasp. I replayed the visitation over and over in my head while *Mingming*, blind, deaf and unfeeling of the drama that had lightly grazed her, plugged on and on, always north.

8

It was by now our seventh day at sea: Thursday the second of July. My last-minute fresh food was almost gone, Jimmy's steak and sausages had long since worked their way back to the start of the food chain, and I was settling into the normal round of sea-going cooking and eating. Over the many months I had now spent voyaging with *Mingming* the overall structure of my diet and provisioning had changed little; there were just one or two gentle metamorphoses in the finer detail, derived from experience and changing preferences.

Sailing a very small light-displacement yacht long distances into remote areas presents some very specific problems as far as food and water are concerned. It is of course impossible to know exactly how long the journey will last and therefore how much food to take. More stores mean a slower boat and therefore the requirement for even more stores; it's a kind of vicious circle. What is more, serious account has to be taken of possible worst-case scenarios. What if *Mingming* is, say, dismasted at the furthest point of her trajectory and therefore has to sail a very long distance under jury rig? How many days or weeks would that add to the voyage? What if the self-steering fails, radically reducing our average daily distance? These are real and pertinent questions, particularly for the skipper of an engineless yacht, and one who has a pathological dedication to total self-sufficiency at sea, but they are impossible to answer with certainty.

To cope with this open-ended provisioning problem I have developed some simple rules-of-thumb. Firstly I measure the straight-line distance of the intended voyage. Let's say this is, as in the case of the Jan Mayen journey, about two and a half thousand miles. I then divide this by *Mingming's* average noon-to-noon distance made good, which has settled in to a remarkably consistent sixty-five nautical miles. That gives me an optimum voyage time of about thirty-nine days. Building in a provision for the constraints of coastal sailing when making our departure and landfall, I round that up to forty-two days: six weeks. I then provision for roughly *twice* that time as far as food is concerned, and *two and a half* times in respect of fluids. So, for this voyage, I had set sail with full food requirements for eighty days and enough water and other non-alcoholic drinking fluids for one hundred days.

As far as drinking is concerned, I survive very happily and without any adverse effects on much less than the recommended minimum. I get by on about two thirds of a litre per day. I am sure that this would be impossible were I not sailing such an easily-handled yacht that enables me to stay below, warm, relaxed and happily free of any excessive physical demands, for almost the whole time at sea. Deck work is dehydrating, as is exposure to wind and sun. Sitting contemplatively in a well-sheltered hatchway using eyes rather than muscles, or stretching idly on a cosy bunk, keep the body's demand for fluid at a low level. Seventy litres will last me for a hundred days. For this voyage I had stowed fifty-five litres of water in various permanently lashed containers from which water was regularly decanted, using a hand pump, into three two-litre plastic bottles kept lashed on the cabin sole and which enabled me to monitor my consumption. The balance of the liquids was made up from a bottle each of lime juice and blackcurrant juice used for occasional flavouring of the water, along with bottles of long-life milk and cartons of flavoured soya drinks. Additional fluid intake also came from the water and oils in my tinned food, all of which were used for cooking, and which were a kind of bonus to the basic calculation. I don't take tea or coffee with me. My preferred hot concoction is bouillon made from a powdered mix; even that I drink rarely.

My main meal of the day is cooked at about six every evening, using three standard components: pre-cooked flavoured rice or dried potato, a tin of fish and a tin of vegetables. This lot is cooked together in my saucepan and takes no more than five minutes, thereby conserving fuel. *Mingming* has a single burner alcohol stove. For a six week voyage I use less than a litre of methylated spirits. I have now taken to buying bigger tins of fish and vegetables. I eat a third to a half of the meal straight off. A little of the remainder is then used for an occasional mouthful during the night, and the rest for breakfast. Five minutes of cooking therefore provides food for about fourteen hours. I also take a supply of long-life desserts. It used to be one for each evening meal, but I now also take large plastic jars of preserved fruit in syrup, one of which will last for about a week.

This system allows me to plan and monitor very carefully. All of the tinned food, rice and one-off desserts are packed in large watertight containers, each one marked with how many meals it contains. At any one point in the voyage I know how many I have eaten and how many remain.

For lunch, taken once I have calculated and plotted our noon position and written up the daily statistics for the log, I have bread and cheese followed by an apple and a slice of home-made fruit cake. The bread is of the vacuum-packed German rye or sunflower or pumpernickel variety. It keeps for months and is extremely rich and nutritious. This is usually well-laced with spreadable butter then jam or marmite before the cheese, of which I take a wide selection from Cheshire and Red Leicester to Emmental and Gruyère, goes on top. The cheese and butter keep for months in a cool un-insulated locker well below the waterline.

This very simple food framework is then supplemented by a range of other edibles eaten on a more random basis: home-made flapjacks, home-assembled trail mix, energy bars and chocolate. I take a supply of muesli too, but regard this as emergency rations.

Mingming has a relatively small internal volume, especially since her fore and aft sections are now foam-filled and sealed. Despite this I have no problem at all stowing all these supplies with room to spare; one of the many advantages, no doubt, of not having an engine and all its associated volume, weight and gubbins. The engine space under the companionway is home to two large food casks containing about twenty meals, plus a selection of smaller self-sealing containers stocked with fruit cake and flapjacks. Unused locker space is filled with foam filled plastic bottles to reduce water ingress and aid buoyancy. As I sleep centrally on the starboard side there is plenty of space in the quarter berth areas for additional stowage. Clothing is stowed in watertight bags on the starboard quarter berth, along with my cameras and, when it is not in use, my sleeping bag. That's where all my rubbish goes too, well-sealed in black bin-liners. I don't throw anything in the sea, my own bodily waste excepted. The port quarter berth is given over to bosun's stores: warps, fenders, spare timber for repairs and so on. I also keep my rarely-used wet weather gear here and, lashed down in the most accessible position, the large bag that holds *Mingming's* series drogue. The solar-fed gel battery that powers *Mingming's* LED navigation lights is also housed at the inboard side of the port quarter berth in a strong well-secured box.

9

We sailed on in a sea of slate. In the flat northern light every wave-face seemed chiselled from hard grey stone. Here was every slaty hue: indigo and green-moss and cold milky-white. Here was every slaty texture: smooth and veined and ribbed and jagged. Here was slate from Cumbria and from Wales and from Cornwall and from Brittany, a kaleidoscopic showroom of hard unyielding slate. The wind eased and we ghosted on, scarcely rippling this quarried seascape. The wind picked up a tad and we tip-toed on into a bank of thick fog. Noon came. We were now half way to Jan Mayen but just drifting north, impelled by a reluctant breeze that had once more subsided to an almost imperceptible and uneven gasping. The waves, such as they were, had lost their hewn and angular look and melted into an igneous flux that rolled us gently from side to side and which, when the humpback whales arrived later that afternoon, gave the perfect mirrored backdrop for the day's second bout of whale-watching.

They came and went so gently I could have missed them. A shimmering square of vapour some way off the starboard beam could well have been lost in the mist-laden air. But there was another! And another! No sound reached us. Still the spouts kept coming, along with, now and then, a brief hint of whaleback, a thin black crescent gone almost before it was spotted. There were perhaps ten or twelve in the pod. I suspected they were humpbacks, but could not be sure until time froze for a second or two as a great fluke rose up and up and even further up and then paused aloft in a thrilling tableau, a mighty scalloped salute to the aerial world, before descending vertically with hydraulic smoothness and an almost unnerving lack of hurry into the depths below.

The pod was evidently feeding hereabouts. For thirty minutes there was no sign of a whale but then the whole initial scene repeated itself, this time just a quarter of a mile off the starboard beam. Now the misshapen boomerang backs of the surfacing whales were clear to see and once more a tail was raised skywards before the pod disappeared for good.

The wind sidled off too. We stopped, and the lack of forward movement now allowed *Mingming* to strike up a maddening clatter as she rocked from port to starboard. Happy nonetheless with the day's double tally of whale encounters, I sat in the hatchway and watched a sea that had now taken on the look of smooth and glinting granite. It was eight in the evening but the sun that from time to time insinuated itself through the uneven weave of misty overcast and thicker fog patches still hung high in the sky. We were now less than a hundred and twenty miles from the Arctic Circle and day had hijacked almost every hour of the clock. Navigation lights were now redundant; there was no real darkness, just a tortuously slow sunset and an afterglow that metamorphosed quickly and seamlessly into the pre-dawn herald of an absurdly early sunrise.

I sat in the hatchway, then, and ruminated on this stretching of the day to its limits, and on my theory that this was no doubt part of the other-worldly charm of the polar regions. My gaze wandered around over the uniform silver of sea and sky and came up short on a huge black log lying half-submerged a good way off the port bow. The log gave off a puff of vapour and lay there unmoving. I grabbed my binoculars from their hook by my left knee and had a closer look. It was square-headed, this hunk of lumber, and its after end, the end that was not giving out an occasional breathy cloud, that is, was crowned with the slightest of rounded protrusions, a sort of knuckle that perhaps a million or a billion years ago still sprouted properly as a fully-fledged dorsal fin.

My long day was now complete. Here was a sperm whale, almost certainly a lone bull, pigmented cousin to Moby Dick himself. Old Ahab had finally met his nemesis. We lay eyeing each other from a respectful distance. Neither of us moved; old Ahab because his ship was trapped, windless, in a narrow rectangle of gently pulsing water; the sperm whale because he was steadily filling his lungs for a long plunge down into the cold underworld. For a few minutes stalemate reigned, the one unable, the other unwilling to make a move and then – Oh joy! – for the third time that afternoon a ton or more of sinewy flesh and blubber arced in the slowest of motions as the huge triangular tail, its fluke straight-sided and utilitarian, was raised high in the air. Again there was a sublime moment of stasis as this great mass defied every expectation and hung there motionless for a second or two in the noblest and most poignant pose in all of nature, before subsiding with scarcely a ripple beneath the placid sea.

Killer whales. Humpback whales. A sperm whale. It was more than I could ever have hoped to meet in a single stretch of daylight. It had raised our intimacy with the sea to a new level. Our yearly wanderings were slowly bearing the most delicious of fruits. In the grand scheme of things they were not much, these encounters, no more than chance and momentary crossings of paths. But that was the point. The more we ranged the seas the more we accumulated these random intersections. They were unplanned, unforced, uncontrived. It gave me the profoundest pleasure that we were all, as it were, going quietly about our daily business at these moments of proximity. As our time at sea mounted up I felt more like a resident than a tourist. It was presumptuous maybe, but in our own little way we belonged more and more to our tiny and ever-shifting patch of displaced ocean. Our progress was leisurely and unaggressive. We had no rapacious intent. Harmony in all things was our watchword. We were not upsetting the locals, but were, on the contrary, making some sort of attempt to integrate ourselves into their lives.

This other world will of course always lie just beyond the limit of comprehension; it is after all not possible to strip away two or three billion years from the march of evolution. From time to time, nonetheless, a corner of the veil is lifted, allowing a momentary glimpse, perhaps even a second or two of less clouded insight, into this strange alternative society. The sub-aqueous world is alien beyond words but tinted with a nagging familiarity. Every encounter with its mammalian denizens evokes a faint and deep-set twinge of longing. Is it possible that somewhere buried within our genetic make-up lies a seed of memory for the ocean we once inhabited; that we envy our cousins who returned to their roots? It seems unlikely. And yet...

10

Overnight the temperature dropped. The wind settled once more into the east-north-east and lost its pussy-footing meekness. Cat's paws were replaced by white caps as, for the first time on this voyage, a cold and weighty blast stirred up a proper sea-going sea. Dense cloud, insipidly grey and uninviting, bore down to mast height and occasionally to sea level, binding us into a tight swaddling of fog. This was more like it! We hadn't come north to drift around in a balmy haze! I dropped a panel of the mainsail to maintain our easy balance. I sealed shut the after portlight and resolved from here on to be more disciplined about retaining what heat I could within the cabin. I shaved, using a tablespoonful of my precious water, and brushed my teeth, using no water at all, and so felt clean and smooth and princely as I sat in the hatchway and took up my morning's work.

I watched the sea. My thoughts drifted in and out of focus. Underlying every reflection was a vein of intense elation. After a week at sea we still had our leading wind. It was now blowing harder than ever, sending us bounding northwards. It looked well-set too, this patch of more virile weather. The Arctic Circle was now within easy reach; just another day's progress would do it. Conditions were at last appropriately sub-Arctic, but *Mingming's* cabin was a haven of warmth and comfort. Already it was clear that the long winter hours spent insulating the hull and coach roof had been time and energy well employed.

Yes, just seven days of sailing and here we were on the very threshold of the Arctic! To the west we were now parallel with the northernmost tip of Iceland; a course due east would bring us halfway up the coast of Norway. Our sea room was proliferating rapidly in every direction. Below us, too, land was falling away; we were now loping north over the deepest part of the Norwegian Basin, a massive trough almost four kilometres deep and not unlike a crudely drawn outline of the British mainland in both size and shape. A sudden thought took me to the chart table and my suspicion was confirmed: we were also lying on a line between the North Cape of Norway and Cape Farewell, the southern headland of Greenland. I realised that perhaps I had become too complacent about the chance of meeting any commercial shipping. I had no idea whether there was much trade between the northern ports of Russia and North America, but if there were, this was the way it would come. For the next day or two I had better tighten up my watch-keeping.

In the early hours of Saturday the fourth of July the wind, still from east-north-east and pushing along great balls of fog like so much tumbleweed, wound itself up a notch and forced us down to just three panels of the mainsail. It was the first significant reefing of our voyage, and for the first time too I allowed myself the luxury of easing off a little from our stringent northerly heading. Jan Mayen was now just three hundred miles ahead, but somewhat to the west of due north. We could now bear off slightly and increase our speed.

By eight that morning we were in the Arctic. I had filmed my handheld GPS as the last seconds of latitude clicked their way to 66° 33'N. I had announced the moment to the whole world with a long blast on my foghorn. I had felt just the slightest welling of moisture in my eyes. All the disappointments of our previous northern voyage now fell away; they would never trouble me again. We had come back with a different plan and a whole new purpose and here we now were, not just inside the Arctic Circle, but with well over a month of sailing time still in hand. Everything now seemed possible. My madcap dreams had solidified to raw reality. Our passage up till now had been remarkably easy. Yes, planning and experience and sheer bloody-mindedness had all played their part, maybe more than I recognised, but it had seemed the simplest of endeavours to bring this tiny yacht this far. I almost felt guilty at not having suffered a bit more on the way. Well, there were still many, many miles of ocean ahead, and plenty of time for all of that.

We were now sailing in the Arctic. It had a crisp and definable ring to it, this newly-acquired geographical status. It overlaid our little adventure with a veneer of the exploratory and the exotic. I now watched the sea, the *Arctic* sea as I was now constantly reminding myself, with something of a proprietary glint in my eye, and so was somewhat miffed after scarcely an hour as a confirmed Great Explorer to see a ship mooching around fine on our starboard bow. Well, maybe I had been right about that shipping lane, but there was no speed or sense of purpose to the vessel's progress. Slowly our courses converged. Examination with binoculars revealed a light blue hull, white superstructure, twin funnels with an S on their sides, and a lot of rust. It had an old-fashioned look to it, this interloper, somehow reminding me of the Isle of Man ferries that in my youth plied between the Pier Head in Liverpool and Douglas on the three-legged Isle itself. We moved closer and I could now make out, astern of the ship, the largest assembly of fulmars that I had ever seen. They were not there in their hundreds, or their thousands, but in their tens of thousands, a tight-packed mass of wheeling agitation that stretched for several miles in the ship's wake.

Where had they come from, so many birds? They must have been drawn from hundreds of miles around. Our own little entourage of fulmars, of which I had always been so proud, was paltry by comparison.

I had been trying to assess our relative courses and work out what avoiding action I might need to take, having long since abandoned the notion that steam gives way to sail. The problem was solved when the ship altered course to due west, thereby lining itself up to cross our bow with no margin to spare. I could now make out huge steel hawsers set from the ship's stern and which were no doubt dragging a massive trawl. This was a fishing boat, but its size and passenger-oriented accommodation and weary air and general unlikeliness suggested it had once had other, more salubrious, lives. Whatever its provenance, this strange craft with its diabolic stern-hamper was now bearing down on us, and I had no choice but to bear away and run parallel with it just a quarter of a mile on its port side. Thus wedded we processed our way west, David and a rust-streaked Goliath. The ship had such a terrific weight to pull that it was scarcely moving faster than *Mingming* and so it was a good half hour before I could haul our wind and cross its stern. I left a healthy margin, but even so the sea was churned into a massive and unnatural turbulence made more unreal by the thousands of bobbing fulmars stretching away on each side and a sky that was packed solid and tumultuous with a swirling mosaic of interlocking flight paths.

I had been unable to determine the ship's name or nationality and we thus parted *incognito*, *Mingming* once more settled to her northerly track, the ghost fisherman disappearing into a fog-ridden west.

I slowly resumed my poise after this rude diversion. Our noon position showed a daily run of nearly ninety miles. Replete after a lunch of bread and cheese and cake and an apple I took up my post in the hatchway, happy in anticipation of an afternoon of lonely Arctic sailing. Out of the fog-ridden west came a shape that resolved inexorably into a blue hull with a white superstructure, twin funnels and a decorative overlay of rust. Our friend was back, heading due east across our track, or so it seemed. She was trawling in a great circle. It was scarcely credible that our paths could cross twice in this way in all of this remote and empty ocean, but there it was. I groaned inwardly and watched her approach. She was still straining along at just a few knots and I realised that we would in fact pass far enough ahead to be able to hold our course. Thus freed from sail handling and hand steering I could study the ship more closely. Not surprisingly, for she had a tired ex-soviet look, she was Russian, the *Armanek Begayev*, out of Kaliningrad. We passed close then once again diverged at right angles. She was the last vessel I would see for sixteen days.

11

I had not yet followed Blondie Hasler's example and thrown *Mingming's* barometer overboard. I could see why he had done it. The movements of that little needle may tell you something significant about the weather to come; then again they may not. That needle has the capacity to create unwarranted anxieties and false hopes. One's mood can soon become slave to its self-important gyrations. It all looks so straightforward: Fair, Change, Rain, Stormy. Ha! The principle may be fine in large scale, but often falls badly short at the level of the tiny slice of atmosphere in which a yacht is sailing. Too many localised anomalies and contradictions breed uncertainty. Uncertainty is of no benefit. The barometer is so much deadweight; better to consign it to the deep.

Yes, I could see why Blondie, an uncompromisingly practical man, had deduced that his barometer was a useless item aboard. My own barometer was by now giving me cause for a mix of mild concern and amusement. It had, it seemed, gone on strike. It had settled in at one thousand and twenty millibars and refused to budge; for eight days it had folded its arms, put up its feet and not lifted a finger. No amount of tapping, cajoling or anti-barometric invective could induce even the slightest tremor of movement. One thousand and twenty millibars. Take it or leave it, mate. I was many a time sorely tempted to unscrew the idle fellow and start him on his own little voyage of exploration to the bottom of the Norwegian Basin, but something stayed my hand. A barometer, for all its shortcomings, added a veneer of serious nauticality to *Mingming's* cabin. It looked the part, if nothing else. I had also rather got into the habit of giving it a regular and officious rap with the knuckle of my right index finger. How would I occupy myself if I chucked it overboard?

Against this backdrop of unflinching air pressure, one thousand and twenty millibars, a reading that would remain constant for at least another two weeks, to the extent that I finally believed my barometer was not simply resting but had expired; against this backdrop, then, scientifically proven by the highest quality French instrumentation, was played out the full range of meteorological drama.

No, a settled barometer did not mean settled weather. As we clawed our way northwards, now indisputably in Arctic waters, and now, at last, truly alone, sky and wind and waves were in constant flux. We sailed through indigo seas under a dome of blue as cold and piercing as it was pristine. Another pod of killer whales came and went. Fog swept in, and rain. We laboured now, close-hauled as the wind backed to north-east, raising fears of being set to leeward of Jan Mayen. We were down almost to storm canvas. A nasty sea built and I made myself comfortable on the cabin sole, wedged in tightly, my back against the companionway, my legs draped forward over food containers. For the first time I shivered a little overnight. An Arctic tern, stupendously long-tailed and at ease in the wild wind, glided overhead. Within a few hours we were almost becalmed once more, stopped nearly dead by a swell from ahead. Now we rotated through patches of sun then cloud then mist. Frustration at our slow progress forced me forward to un-gasket the spitfire jib. On cue a series of rain squalls marched through then left us mouldering. A little breeze came in, back to east-north-east. A puffin, first intimation of approaching land, whirred round *Mingming* three times then headed off west. Curiosity impelled him back for yet another circuit before he went off for good, this time to the south. He was soon followed by a black and white cigar, an unmistakably pot-bellied Brünnich's guillemot. Hours of constant fiddling in a faint breeze from north-west brought us to 70°N. For the first time in eleven and a half days we were on port tack. The wind increased. The wind dropped. The sun came out. The sun disappeared. On it went and at two in the morning of Wednesday the eighth of July, after exactly twelve days at sea, the tall white sails of a fleet of ocean racing yachts appeared in the distant mist ahead.

At first there was just a single triangle, the thin and narrow-footed spike of a hard-sheeted genoa seen from ahead. It seemed that we, *Mingming* and this ghost yacht, that is, were on reciprocal courses. We would pass beam to beam. She had obviously just left Jan Mayen and the thought deflated me; our delicious solitude had once more been wrecked. Is there nowhere on this earth where a man can be truly alone? From time to time I lost sight of the approaching column of white in the shifting mists, but it was clear that we were still at a good distance; any convergence was hard to detect. The fog lifted a little and suddenly there was a whole fleet crowded into a narrow vector ahead; three then five then six or more vertical streaks of snowy white. For a second or two I was stunned. These sails were set on the loftiest of masts, all of a matching height. They had the look of a pack of Open 60s battling it out. Was there some Arctic race going on that I had not heard about? I stared at this most unlikely scene, still far ahead and somehow misplaced and unreal, until a slight solidifying and darkening of the air around the yachts caused a total reinterpretation of the visual data and with the greatest of joy I realised that what I was watching was Jan Mayen itself. We were there! The tall white sails were snow gullies piercing the now visible cliffs of Jan Mayen's South Cape. Snow! At sea level in July! I have made many landfalls in my life but nothing matched the rapture of that moment. I tingled with a deep-seated satisfaction. Within less than twelve months *Mingming* had taken me from Terceira to Jan Mayen; we had traversed over thirty degrees of latitude from sun to snow.

I stared at those distant headlands. They were still low on the horizon and grainy with a mist that was once more thickening. How I loved their hunched blackness, their wildness. They lifted my heart, those snow-streaked bluffs, immutable in a cold ocean. I loved their stubbornness, their unspeakingness. They took my breath too, those headlands. They made me feel more of a man and less of a man; I had reached this far, yes, and that was good, but besides the mass and scale and age of those cliffs I was nothing, less than nothing. They were humbling, those headlands. They put an impertinent sailor in his place and that was no bad thing.

Jan Mayen now disappeared behind a screen of fog. I didn't care. We had made our landfall and had as much time in hand as we wanted; time and plenty to savour our arrival.

12

At seven thirty, more than five hours after our first sighting of the island, the swirling mists momentarily parted and created a chance corridor of visibility ahead and fine on the starboard bow. It lasted for scarcely a minute, this unlocking of a narrow segment of the wider world, but those few seconds were enough to reveal a scene so extraordinary that after some weeks I began to wonder whether I had only ever imagined it. The picture was clear in my head, but had I really seen it? I was sure I had followed my usual practice of taking a quick photograph – even the worst of snapshots is better than nothing – but trawling through the saved images on my camera viewers drew a blank. It was only careful study of my photographic record of the voyage on a big computer screen, once ashore again, that finally confirmed that I had not been dreaming.

What had opened up ahead was the northern end of the island. A layer of thick cloud stretched across at a height of perhaps a thousand feet. Below this lay the lowest segment of a massive and symmetrical cone, the base of Mount Beerenberg. This band of mountain was heavily snow-covered, in many places down to the waterline. Steeper cliffs and crevices patterned the snow with a rugged black mosaic. To the west the lowest slopes merged into the island's central lowlands; to the east they trailed gently down into the sea. The sheer presence and physicality of this great monolith rising fully-formed out of the ocean was of itself impressive enough, but it was a single happy moment of interplay of the higher cloud cover that added, almost literally, the icing to the cake. A gap, fuzzy-edged and somehow begrudging, had opened up at somewhere between three and four thousand feet and there too was the mountain, its steepening eastern slope still thrusting skywards, its snow cover still streaked vertically with narrow shoulders of bare rock. That brief glimpse of an upper portion of the volcano put its size and shape into context. In my mind's eye I continued the line upwards and joined it to a similar one from the west and thereby saw, behind the countervailing cloud, the full outline of this lofty triangle. Seven thousand feet straight out of the sea! We were sailing into the upper reaches of a wintry Fuji-san. Here were the topmost slopes of the Munch or the Jungfrau transported wholesale into the Arctic Ocean.

For a moment my spirit soared too along with those skyscraping contours but then they were gone. Cloud and mist conjoined and the show was over. It had been the briefest of revelations, ethereal, ghostly; small wonder that later I doubted it. For the next thirty-six hours or so we were to sail close in to the island but would never again be treated to anything so sky-borne and precipitous.

I had no clear notion of what I would do once we arrived at Jan Mayen. Much would depend on the conditions on the day. There are no sheltered anchorages, and even if I did manage to anchor I had no means of getting ashore. I was also hampered by the lack of a detailed chart. I knew, from many readings of Bill Tilman's disastrous stay at the island with *Mischief*, that there were rocks off the southern tip, but that the east coast was generally clear of hazards. My aim was simply to bring *Mingming* as close inshore as I dared and see what happened.

I held a course that would bring us in to the centre of the eastern side of the island. As we closed the land mass on its south-west to north-east axis the mists cleared, laying out the island in a shallow curve. At the northern end low cloud persisted, cloaking Mount Beerenberg, but to the south growing patches of raw sky of a blue dyed almost to icy white were imposing themselves over the jagged peaks that now ranged along our port beam. Ahead the softer contours of Jan Mayen's narrow waist were disturbed by the great fist of a misshapen headland, dark-hued and canting to starboard, that stuck out in such contrast to the coastline that at first I took it to be an offshore island. I later learned that it is in fact called Egg Island, though joined to mainland by a causeway of black volcanic rock.

The wind backed to west, an offshore breeze, giving me the confidence to continue our run in closer and closer. For a while we lay becalmed and I studied every visible inch of Jan Mayen. I wanted to impress each and every curve and crevice and contour into my mind's eye, indelibly; to make this picture part of the fabric of my memory. It still seemed so unlikely, our presence here, so dreamlike. I had somehow to capture this evanescence, to wrestle it down and stake it out and record it and measure it and classify it. Otherwise it just might slip away for good.

For here was the first scene we had encountered that was truly Arctic. It was not Arctic merely by dint of some midsummer snow and ice. It was not Arctic simply because of its mountains, all toothed and serrated and scored wide and deep to the waterline by the moraines of extinct glaciers. It was not the sky, wild with buzzing flocks of puffins and guillemots and fulmars and skuas and terns. It was not the light, washed out to piercing limpidity; nor the air, crisp and cool as fresh-starched linen and as sweet to smell and touch. Nor was it the mist that now wisped soft as mink around the southern cols, crystalline and diaphanous, almost blinding under a strangely angled sun; nor was it that mist's stubborn northern counterpart, the dome of unmoving grey stratus that capped Mount Beerenberg. Nor was it either the sense that at any moment something momentous could stamp a final seal of enchantment on the day: a humpback whale breaching skywards; a belching of fire from a dormant crater; an iceberg nosing into the bay. No, there was not one detail that was definitively and exclusively Arctic, but in combination they left no doubt as to where we were.

The breeze picked up a little and we nosed our way tentatively towards the shore. We were heading towards a spot just south of Egg Island. I knew that tucked somewhere in the gentle slopes thereabouts was the Norwegian scientific station that housed the island's transient population of eighteen or so, but I never managed to locate it. From time to time, though, I saw signs of life and activity – moving plumes of dust from unseen vehicles on the dirt tracks that link the various scientific huts. At one stage I wondered about assembling my handheld VHF radio and announcing our presence to the station commander. That was obligatory if we wanted to anchor, but otherwise there seemed little point. With no inclination for fuss or fanfare I preferred to make a silent visit and be on my way.

With the binoculars I could now make out a curve of blue-grey beach. Whether it was sand or shingle was impossible to tell but it had all my attention, this narrow strip between the sea's edge and the low plain behind that soon turned to soft-edged hills. This was, almost certainly, the spot where Tilman, with the help of the Norwegians, had beached *Mischief* in a doomed attempt to repair her after her holing. That was in July 1968. The main problem he faced was the weight of ice floes pressing onto the beach, damaging *Mischief* even further. She was eventually towed off by a

Norwegian supply ship but her make-do pumping arrangement soon failed and she sank.

Summer ice floes have long since gone from hereabouts.

We moved gently in towards the beach in the lightest of zephyrs. About a mile off I eased the sheet and we began to run north-east, parallel with the shore. Anything closer would have been too risky; my insurers had stipulated one exclusion on my policy: *removal of wreck from Jan Mayen.* Care was needed.

We ran past the contorted nodule of Egg Island, its upper contours lost for a moment in a swirl of low cloud. To the north of the causeway linking it to the island proper was another smaller beach of volcanic detritus. Perhaps it was here that *Mischief* had been hauled partially ashore by a Norwegian digger. The beach soon gave way to the squat and untidy cliffs that marked the base of Mount Beerenberg. In places the smoother volcanic slope ran straight down into the sea; elsewhere erosion had carved sheer faces, their tops irregular, haphazard. Up close every nobble and indent of the mountain's base was in clear delineation, this clarity enhanced from time to time by shafts of low-angled sunlight that had found their way through the shifting cloud mass above. Snow lay in myriad patches shaped by the lie of the land; every dimple that lessened the sun's effect housed its own peculiar pattern of white. The un-snowed areas gave off the merest hint of green sward; something was growing there, probably a hardy mountain grass of some sort. Cloud, more ragged up close than I had at first imagined, still persisted. Once or twice a chance clearing gave a quick glimpse of a higher outline, but nothing above a couple of thousand feet, and nothing that allowed once more a sense of the whole.

On we ran under the lee of this stupendous mass. I could not imagine a greater or more unlikely joy than to be here in little *Mingming.* Our presence cocked a snook at every sailing convention, but that was of little relevance. What mattered was that here at Jan Mayen, as we sailed softly along the base of Mount Beerenberg, was every stimulus to pique an ageing sailor's spirit: solitude, distance, wildness, grandeur. I could not have been more content.

13

Keeping just a mile or two offshore we crept on up towards the North Cape. The wind was failing and by four the next morning it was gone. For twelve hours we lay there, wafted just a little this way and that by an insubstantial tide. The previous day's sparkle had dulled to a dour and overbearing grey. The cloud cover over Mount Beerenberg pressed lower and lower, squeezing the volcano's visible base into a narrow layer of black and snow-flecked cliff. This great tea-cosy of cloud thickened too, and darkened, and refused to budge, and so added to the frustrations of our immobility, for I longed to see the mountain properly, from tip to toe, revealed, naked. It wasn't to be.

For twelve hours we lay there, then, in a day suffused with monochromatic idleness. Fifty or so fulmars kept us company, they too untypically lethargic, dozing with heads under wings, or pecking lazily at surface titbits. A couple of minke whales rolled their long backs through two identical and serene curves and disappeared, and a black guillemot, its wing patches of a white too brilliant for such a subdued day, its flight too energetic and urgent for the prevailing mood, hurried past.

I sat in the hatchway and watched the grey mass over Mount Beerenberg, alert to the slightest hint of a break in the cloud. Nothing moved. I studied the North Cape itself and found it disappointing. It was no more than a low finger trailing off into the sea. The faintest breaths of wind came occasionally from here or there, boxing the compass but never amounting to anything. I took a nap.

It was late afternoon before we were on the move again, driven by a breeze that started lightly from north-east then backed quickly to north-west and then west, strengthening all the while. For the moment this suited me fine. Eventually I wanted to head west, but I still had a yen to sail a little further north. We had now reached 71°N, but that struck me as an awkward, in-between sort of number. 72°N somehow had a more settled and satisfying feel to it; it would be a good latitude to mark the northern extent of our voyage.

We pulled away from the narrow tip of Jan Mayen and gradually opened up the cliffs of the western coast, receding darkly south-west beneath their own blanket of static cloud. We were joined by a northern bottlenose whale, a burly second-row forward of a fellow, bluff-headed, somewhat laboured of movement, who evidently took a shine to *Mingming*, for he played around us for a while, surfacing alongside and ahead with an ungainly roll. There was something of the pilot whale about him; he was bigger though, and lighter of hue, and nowhere near as graceful.

Sailing full and bye on port tack we resumed our quest for northing. Within a few hours we would notch up two weeks at sea, fourteen days and half-nights and now no-nights of an obsessive polar trajectory, our straight line disturbed by only two deviations, the first an almost imperceptible jink past Fair Isle and Foula, the second a three-day slant ever-so-slightly west to bring us to Jan Mayen. We were now back on track, cutting our understated little furrow directly for the end of the earth. It was not to last long, this final advance to a euphonic latitude, just twenty-four hours, but it felt good to leave land behind once more and push on out into the open ocean. Over a fair range of longitude nothing by way of anything terrestrial now lay between us and the North Pole. We had shaken off every last vestige of mud and sod and rock. Our world was now wholly and unequivocally watery. It may seem a small thing, this passage beyond the final outcrop of firm earth, but it was a heady moment of the sweetest exhilaration. We had crossed some sort of threshold, entered a new and higher plane of solitude and remoteness. We were now truly on our own, escapees to a far wilderness. I thrilled at the thought. How I would have loved to have sailed on and on, deeper and deeper into the heart of this other distant place.

For twenty-four hours we headed on north through patches of mist and thicker fog and light showers, their procession laced with brief interludes of anaemic sunshine. All around, the workings of nature had reached their most industrious. Tight-packed parties of Brünnich's guillemots and puffins and little auks hurtled this way and that, bands of impeccably-dressed salarymen racing to important meetings to conclude contracts in machine-tooling or electronic circuitry. The little auks zipped along like steroidal hummingbirds, all flash and whirr. This high-level activity low over the sea raised a thousand intriguing questions. How and on what basis did these groupings form? How long did they last? Who decided which way they would fly? Why the hell was every gang heading in a different direction as if each member's life depended on it? What were they all up to? Of course everything revolved around the only two imperatives of every life-form: food and reproduction; they were certainly not out visiting or sight-seeing, or off to away-day jollies, these criss-crossing squadrons, but there was something anarchic and slightly mad about their desperately intent gyrations. Did they really know what they were about? Was there a master plan? Did they have a *Mission Statement*?

At six-forty on the evening of Friday the tenth of July we

reached the most northerly position of our voyage: 72°N 7° 23'W. The surrounding seascape declined to rise to the occasion; all was a uniform wet-slate grey above and below. Our fulmar escort had dwindled to just three or four. I filmed the moment and once more let off a ceremonial blast of the foghorn, but I had forgotten to pump it up and all that came out was the last gasp of an expiring bull-frog. Never mind; we had made our northing, aided by a most benign run of winds, and inserted ourselves unequivocally into the Far North.

It was time to turn west. Within five minutes I had put *Mingming* about and adjusted her, now close-hauled in a veering north-westerly, to her new heading. This changed orientation was immediately unsettling. We were heading for land. The imaginary vista of infinite ocean was gone. Ahead lay Davy Sound and King Oscar Fjord and Liverpool Land and Scoresby Sound itself. Two hundred and fifty miles of plain sailing would bring us to that barren coastline, but the sailing would not be plain and I knew well enough that we would never see its cliffs and headlands and crowning glaciers. That coastline is well-protected against the advances of a presumptuous sailor. Long before its iron-bound bluffs hove into view we would be stopped and threatened and undoubtedly rebuffed by a much greater and more insidious danger than an endless line of towering rock. Yes, I was unsettled alright, though my apprehension was hung about too with tendrils of the keenest expectation. We were now heading west, and our voyage, if I knew anything about it, would soon reach a kind of climax. At long last *Mingming* was about to sail into ice.

14

For two days we headed west on a normal ocean. The barometer had still withdrawn its labour, and remained unmoved by weather that was back and forth 'twixt fair and foul and had me reefing and un-reefing and reefing again every few hours. Great swathes of fog came and went. A band of clear sky of the palest azure taunted us from low on the north-western horizon, always there but never a jot closer. The wind maintained its bounteous mood, now hauling round into the north. I eased the sheet and *Mingming* leaped happily on.

We were sailing on a normal ocean, but the feel of the world was in flux. Our fulmars were almost gone; just one or two birds now kept us company, half-heartedly. In their stead, lone kittiwakes passed regularly by, flying north on shallow and unhurried wing beats. A Nelson's Column of a whale spout pierced the mists on the southern horizon. Unless I had misread the distance and scale it could only have been a blue whale, but a trail of vapour, however tall, was not enough to go on, and I'll never really know. There was no doubt, though, about the humpback whales that were soon proliferating hereabouts. Occasionally a crooked dorsal profile broke surface, confirming what the low and rounded blows had already suggested. They were sociable, these humpbacks, ranging round in pods of four or five or six and coordinating their rhythm of surface and dive. I had no way of measuring it, having forgotten to bring a thermometer, but the sea was cooling rapidly as we broached the East Greenland Current. We were now in water that a few months earlier was crusted with solid pack-ice; its residual chill still lingered.

Just after six in the evening of Sunday the twelfth of July, within a whisker of forty-eight hours after turning west, I was surprised to see a small vessel low on the north-western horizon. It had a boxy, fishing boat look about it, but not for long; proximity and a chance patch of sunshine soon transformed it into a gleaming cube of ice. Ice! I had not expected it this far out. Only a few hours earlier I had written in my log that we would probably have to sail another fifty miles or so before our first encounter. Well, here it was – a single floe; in the scheme of things a rather unimpressive agglomeration of Arctic pack. That may be so, but how I loved that lone lump! I studied it long and hard with the binoculars. How it flashed and sparkled as the sunlight hit it! How pretty it was, and sculpted, and... and icy! There could never have been a more beautiful wedge of frozen water! Ever! Yes, I was absurdly proud of this frosty block. My first! We had made it! Wow! This was almost like real Arctic exploration!

This exclamatory excess soon petered out as I spotted another flatter floe further off and began to consider the implications. We were still a hundred and twenty miles or so off the Greenland coast, and here was ice already. Nearly three weeks had passed since I had last looked at a satellite analysis of ice concentrations. I still had a rough sketch in a notebook, showing the thickest patch much closer inshore, a squiggly u-shape east-north-east of Scoresby Sound. How accurate was that now? I had no idea, but having observed over a long period how quickly these patterns change, I suspected that it could well be of no value whatsoever. In any event, the satellite rendition only showed pack-ice still at ten/tenths cover. I had yet to find out what level of ice density would be too threatening to *Mingming;* I had yet to discover the extent to which weather conditions would impact on our ability to negotiate our way through any heavier concentrations. The only certainty was that as we progressed west we would meet more and more ice. Those two floes were the first intimations of a grave and ever-present danger. From here on I would need to be at my most alert.

Fog closed in and for the first time on this voyage I reduced sail to slow us down while I took a short evening nap. The wind hauled round to north-north-east, a perfect quartering breeze, and I dropped two more panels to restrict our advance to the most gentle of paces. Time and speed were now of no relevance. We were nosing our way almost blindfold into a kind of mine-field. This was no place for brawny rush; what was needed was the gossamer and exploratory touch of the detector and the de-fuser.

We drifted along, then, unhurried, through mist that now bound us tight, now relaxed a little, revealing a few hundred yards of empty seascape, then contracted in once more. Under-canvased, the mainsail swung slightly aft with every passing swell, then thudded softly forward again. The mainsheet blocks creaked with each re-tensioning, and so we eased our way towards the unknown to the faint beat of drum and fife, a detachment of greenhorns headed for their first skirmish. I peered forward through the late evening murk. Nothing. I slept for ten minutes then looked again. Still nothing. The fog thinned a fraction and there ahead, receding into the gloom, was a scene to make a heart leap with fear and swell with joy. The whole arc of the visible west was spread with a pattern of floes. Their random and relaxed spacing left plenty of clear water. We had the lightest of breezes and a smooth sea. My mind was made up in a flash; we would sail into them and through them and see what happened. If the ice became too thick we could sail back out the way we had come. I lowered the mainsail down to a single panel, enough to keep us ghosting forward with steerage way, little enough that any collision would be at minimal speed. I disengaged the self-steering and took over with the hand-steering lines. Easing forward at just half a knot we sailed into the Arctic sea-ice.

15

It must have its own chapter of our tale, this little patch of ice and our passage through it. For this was the moment I had dreamed of and it could scarcely have been more perfect. This hour was the pinnacle of our voyage. It was this moment that justified and explained and excused the impudence of our endeavour.

I had imagined this scene under a canopy of brilliant blue, but here was something even better. It was nearly midnight, and the light was so filtered and subdued by the heavy cloud that pressed down to sea level that there was no sense of its source. Every object radiated its own weak luminosity. The ice floes glowed. There was no glint or shimmer, no hard shadow, no clear-cutness about them, just a delicate and eerie glow, and the softness and the stillness and the strange light that hung over the ice brought an unworldly and suspended feel to this last hour of the day. We had sailed straight into the heart of a distant poem:

And through the drifts the snowy clifts
Did send a dismal sheen:

Slowly we came up to the first outrider of the pack and passed to leeward of it. From a distance it had seemed to be a solid chunk of canted ice, but was nothing of the sort. Wave action had scoured it away at sea level, biting deeper and deeper into the floe and sculpting it to a massive and distorted mushroom. Its top, ragged-edged and leaning crazily, was held aloft by a central stalk of thick green ice. It was heavily-rooted, though, this singular toadstool, supported by a massive sub-aqueous platform washed smooth by the sea. This underwater portion was of considerably greater diameter than the aerial sculpture it carried and formed a kind of moving reef; small waves lapped at its edge.

We moved on into denser pack and a wonderland of chance and unconscious creation. Every floe was a unique statement. The underlying thrust was perhaps the same, but the action of wind and wave and the mechanics of melting had applied themselves in a different way to each starting block of ice and compacted snow, and produced unending variations on a central theme. I suspected that we were viewing this exhibition of dynamic sculpture at just the right moment; any earlier and the pieces would not have reached such delicate subtlety; any later and they would have crumbled back into the sea. For here were the most extraordinary shapes and arrangements. Time and nature's unthinking fingers had spun hard ice into the lightest and most insubstantial of filigrees. Here were traceried patterns of wafer-thin ice, finely-worked oriental screens, inverted chandeliers of the purest crystal, rows of tiny Doric columns supporting unlikely pediments of triangulated snow. One floe had created a marvellously balanced pair of mushrooms, one at each end of a thirty foot interlinking reef; they see-sawed along like Siamese twins. The water was riddled too with cast-offs, renegade escapees from the main bodies, some now smoothed to ice-boulders, others still sporting twisted antlers or picket fences or the spread fingers of a frozen hand.

The slabbed upperworks of the bigger floes bore all the scars of a winter of close-packed pressure. Here was one forced almost vertical. Here was another with its back split, one half riding up the other. Every floe had been forced and frozen into a strained and unnatural posture. There was nothing brutal about this, though, for the weight and awkwardness of every slab was relieved by an accompanying detail of the rarest beauty: a rim of spun sugar, or a sprouting rhubarb leaf of veined and curling ice, or the thinnest of cornices projecting far out over the water.

I steered through them and grew bolder. Up close the ghostly green light that seemed to spread from the heart of each floe resolved into a finely calibrated spectrum that depended on the depth and thickness of the ice it suffused. Another fragment sprang to mind:

And ice, mast-high, came floating by,
As green as emerald.

Yes, here was emerald green, and every gradation through to a turquoise that itself transmuted to azure and then paled to a cool and milky blue. I had never before seen such soft and subtle colorations. Here were huge and precious stones, priceless and transient, cut by the waves, an ocean-load of *Koh-i-Noors*.

A slight bump on the port bow warned me not to become too complacent. We had hit an outsize jewel, barely awash and unseen. It was the most innocuous of collisions, but enough to remind me of the weight and hardness of even the smallest ice-lump. They may well radiate the most ethereal beauty, these floes, but they were deadly too, and it was this overlay of danger that added the final thrill to the moment. Every one was an Ice Queen - remote, ravishing, implacable, cruel. I could look but I mustn't touch; even the slightest caress could lead to a cold and watery retribution.

The floes stretched away to north and to south, the most

distant finally merging into the fabric of the midnight mist. I had been so taken with the intricate detailing and baroque craftsmanship of the closer individuals, and so absorbed in the whole new palette of unearthly colours that they presented, that I had not yet really looked, as it were, at the bigger picture. It was a scene of the most heart-warming desolation. Blocks of sculpted ice moved silently through a smooth and frigid sea. Fog weighed down, heavily. No sounds came, save the rhythmic creak of *Mingming's* blocks and the faint heave of water breaking to its own beat on the nearest floes. We had transgressed some boundary, over-reached perhaps, into a world of delicious indifference. There was no help here, no blather, just the cold heart of wildness itself, wordless and unmoved. The floes bore the scars of their long winter and before long they would re-form and re-pack and crush themselves together for another endless night. The scene was hung about with the residue of winters past and the march of winters future. We had no place here, little *Mingming* and I, in this frozen ebb and flow. We had broached the outermost limit of our possibility.

A sudden movement and splash somewhere off to starboard had me reaching for the binoculars. A small seal lay on one of the floes. Its companion had just slid off into the water. We had no place here, but it was nonetheless home and hearth to warm-blooded life; even here the vacuum had been filled. I watched the dark shape stretched motionless on its bed of ice and for once felt no link or complicity. It was too alien to comprehend, this mode of life on the floes.

The ice thinned out and we were once again in clear water. The wind strengthened. The fog bore down. I did not dare sail properly or sleep for long. We were into the ice; it could now be anywhere, in any concentration. I dropped the mainsail and lashed it down, then slept for four or five hours, but in blocks of just fifteen minutes. Four times an hour I hauled myself out of my swaddling and checked the outside world. For the whole remaining night it remained thickly grey and ice-free. With such poor visibility I was not reassured. For all I knew the pack-ice might now lie all around, just beyond the limit of my vision. We had entered the labyrinth. Two questions occupied me. How much further could we sail west? Would we ever find a way out?

16

By every conventional standard our little voyage had now attained a measure of foolhardiness. I was sailing into the ice, single-handed, in an engineless and un-strengthened yacht. I was also close to breaching Greenland maritime regulations that require vessels navigating within a certain distance of the coastline to send six-hourly coded radio reports of their position and accompanying weather and ice conditions. We had been at sea for two and a half weeks and so were well beyond the point where even an approximate guess at our location could be made. We were the tiniest speck on a distant and icy ocean, unseen and unannounced.

None of this concerned me in the least. I had never felt so liberated. I was bound by nothing: no person, no institution, no rule, no expectation. My life was mine to push to whatever limit I decided; I could come, or go, as I pleased. I was starting to nibble at the edge of a higher level of freedom, and the more I pondered on it, the more clearly I saw that this freedom grew out of the two most important pre-conditions of my voyaging.

The first was the deliberate avoidance of any means of long-distance communication. How can a man be free if he is enslaved to a daily satellite telephone call? What kind of liberty is delivered from an email inbox? How can a man lose himself in sea and sky if he is worried about when he'll get his next weather fax? They may all be wondrous technologies, these streams of data winging through the ether, but they bind a man into an insidious and stifling net. They are birdlime for he who would fly. They export the dull hand of the daily land-bound routine out onto the waves. They engender an unthinking and unending series of Pavlovian response and counter-response. They keep half of you at home and what use is that to a man who would go places? They are the kiss of death for the seeker-out of the wild and the exotic. They are a negation too of the spirit of single-handed adventuring, for how can a man know solitude unless he is truly alone? And how can a man be free unless he can confront his own solitude?

No, I was no longer party to a world of six-hourly radio reportage; all that was well astern. I had entered the realm of self-determination pure and simple. What is more, I had earned the right to that self-determination through the second and even more crucial pre-condition of my voyaging: total and uncompromising personal responsibility. I go to sea by my own choice and I am prepared to live, or die, by the consequences of that choice. If I get into difficulty then I have to shift for myself. I do not assume any right to be rescued. I have no means of calling for help. That is as it should be. I am not a professional mariner, just an insignificant leisure sailor. I have no right to put other lives at risk if things go wrong.

If I had sailed into the ice carrying some means of attracting help – an EPIRB (Emergency Position Indicating Radio Beacon), for example – and been prepared to use it, then I could justifiably be branded as stupid and irresponsible. I would have been implicating others into my actions. I would have compromised too that precious freedom that I was seeking, for freedom is born of absence of all dependency.

No, as we moved into the ice I was gloriously clear of temporal ties, my life stripped down to the barest of essentials.

I had become a kind of sea-borne monk, confined to a tiny and unheated cell, silent as a Trappist, ascetic, contemplative. I had no illusions though. There would be no divine intervention to get me out of any fix.

17

By breakfast time the fog had lifted and I set sail under a bracing sky. Once more something about the world had changed; here was a blue-black sea scoured by a brisk and bitter wind straight out of the north. There was no half-measure about the cold; above and below all was near freezing. I pulled on a pair of ski trousers. We headed south-west, slanting in towards the Greenland coast through a procession of widely-spaced floes. There was nothing threatening about the bigger fellows; I could pick them out a mile or two ahead and keep well clear. It was the little chaps that worried me. The sea was littered with bergy bits, some no bigger than medicine balls. Many had lost their superstructure through melting and erosion, and so floated along level with the surface. They were devilishly hard to pick out, these lumps of ice, and they were very dangerous. The breeze was picking up, creating a more turbulent sea that broke forcefully on the bigger floes, sending showers of spray skywards and reminding me that to be pinned to the windward side of even the smallest berg would be catastrophic.

Ah, but wasn't it great! What a wonderful and uplifting thing it was, to sail through this frozen waste in the tiniest of sailboats! I sat in the hatchway, careless of the cold, entranced by the scene and the idea of the scene and the idea of us being in the scene. Yes, a long-held dream was now a reality and this fusion of thought and fact created something that was bigger than the sum of its real and imagined parts and had me swelling with the greatest happiness. It was a moment of fulfilment, and it was shared by two humpback whales that appeared close on our starboard beam, heading north with a great puffing and rolling. How their backs gleamed in the crisp and limpid air! How the ice sparkled, spread like rare diamonds along the rim of the world!

By noon we were in 71° 08'N 17° 04'W, which had us just eighty-five miles off Liverpool Land on the Greenland coast. It was our eighteenth day at sea. On we ran through buzzing flocks of little auks and Brünnich's guillemots and the occasional black guillemot. The ice thinned, leaving us almost to a clear sea, and for a while I thought that perhaps we had seen the last of it. Maybe we could make it to the coast after all. I pulled out the pilot and spent an hour or two investigating the bays to the south of Scoresby Sound. There were anchorages here in the right conditions, but the conditions are seldom right, and the ice has a habit of crowding into bays and making life difficult. Nevertheless I did my homework and boned up on the possibilities, but I knew I was just going through the motions.

I did not really believe that we could ever get ourselves within sight of that glowering coastline and I was right. So far we had had an effortless run through the ice, but all that was about to change. The wind blew more viciously from the north, bringing with it a dense swathe of low and misty cloud that soon turned to rain. Something of an awkward cross-sea had been building since morning, encouraged by an inexplicable swell from the north-west. The day was quickly losing its glamour. We were once again meeting occasional small ice-bergs, but their mystique and sparkle were gone, replaced by dull menace. They still glowed, unnaturally, even as the rain came down harder, but that only seemed to underline their threat. We were now running almost straight off the wind under a couple of panels and I had the sailor's unease of bearing down onto dangers unseen.

Once again the floes thinned to nothing and in the late evening I took a short nap. Ah, sleep, it is a wondrous thing, but when I checked the sea just a few minutes later I was glad I had set my alarms, for we were not far from running into a sizeable berg straight to leeward. It was a small island, this chappie, white and pure and innocent, and had I slept for another three or four minutes our acquaintance would have become intimate, and I would have experienced firsthand the lift and break of wave on its windward shore. I reduced sail even further and hand steered round it, but now the sea was awash with lumps of ice of all shapes and sizes and within no time one had lodged itself under *Mingming's* starboard quarter. It would have passed muster as a flying saucer, this lump that was now graunching along *Mingming's* hull. It was topped by a little dome, about eighteen inches in diameter, and it was only this perfectly symmetrical observation point that lay above the water. The saucery bit was submerged and was a good six or seven feet across and it was this that was trapped beneath us. I threw off the main halyard and at the same moment a passing swell rolled us off and away from our icy assailant.

Within half a second my mind was made up; it was time for a tactical withdrawal. These were not the conditions to be flirting with ice floes. I would make sail and head due east for a while into clearer water. But I had to go on deck first, to retrieve the main halyard which I had forgotten to cleat and which had run forward to its block at the base of the mast. I quickly pulled on a waterproof nylon parka, as the rain was by now torrential, and hauled myself through the hatch. It was a miserable enough day out there, what with freezing water above and below and frozen water all around, but not sufficiently apocalyptic to prepare me for the view down to leeward. My height of eye was now raised four or five feet and I could now see what up until then had been hidden below the horizon. It was not much to look at, this new seascape, but it was enough to send a short shock through my nervous system and enough to confirm that my decision to take evasive action was not a second too soon. Across the southern limit of my visibility, end to end, just half a mile or so to leeward, stretched a thin and unbroken line, pale and innocuous-looking. We had been heading straight for it. In 70° 45'N 18° 0'W, eighty miles or so east-north-east of Scoresby Sound, we had finally met up with solid pack-ice.

It was neither the day nor the time nor the place for sight-seeing. I hauled up three panels of the mainsail and got *Mingming* set on a fast beam reach due east. There was no guarantee that we could escape. For all I knew we might have sailed into a shallow bay in the ice, or a deep bay, or a long and wide lead from which the only exit was back to windward. For two hours we thumped and rolled quickly east, covering ten miles or so, with no signs of ice, and it was only then that I started to ease off a little. It was now blowing a good Force 6 and still raining heavily. Poor old *Mingming* was not accustomed to such hard usage. Feeling a little more relaxed I reduced sail to just a single panel. We ran gently off to the south-east.

18

Every voyage has its dog days, and mine began there and then; for forty-eight long hours my mood slumped into the blackest of holes. What brought this on is impossible to say. I ought to have been deliriously happy. We had seen the ice. We had sailed through it. We had escaped it too. Every little ambition had been fulfilled, but the world had become hateful. Perhaps it was because we were now homeward bound. There were still new waters to sail, discoveries to make, but nonetheless we were heading south; those degrees of northerly latitude that had so absorbed me were slipping rapidly away. From here on everything would be downhill. Perhaps it was the weather, uniformly black and cold and rain-choked; even the sea had turned to a dark and inky sepia. Perhaps it was the suspicious creaking that resounded through *Mingming's* hull every time the tiller, and therefore the rudder, moved. For a long time I worried that our short interaction with the flying saucer had damaged the steering system.

Or maybe it was nothing more than the simple imperatives of flesh and blood. My biochemistry had been well dosed with feel-good stuff for some weeks. Now it was the turn of the other lot. Action had transformed to reaction. I was adept at maintaining a harmonious balance at sea, but it was still too much to expect unwavering equanimity throughout every single phase of a long voyage.

Whatever the cause, I slipped into a foul mood and stayed there, and with each hour grew more sullen and despondent. I lost interest in the voyage. The ship's log became monosyllabic. My notebook lay unopened. I no longer much cared which way we were heading. Our course was taking us towards north-east Iceland and that wasn't particularly the way I wanted to go but I let us run on anyway. This indifference made me feel worse. I buried myself in my sleeping bag and tried to keep warm and tried to forget the relentless passing of the waves outside.

Ah yes, those waves. How I started to hate those fucking waves. Do they never stop, those mindless, endless, stupid waves? God, how I hate the sea, and being at sea, and anything and everything to do with the sea. I don't even want to look at the sea but there is nothing to look at but the sea. They are mesmerising, these waves that just come on and on, day after day, lifetime after lifetime, age after age, for ever and ever. Waves, wretched inexorable untiring waves, billions and billions and trillions and trillions of the damned things, on and on, just rolling along all day and every day, on and on and on. Christ, I could write an Encyclopaedia of Bloody Waves. I could describe and catalogue and categorise every wave ever known to man. It would have three hundred and fifty-seven thousand entries, my Encyclopaedia of Bloody Waves, and run to two hundred and eighty-nine volumes. That's waves for you.

And clouds. They're not a whole lot better. Like waves, they just keep coming and coming. What I can't stand about clouds is their puffed-up self-importance. *Look at me! Aren't I a great cloud?* There's something collusional about waves and clouds. It's the way they just keep spewing out over that windward horizon. Oh yes, they're in cahoots all right, waves and clouds. They run to the same rhythm. Faster the waves, faster the clouds. On and on they come, streaming over the edge of the world like newsprint off some gargantuan press.

And why oh why is it always bloody fulmars following us about? Have they got nothing better to do, these silly lickspittle fulmars, than to ape every petty twist and turn of our hollow peregrinations? I'm sick of fulmars. Why oh why is it always, always bloody fulmars? What would I give for a pair of sea eagles or a flock of humming birds? An Egyptian vulture would break the monotony. How about a flying fox or a pterodactyl or a Sopwith Camel or two? Even a common-or-garden house sparrow would do. Or a blue tit. Anything for a break from fulmars, fulmars, fulmars. God, I hate fulmars.

Oh yes, the dog days had really got a grip and I brooded darkly on waves and clouds and bloody fulmars. All that nautical get-on-with-it briskness had evaporated. It took an hour to find the will to clean my teeth. My noon position was five or ten or fifteen minutes late but we were in the middle of nowhere so what did it matter? My bladder was exploding before I would shift myself to open the hatch and retrieve the toilet bucket from the cockpit. Well, a man can't always be as tiresomely chipper as a young Hornblower.

And it was worse than that, for that vapid cabbage-grower of a ship's boy was forever whispering in Old Ahab's ear, whining and whispering, and conjuring up images of sunnier climes and hot showers and warm beds and foaming pints of fresh-pulled ale. Yes, that nasty little turncoat, that pimply weak-willed son of a hay bale was all for heading straight for home there and then. *Just think of it, sir. Home in ten days. Fresh toast with a nice boiled egg for breakfast. Lovely. Beats hanging about in this godforsaken hole, don't it, sir?*

Yes, the dog days can gnaw away at the last threads of a man's resolve, and I came within a whisker of capitulating. It would have been so easy to sail on to the south-east, to take the direct line back to northern Scotland and home, to convince myself that we had done more than enough for one voyage. For two long days the battle of wills raged on. I stared at the chart and measured distances and weighed pros and cons. The choice was stark. We could hold our course and sail direct for home, skirting around the north-east tip of Iceland. This option gave a straight-line distance of about six hundred miles. Alternatively we could alter course to the south-west, a ninety degree shift in heading, and pass through the Denmark Strait between Iceland and Greenland. In so doing we would effectively circumnavigate Iceland. A passage through the Denmark Strait had of course been the final objective of the voyage, but from where we now were it was a huge detour, almost doubling the distance home. We would have to sail well to the west, to at least twenty-five degrees of west longitude, taking us as far from the Moray Firth as Jan Mayen. It was almost like starting another voyage.

By early morning on the sixteenth of July we had been at sea for nearly three weeks, half our allotted time. I could no longer delay a decision on what to do. Another day's sailing on our current heading would put the west-abouts option beyond reach. The nasty procession of rain and fog continued unabated, encouraging dark thoughts and indecision. At least the wind was favourable for whichever choice I made. Yes, it would have been so easy just to run on and let that young clod-hopper of a foredeck hand have his way, but at four that morning I pulled myself out of the pit of indifference into which I had fallen, gave myself a metaphorical kicking, slapped myself about a bit, and reasserted my grip on the voyage. I altered course to the south-west. Ahead, some two hundred and fifty miles away, lay Straumnes, Iceland's north-westerly headland. We would pass close by then head south through the Denmark Strait.

Inevitably I felt better, having taken up the challenge of the longer and more difficult route and re-established some direction and purpose to the second half of our voyage. I had little expectation that it would be easy, this great loop back towards the Greenland coast and around Iceland, followed by a long haul east to Scotland. Winds had been predominantly easterly for the whole voyage; if that continued, the last leg could be very tough. We would be spending much longer at sea, especially in the critical zone between Iceland and the British Isles, in the track of the North Atlantic depressions. There was little chance that we would retain the settled high pressure that had been with us so far. Yes, deep down I had all the intimations of what was to come, and I wasn't wrong. Over the next month every worst fear would be handsomely fulfilled. The real dangers and trials and tribulations of our voyage were all yet to come.

19

My mood lifted and so did the weather. With an easing north-easterly we ran to the south-west under skies that within a day or so had lost their stifling layers of low cloud and transformed to a limitless and liberating blue. Two fat vessels hull down on the port beam soon separated into four vessels, fishing boats working in pairs. I was by now hand steering with the whipstaff, the following wind being too fickle and inconsequential for the self-steering gear, and so was able to keep us moving along, which was just as well, for the fishing boats were edging closer, threatening an uncomfortable contact. For six hours we danced a stately quadrille, or maybe a sort of pavane, five little ships backing and forthing over the wide ocean, bowing and curtseying, until finally one of the boats, a substantial fellow with a jaunty maroon hull and a white superstructure, made a trawling pass close across our stern and I was able to read his name and his provenance: the *Godmundur* of the Vestmann Islands. A real Icelander! *Mingming* and I struggled on while our dance partners kept up their circling astern until they were gone save for the low thrumming of their engines that was almost beyond hearing but infused the stillness of the day with a soft and vibratory undertone.

For twenty-four hours, twenty-four hours in which the sun traced the oddest of trajectories but never dipped totally away from sight, we ghosted parallel with the Icelandic coast sixty or seventy miles to our south, and covered little more than thirty miles. Once more happy in my work I sat in the hatchway and looked for what I could see. A humpback whale spouted close to port then disappeared with a flourish of its mighty fluke. The occasional seal, square-headed and rough-muzzled, watched our passage, the flaps of its wide and lozenge-shaped nostrils twitching inquisitively. Parties of Arctic terns swished and bounced elegantly north in a creaking welter of constant and companionable chatter. *Mingming* charmed them; they hovered over the cockpit and tried to alight on the thin top edge of her wind vane. For all their streamlined and balletic grace they were fearless, these sea swallows, aggressive even, joining unhesitating battle with passing skuas and soon sending those bully-boys packing. From time to time the sea erupted as a white-beaked dolphin went through its routine, a quick succession of prodigious acrobatic leaps, each ending with the foamy splash of an any-old-how landing, usually flat-sided and all skewwhiff. A few kittiwakes had joined our fulmar escort and they, by contrast, had developed a most precise and delicate technique for settling on the water, descending gently with outstretched and unmoving wings and timing the last few inches with unerring accuracy to give a gossamer landing; a simultaneous folding of their wings created a seamless transition from flying to floating.

Somewhere not far to our south lay the only bit of Icelandic territory within the Arctic Circle, the tiny uninhabited island of Kolbeinsey. For a while we headed almost due west to be sure of clearing it, then gybed to run straight for the north-west tip of Iceland.

Midnight brought us to Sunday, the nineteenth of July, and the start of our twenty-fourth day at sea. The sun hung low and red, but still well clear of the horizon, and so, like a daft tourist, I photographed it. *Look at this one! Taken at five past midnight! See that, that's the sun!* I had my come-uppance, though, for within a couple of hours it was gloomy enough to demand the use of *Mingming's* navigation lights for the first time in nearly three weeks. Our eternal day was slipping away.

It did not last long, this hint of darkness, and we were soon bounding along once more with a following breeze under a bright and cloudless sky. I changed the blade in my razor and so scraped my cheeks and chin to alabaster smoothness. Inspired to even greater things by the unaccustomed excellence of my *toilette* I delved deep into my wash bag for a small pair of scissors and spent a rejuvenating five minutes or so ridding my nostrils and ear-lobes of all unsightly hair. I took special care over the subsequent teeth cleaning, scrubbing and spitting with unusual vigour, and so emerged from the hatchway all fresh-faced and sparkly-toothed and ready for any Viking maiden who might just climb aboard.

On we ran, quickly closing the topmost point of the many-fingered hand that thrusts out from Iceland's north-west corner. With every hour our fulmar escort swelled, and was joined by an almost equal number of kittiwakes, their brilliantly laundered plumage of an altogether higher grade than the mucky off-white of the fulmars. I felt almost guilty at all this attention and activity. Here were a thousand avian brains somehow programmed into an endless round of take off and land and an imperative to stick close to this...whatever it was they conceived a boat to be. Here was a well-rehearsed routine under-pinned by some vague expectation of an eventual reward: the last pickings of a fisherman's by-catch. These birds were happily untroubled by the least power of reasoning. *Mingming* was a cause that never, ever produced the long-awaited effect, but still they stuck with us, trusting and gullible. How I wished I could have emptied a bucketful of fish heads overboard and so given some sense or justification to all their wasted effort. How I would have loved to have seen the primal screech and fury and in-fighting that a pail of blood and guts would have set off amongst this lot. It would have warmed my heart to have paid our dues, at long last, to these constant attendants, for the more they stuck with us, and the greater their numbers grew, the more I felt like a kind of fraud. *You are hereby charged with the wilful impersonation of a fishing boat and the disruption of the feeding habits of eighteen thousand two hundred and thirty-three assorted seabirds. How do you plead?* Guilty, m'lud. Most horribly guilty.

Leaving the Arctic bird population to sort out its own dinner arrangements I went below and cooked up a pan of rice and tinned kippers and peas, a concoction whose excellence was exceeded only by the preserved peaches and home-made fruit cake that followed. By now feeling thoroughly at one with the world I once more checked the horizon and there, stretching from the port bow to a point somewhere out on our port beam, were the jagged peaks and snow-clad slopes of north-west Iceland. How it thrilled me, this low amphitheatre curving around the south-westerly quadrant. It was almost two years to the day since our first brief sighting of Iceland, a far-flung and niggardly glimpse of rock and ice through a veil of heavy cloud. Now we had it laid out end to end in crystal clarity. We were hurtling landwards with a fine following breeze. What's more, our approach to Iceland was *from the North.* Every circumstance had been reversed. A satisfied spirit conjoined with a satisfied stomach and so I sat in the hatchway as satisfied and as self-satisfied as it is decently possible for a man to be and with the help of binoculars traced the curves of the Drangajökull, Iceland's northernmost glacier that dominates the Vestfirðir, the north-west fjords, now fast approaching, and contemplated my good fortune, and considered the thought that there is nothing sweeter in all of this short life than to be alone on a stretch of ocean way beyond the back of beyond.

20

We were fast approaching land and I was about to do something stupid. Within the next twenty-four hours my smug mood would undergo something of a transformation. Such is the sea; it is no place for complacency. To be fair to myself, I was in two minds about a course of action that in retrospect I characterised as un-seamanlike. I almost didn't do it. I hesitated. For a while I even changed my mind and decided not to do it. But then I did do it and I should have known a whole lot better and so I have no excuse. Thinking back over the forty-eight days of this voyage, this is the one moment that embarrasses me and that I have swept away into one of the dustier recesses of my recall. It would be easy to gloss it over, or to present it in a different light, or even to turn it into something bold and virtuous, but that is not my way. I have to come clean and come clean I will.

We were fast approaching the tall and toothed headlands of north-west Iceland, then, and one question occupied me. How close in should I go? Here I was faced with something of a dilemma. My instinct was, as ever, to keep a good offing. No harm would be done if we were to pass the north-westerly cape, Straumnes, at four or five miles distance, striking a tangential line back into open sea to the west of Iceland. This would keep us away from inshore tides and races; we would at no time have a dangerous coastline under our lee; we would just graze the land mass in the briefest and most unthreatening manner.

All that was just as well, but another consideration was imposing itself into the argument. *Proof.* I needed a good and incontrovertible photographic record of our voyage. I needed strong evidence of everything *Mingming* and I had done, for here was one of the problems of the single-handed sailor who prefers to keep the sea and who eschews all communications and tracking devices: *how do you prove you've been where you say you've been?* I wish this weren't a consideration. For several years it had never crossed my mind, but one or two comments, made half in jest, had shocked me, and made me realise that this was something I needed to take seriously. Without good photographs or video footage of north-west Iceland, what real proof would there be that we had passed through the Denmark Strait? I had no idea what visibility would be like down the west coast, and whether there would be another opportunity to take good photographs. It was extremely unlikely that I would have the time or the will or the desire to try to bring *Mingming* into one of the Icelandic ports such as Reykjavik; that would be difficult and dangerous for an engineless single-hander, and held no attraction anyway.

All this in its turn raised another difficult question: *why should I care what anyone else thinks?* These voyages are intensely private endeavours, which thankfully attract little interest or attention. I go to sea to see the sea, not to build a personal brand; third party opinion is, on the face of it, irrelevant. But I also go to sea to write about the sea and I do care very much about what you, dear reader, think. You have invested time and energy to share our little escapades. You have found your way aboard and down the hatchway and into *Mingming's* cramped and cosy cabin. You have sailed many thousands of miles along with us, north and south, through calm and storm, and become a strong and silent and resilient member of our tight little crew. You have shared our night watches and our day watches and spooned your grub from the pan along with the rest of us. You have known all the discomfort of a hard and narrow bunk. You have tested the boundaries of personal hygiene. You have thrilled at distant landfalls and proximate ice, and sworn like a good sailorman at waves and clouds and fulmars. Oh yes, you have always been there, dear reader, watching and considering, sometimes nodding in approbation, sometimes tut-tutting, always at my shoulder, a valued fellow to have aboard (more so than that wheedling drip of a country cowherd), and therefore worthy of the highest respect. I care what *you* think, faithful and long-suffering reader, and almost came unstuck because of it.

For a while I had been studying the Iceland Pilot, and in particular the north-west fjords. Whilst the fjords themselves looked difficult to navigate under sail alone, there was a bay, Aðalvík, immediately to the south of Straumnes, that caught my attention and set me wondering. It was five miles across at the mouth and narrowed with a gentle curve to the north-east. At its head was a fine anchorage in softly shoaling sand. Perhaps we could creep into the bay and lie to anchor. The Pilot promised whooper swans and red-necked phalaropes, grassy slopes, waterfalls and a cool down-draught from the Drangajökull. Earlier settlers had abandoned the bay; just one or two summer houses remained. It seemed somehow idyllic, and the more I pondered on it the more attractive it seemed, and I decided that if conditions were right we would indeed enter Aðalvík and cast our hook into the sands of Iceland.

All night we ran towards the line of high cliffs under a clear sky. Hereabouts was evidently a fruitful breeding and feeding ground; above, huge squadrons of puffins and guillemots swarmed north and south, tightly-packed and intense in their work. The sea too heaved with guillemots, thousands of pairings of adult and chick. *Mingming* drove on through them, causing quick scuttlings and angry squawks and once a doleful wailing for a lost offspring caught, I fear, under *Mingming's* advancing prow.

By five in the morning we were running parallel with the coast, just five miles off. Here was a strange fusion of hard and soft, for the rock formations had a razor-edged and brittle and unyielding look to them, but glowed pink in the morning sun. Most prominent was the headland Horn, a towering bishop's mitre, its height accentuated by the vertical corrugations that I was seeing for the first time and which characterised all the sea cliffs of north-west Iceland. These perpendicular knife cuts in the rock were offset by a horizontal layering that further on became a kind of intricate terracing, all of these together creating the most extraordinary and beautiful sculptural effects. Here were the great domes of Angkor Wat, but now linked side to side, and more subtle, and more intricate, and showing once again that the aleatoric workings of nature will always, in time, outstrip all of man's greatest creations. Further back the land rose to a long and uneven ridge, its slopes patched and streaked with snow and ice; to the east the brilliant white whaleback of the Drangajökull slipped quietly away. Another odd discovery added to the headiness of the moment; the Arctic Circle lay between us and the land. For the moment we were sailing almost due west and so would retain our Arctic status for just a little longer.

A few streaks of cloud from the north-east were the first warning of a rapid change in the weather. I had been anticipating perfect conditions for both photography and for our entry into Aðalvík and so was dismayed when within an hour the sky had deteriorated to a thick mass of low cloud.

The higher inland peaks disappeared and then the tops of the cliffs and before long the cliffs themselves as rain swept in, whipped on by a cold and vicious wind. We were by now of course in shallow water and were soon driving on, well reefed down, in a short sea, turbulent and white-capped. Muscular headlands, bulging black shoulders, their peaks now always hidden, came and went with each passing squall. Each pair of bluffs guarded a shallow bay, and by some quirk of the conditions shafts of sunlight occasionally illuminated an amphitheatre of rock and green sward and snow-filled gullies. The shifting scene and the shifting light and the bulk and height and grimness of the closer cliffs and the weight of the clouds that cloaked them created something wild and grandiose. It must have set off some deep-seated memory of an image or a feeling, something perhaps from childhood, for I had the strongest sense of having sailed into an Arthurian legend; there was something literally fabulous about the whole moment and I would not have been in the least surprised to have seen a hand reach out from the very waves and grasp a fabled sword.

All this drippy romanticism was a fine thing, but the navigator in me was growing restless and unhappy. In the clearer moments I had now picked out Straumnes itself, the last and most imposing headland of this line of coast. Beyond, the land turned southwards and so was out of sight; the lower portion of Straumnes from time to time showed itself in silhouette against a distant line of clear sky. At its base, just visible with binoculars, was the lighthouse, the tiniest of needles set almost at sea level. We were angling in closer and closer. The wind was still rising; I had by now reefed *Mingming* down to just a single panel of sail. A fine old sea was running. Nothing on the charts or in the Pilot suggested that there might be a tide-race hereabouts, or overfalls, but it was getting nasty nonetheless. Every instinct in me screamed to move offshore and create some sea room and eventually I gybed to take us away from these cliffs and shoal waters.

For five minutes or so we ran towards open sea and then I gybed back and reset our course for Straumnes. The navigator had been over-ruled. It was quite possible that if we ran straight on out into the Denmark Strait, to sea room and to safety, we might never see the Icelandic coast again. It was clear that a good blow from the north-east was coming on, which would force us well out to sea. I had a few photographs and some video footage of what we had seen so far, but in the main it was murky, distant stuff. I wanted close-ups, good screen-filling images showing every last geological detail. I wanted bold photographs that had us properly linked in to the land. I wanted, dear reader, to take you by the scruff of the neck and bring you face to face with every nook and cranny of these monumental cliffs. I wanted to sail in, between the headlands, and be surrounded by Iceland. I wanted, just for once, to get a true sense of this bit of earth, of the look of it and the lie of it and the very smell of it.

And so I set sail for Straumnes and the worst day of our voyage.

21

For a while it was fun. I had thrown off all caution and started to enjoy myself. Angling in more steeply and deliberately towards the coast, we now had the wind almost on the beam, and so were rolling and plunging and taking the occasional slap of a breaking crest. Ahead, the two thousand foot buttress of Straumnes, still black under the lowering cloud, loomed higher and higher. Twenty-four days at sea had altered my perception of *Mingming*; she had swelled to palatial proportions. All that was now reversed. The scale of this great monolith soon stripped away any illusions and reduced us back to our true and feeble insignificance. As ever it was this moment, the instant at which all the delusional constructs evaporated and I could see us for what we really were, that brought a rush of the sweetest exhilaration. It may have been a kind of madness that had brought me to such an outlandish place, borne on the waves in the most unlikely of little yachts, but out of that madness came the occasional moment of clarity so piercing and uplifting that I would trade half a lifetime of the dull and the commonsensical for just those few seconds.

Ah yes, how magnificent it was, to career through that angry sea, helter-skeltering into a face of sheer rock! As we closed the coast the headlands to the east formed up in line astern and before long we had opened up ahead the first glimpse, round the corner, as it were, of the south-going land; here now was Ritur, a huge beehive of a bluff, and now I had my bearings laid out nicely, for it was between the twin outposts of Straumnes and Ritur that lay the bay we were about to enter.

I started filming and became over-confident in my work, unable to resist the idea of panning right round to windward to show the seascape of boiling white crests bearing down on us. One hit us and sent a thick shower of sea water curling over the boat, dousing my unprotected camera. I switched it off and ducked below to dry it off with kitchen roll but the damage was done; when I resumed filming the camera was dead. Nothing. Oh no! No! No! No! If the water had scrambled the circuits completely I might have lost almost two hours of utterly irreplaceable footage. No! No! No! I screamed and groaned and cursed my stupidity. How could I have been so careless? A few seconds' idiocy had probably destroyed the most compelling visual record of our voyage. Stored on the camera's hard disk were moving images, in both senses, of killer whales and humpback whales and the mountains of Jan Mayen and our arrival at 72°N and our passage through the ice floes. Oh no! The ice! Most of my visual record of the ice was on film; I had been so entranced that I had forgotten to take still photographs. Had I lost that once-in-a-lifetime footage?

Feeling sick to my stomach I put the camera away below and tried to focus on the navigational business in hand. We were just a mile off Straumnes and closing it fast. At its foot the tiny needle of a lighthouse was resolving into something more bizarre: an ochrous yellow pyramid. I couldn't give it my full attention. I was still reeling at the possible loss of all my film. After sixteen days within the Arctic Circle we had just crossed back out but the moment had gone unnoticed. Ahead I could now see the sail of a yacht running south close inshore. I dragged up enough interest to get out the binoculars and study it more closely. It looked like a Tradewind 35 and seemed to be flying a Red Ensign. On any other day I would have tried to make contact with my handheld radio, but I was in no mood for jolly conversation. It crossed our path half a mile ahead and continued on down the coast, squared off under mainsail only.

Aðalvík was now opening up as we rounded Straumnes and I could now confirm what I had suspected; the mass of low cloud that had poured in had met some kind of barrier as it reached the land. The bay and all the mountains behind it still lay under the clearest blue sky.

It ought to have been a wonderful moment. As we advanced under the lee of Straumnes we escaped the full blast of the north-easterly and the sea smoothed off. The southern arm of the bay, a sweep of grassy slope rising sharply at its seaward end to form the great cone Ritur, was devoid of snow and ice save for a single dab of white, and so looked soft and summery and absurdly inviting. Beyond Ritur four more headlands of the Vestfirðir, four stubby and symmetrical fingertips, their tops flattened to a precise horizontal line, each one reduced in height by an unerring perspective, stepped their way south and signposted their respective fjords: the Ísafarðjardúp, the Súgandafjörður and the Ónundarfjörður. Hard on our port beam the cliffs of Straumnes still dominated, maintaining their height and their intricate patterning well into the bay. Only at the seaward end, just inside the lighthouse, was the symmetry broken; here the lines of terracing were obscured by a monstrous patch of steep grey scree.

It was the head of the bay that should have warmed my heart. I could see a long curve of unbroken sandy shore that rose to undulating green slopes. Here was still a good residue of winter, for the slopes were striped with snow patches, formed by the lie of the land into horizontal striations, a sort of zebra patterning in white and moss green. At one point the sand continued on up from the beach to form a khaki-tinted hillside, its smoothness broken only by the odd patch of low vegetation. The waters of the bay, of a limpid blue I had not seen for weeks, glinted merrily in the late morning sun.

Yes, it should have been a wonderful moment, our entry into Aðalvík, but the day was already ruined and it was about to get worse. As we made our way up the bay the breeze grew lighter and more fickle. By rights we should have had a strong headwind; I had anticipated a lively beat up to our anchorage. About a mile or so inside the bay we lost the wind completely. Astern, out to sea, I could see the lines of rolling white caps; ahead, close in to the beach, was a long streak of darker water flecked white by a healthy breeze. The north-easterly was still blowing, but even in this wide bay the height of the surrounding cliffs and hills was enough to play havoc with the normal air flows. We had hit a dead spot.

I was not unduly concerned; I did not imagine it would last for long. I was slightly embarrassed, though, for we were not alone in the bay. A little creel boat with a bright red hull and a deck totally enclosed by a boxy white superstructure had chugged in from seawards and was now engaged in some sort of harvesting activity just half a mile to our south. Had we been lying there serenely it might not have been so bad, but despite the absence of wind we were hobby-horsing violently in a short and steep chop. The waves were dancing with an unnatural energy brought on by cross-currents and the scend curling in around the headlands. *Mingming* was bucking back and forth, maddeningly, helplessly, noisily. I could not imagine what the skipper of the fishing boat made of this weird little interloper into his territory.

For an hour or so I worked *Mingming* one way then the other way, trying to find some wind and some forward momentum, but it was hopeless. By now I was in the cockpit, hand steering, although that term rather exaggerates the notion that I had any real directional control. Rather we were describing an endless series of random and misshapen circles over which the rudder had only minimal influence. Any attempt to hold us up to windward would end with us either falling off completely, or being pushed round onto the other tack by a mix of wave action and wind shift. The wind anyway was as circular and unpredictable and ineffective as our course.

Frustration turned to worry. I had not the slightest idea what the tides or currents did hereabouts. We were completely at their mercy. Fortunately I had kept reasonably well clear of the cliff face that spanned the northern arm of the bay, but as our immobility and helplessness increased it overbore ever more threateningly. Round and round we went, going nowhere, locked in a vice of unfathomable forces. By the end of the second hour I was beginning to curse my foolishness in bringing us in so close to land. All around was a scene of rare magnificence, a vista to lift the spirits of the most unimaginative of dullards, but it was impossible to savour it; all it did was taunt and mock me. The day was turning more bitter by the minute.

For yet another hour we waltzed a series of tight gyrations and moved not an inch. I could gauge our progress, or lack of it, by the position of an orange rescue hut that showed just beyond a shoulder of cliff on the northern side of the bay. It moved in and out of sight to the minimal ebb and flow of our movement and never came a yard nearer. By now I had in any case given up all thought of advancing further into the bay. I'd had enough. I was desperate to be out of there, away from this trap, away from all this siren beauty, away from land, away from this double-dealing and trickery and the bloody-minded interactions of rock and wind and water. I'd had enough all right and longed to be back once more to the simple certainties of endless sea and sky.

Lunchtime arrived but I did not eat. Instead I rowed. There was no other option. I unlashed *Mingming's* fine new sweeps and set to rowing us back out to sea. They were heavy, those fine new sweeps, and so was *Mingming*, still pretty much in maximum cruising trim, and every stroke took a supreme effort of muscle and will. I pushed and strained and grunted and within no time had sweat cascading down brow and cheeks and body. The trick was to get *Mingming* moving and then keep up the momentum with continual and rhythmic strokes; in other words to keep going - once she lost way *Mingming* was immediately back to her slow spinning and therefore needed re-orienting before any serious progress in the right direction could be made. For an hour I laboured manfully and called on every last physical reserve to try to push us through the steep wavelets and overcome the circular current that was holding us fast. I worked until my chest throbbed and my heart literally ached and until I felt nauseous with the effort and until I gave up because, according to our bearing on the orange rescue hut, we had not moved one single solitary fraction of an inch.

I have scarcely ever felt as bad and as searingly unhappy during any other moment in a lifetime of sailing. All balance and harmony and composure had been comprehensively obliterated. Vanity and over-confidence and poor judgement and the weak-willed abandonment of my simple navigational rules of thumb had landed me in the direst of fixes. And no, I am neither being unduly harsh on myself nor simply striving for some convenient literary effect with all of this self-criticism. As I have underlined many times, minimal ocean sailing is an uncompromising business. There is no place for half-pie heroics or seat-of-the-pants risk taking; it is about sound judgement based on sober analysis. Even at the time there was no limit as to how furious I was with myself for compromising the success of our voyage. I had lost two hours of precious film and now was trapped helplessly within little more than a stone's throw of a rocky shore. My prolonged exertions at the sweeps, a sudden explosion of work after weeks of physical tranquillity, had left me feeling ill. A day that had started with calm expectancy was now torn to shreds.

I made a third-rate job of re-lashing the oars and went below. My sweat was now cooling, setting me all a-shiver. I gulped down some water. I lay on my bunk and calmed myself with deep breaths. My chest ached. *Mingming* still hopped from one foot to the other in the chop, her mainsail banging from side to side. I wanted to close my eyes and sleep and forget. Anxiety brought me to the hatch. For an hour I sat there, immobile, vacant. A patch of darker water swept in from the head of the bay. Wind. *Mingming* heeled gently. I grabbed the steering lines and paid out the mainsheet. We were moving. The north-easterly had found us once more. We ran out between the headlands Straumnes and Ritur in a freshening half-gale of wind and came home to the wide ocean.

22

Are you still with us, dear reader, or have you grown weary of it all? Were you tempted to jump ship and swim those few yards to land and leave the sea forever? I wouldn't blame you. It is not always fun, this ploughing of a lonely furrow through distant waters.

If you have kept faith and are still aboard then I embrace you heartily. I need you now, for our voyage is far from done. Just think! We are still eight hundred miles from home and must surely sail a thousand miles before the hills of Banffshire heave once more into view. They will not be easy, those thousand miles. Let me be frank: there will be times, dear reader, when we will despair, you and I, of ever seeing those hills again. It will seem, I promise, that every last atom of the world has conspired to bar our way. Our voyage will drag on, day after day after day. We will meet frustrations beyond imagining; every one of those thousand miles will be wrestled from the iron grip of an implacable Nature.

I tell you this now so that you are under no illusions. Don't say I didn't warn you! I believe you have the stomach for it, faithful reader, but if you are unsure, and hanker perhaps after the easy way home, I won't hold it against you if you turn straight to the last few lines of our tale, as yet unwritten, but no doubt along the lines of *and so we came safely into harbour and lived happily ever after*. No, I won't hold it against you, but I will be sad for you, dear reader, for you will miss the point of the whole endeavour; our sailing may be simple, but is seldom quick and never easy.

We ran out into the Denmark Strait, then, with a furious following wind, a nasty squally wind that only cleared itself of sudden holes and violent shifts once we were well offshore. It was hurtling down from the slopes of the Drangajökull, this icy blast, and was as Arctic and as glacial as anything we had yet encountered. The great mouth of the Ísafarðjardúp, the inlet leading to the Vestfirðir, the north-west fjords, opened up on our port beam, but I wanted no part of it. Further south the land rose sheer out of the sea to form a table top that stretched as far as vision would allow. Giants had clearly been at work here, setting the land to rights with spirit levels and outsize smoothing planes. A fishing boat crossed our path, making for the Ísafarðjardúp and pitching heavily into a head sea. We sped past, away from the land, with just a few inches of sail set, and pushed on by waves that turned an inky black as the evening wore on. Heavy cloud bore down once more. I lay shivering in the cabin, unhappy, unwell and worried that I may have caused myself some lasting physical damage. The wind rose further; by eleven I had lashed the sail bundle amidships and by three the next morning had been forced to put on an extra lashing. The seascape aft was a welter of churning white.

It was a cruel weight of wind that pushed us offshore, but it did not last for long; every hour of the new day brought a steady easing, forcing me to the hatch to raise another panel of sail. We were now forty-five or so miles out into the Denmark Strait or, as the Icelanders would have it, the Greenland Sound, but had not yet lost our connection to the land; to the west the Icelandic plateau showed a degree or two above the horizon, a precise stratum that only dropped away as it curved to the north into the Ísafarðjardúp, and to the south into the Breiðafjörður, the massive bight that eats into the Icelandic west coast. At the southern end of this indent a long and mountainous peninsula pushes once more to the west, bringing a finger of land back out into the Strait, and reaching a kind of apogee at its seaward end, where the great dome of the Snaefellsjökull, the Snow Mountain Glacier, rises to four and a half thousand feet. The sky had cleared by midday, and it was not long before the glacier's upper slopes, garishly white in the afternoon sun, rose skywards far on our port bow.

For two days the Snaefellsjökull dominated our passage southwards through the Denmark Strait. It was a constant presence and as it passed from bow to beam to quarter, close enough to impress, distant enough not to threaten, solid and calm and supremely detached, it helped restore some equilibrium to my shattered spirit. For a while we lay once more becalmed as the north-easterly snuck off. I had decided that I had best not touch my video camera while still at sea, but anxiety about the possible loss of all my film still gnawed away at me. The camera had by now had a while to dry out, although sea water, once it has affected fine circuits, never properly dries; the salts it deposits continuously attract moisture. In the calmer and marginally warmer conditions I decided to switch it on and see what happened. The tiny green 'On' light glowed! The screen lit up! I had a go at playing back some earlier footage. Yes! It was still there! I attached the fancy microphone that fits onto the top of the camera. Everything went dead. Nothing. I took the microphone off and started again. Once more everything worked. I closed my eyes and hugged the camera to myself, rocking back and forth in sweet relief. There was obviously a problem with the microphone connections, but the camera was still functioning and, more importantly, the hard disk was still intact. Well, it was the preservation of the images that mattered. I put the camera carefully away, well wrapped and protected in its waterproof bag; I would not risk using it again during the rest of the voyage.

The north-easterly picked up once more, driving us south through the Strait under skies once more laden horizon to horizon with a dense layering of cloud. The Snaefellsjökull and the line of peaks to its east sank down to the very wave tops then dipped out of sight. The land was, to all appearances, gone, but I knew well enough that this was a kind of illusion. Not far ahead lay trouble: land, plenty of it, lurking just beneath the waves. The south-west corner of Iceland continues out into the sea for forty miles or so, creating a line of shoals and skerries and dangerous water, the so-called Reykanes Ridge. I was aiming for a narrow gap at its centre, a deep water passage just a couple of miles wide, but as we bore down on it my anxiety grew. The wind had wound itself up to a fine old Force 6 and looked to be threatening more. A turbulent sea was building. It would only get worse as we moved into the shoal water of the Ridge. I could either stand on into the passageway, which beyond a certain point would become an irrevocable commitment, irrespective of the conditions, or else I could bear off and run to the south-west, parallel with the Ridge, and skirt round its outer end in deeper water. This second, safer, option, would take a day or so longer.

For several hours I agonised over the decision as we raced towards those hidden rocks. How desperately I wanted to be through them, with a clear run for Scotland and home. Just a few more hours and we would be out of the Denmark Strait and set fair for the south-east with only the Faroes in our path. It blew harder and with a resigned and heavy heart I squared away to take the long way round. It was not worth risking a mishap in that narrow channel. For a whole night, then, for a full twelve hours, we ran down the northern side of the Reykanes Ridge, just a few miles off, our course taking us away from home once more. At six on the morning of Friday the twenty-fourth of July, our twenty-ninth day at sea, we rounded the seaward end of the Reykanes Ridge and, in a breeze that was failing fast and leaving us to a nasty slop, set a course for the Fair Isle Channel.

23

Relative to the British Isles, Iceland is not as far north as popular imagination would have it. Yes, it lies in higher latitudes, but is much further west than north. Britain's most northerly point, Muckle Flugga, lies in about 61°N, while Iceland's most southerly land, the Vestmann Islands, are located just above 63°N, less than a hundred and fifty miles nearer to the Pole. Iceland's frozen nature is not so much down to its higher latitude, but to a location that robs it of the full warming effects of the Gulf Stream and that at the same time exposes it to the cold East Greenland Current. Our course back to Fair Isle therefore required us to sail almost six hundred miles east, but less than two hundred miles south. As we approached the Faroes we would be subject to an increasing north-easterly push from the North Atlantic Current, the last vestiges, in effect, of the Gulf Stream.

As we rounded the Reykanes Ridge and shaped our course to the east-south-east and home I felt a flood of exhilaration. All the objectives of our voyage had been fulfilled: Jan Mayen, the Greenland ice, the Denmark Strait. Of all the possible routes that I had dreamed of in front of a winter's fire, we had managed the longest and the most challenging. Mixed in with that exhilaration, though, was a tinge of foreboding. The main driver of our success had been a long run of settled easterly weather. Winds had been predominantly east to north-east for nearly a month; we had scarcely had a sniff of anything from the west for all of that time. It seemed unlikely that this would continue, especially as we moved south into the track of the North Atlantic depressions. We were surely due a good south-westerly wind, a fine breeze just aft of the beam that would spur us quickly home. Nevertheless, as I looked at the chart and considered that long haul east and thought of the unerring easterly winds of the last month, my joy at lining up for the last leg of our voyage was tempered by a nagging suspicion that a smooth run home was not a given. Nearly a quarter of our total distance was still to be sailed. The rounding of south-west Iceland and the opening up of a clear route back to Scotland may have given the impression that we were nearly home, but in reality there was still a long, long way to go. What's more, most of it would be through, or skirting, those jewels of the Shipping Forecast: South East Iceland, Faroes, Bailey, Hebrides, Fair Isle, names that resound in the head like tolling bells and seem somehow incomplete without their usual preface of *'There are warnings of gales in...'*

As we cleared the Reykanes Ridge, then, the breeze fell away and left us languishing. There was a cruel irony here, for the sky above was by now a trade wind sort of sky if ever I saw one, a blue and puffy-clouded sky that promised much and gave us next to nothing. What little it did give came at first from the north, raising my hopes of quartering winds and fast passages, but it soon abandoned us, this putative northerly, and took to rotating idly around the compass, and disappearing altogether for longer and longer periods, until, after a day or so, what little puff was left came straight out of the south-east. This faint and patchy zephyr from dead ahead was not enough to power the vane steering, so I rigged the whipstaff and hand steered for hour after hour. In the calm and clear conditions land was once again visible to the north and north-east, first the Eyjafyallajökull, yet another distant glacier to add to my growing list, then the darker foreground smudges of the Vestmann Islands. The wind gave up completely and I sat in the hatchway under a slatting mainsail and watched Iceland. I felt sure that I could smell it too; for some unfathomable reason the air was infused with the faintest hint of almonds. A leach's petrel bounced past, a welcome diversion from the usual crowd of bickering fulmars that now crowded in close and delivered the final insult: they could keep up with us with no more than a lazy paddling. At times it was worse; the more adventurous ones made excursions right around *Mingming*, examining her topsides and her sheer and the cut of her light weather jib with a critical eye. A juvenile arctic tern, perhaps separated from its kin and looking for some maternal love, flew in and settled right alongside a friendly-looking fulmar and was promptly pecked and screamed at. It took off and alighted again at a more respectful distance and so we all lay there together, eyeing each other and going nowhere.

There were compensations, though. For five days since that disastrous day at Aðalvík I had eaten little; dismay had crushed my appetite. My sleep too had been fitful. Now I made up for it with an orgy of gorging and rest.

The deterioration in the weather started slowly and at first I did not take it too seriously. We had been at sea for a month and had been through one short half-gale at worst. Two days of crippling calms and scarcely discernible air flows had dulled the edge of my expectation. A rising wind from east-north-east, almost a leading wind that brought with it a grumpy, frowning sky, was at first a happy change. We were on the move at last. We pulled away from our fulmars, leaving them bobbing in a wake that soon transformed from the occasional bubble to a foamy swathe. They gave up their paddling and took to the air, still intent on sticking with us. I had learned my lesson many times and went forward early to gasket the light weather jib, now redundant as we slogged to windward under four, then three, and before long just two panels of the mainsail. My noon position showed we had covered just thirty-eight miles in twenty-four hours. The crosses on my chart were pitifully close. A torrential downpour emptied the skies of cloud, and for a while I thought that maybe we had seen the last of this little blow, but before long a mucky skyscape reasserted itself and the wind got up still further. We were now down to just one panel, fore-reaching awkwardly into a head sea that was looking increasingly unfriendly.

I cooked my evening pan of food, ate the usual portion, then sat in the hatchway, well-protected by the folding hood, and considered the outside world. The conditions had now been worsening for twelve hours or so, and as I watched the waves bearing down on us and past us and away from us towards a distant Greenland coast I finally understood that this patch of bad weather would be neither short-lived nor inconsequential. The wind and the seas had built to a weight that meant business and every few minutes were growing palpably more intense. I realised at last that things were going to get a lot worse before they got better. This was a storm that had crept up on us almost unnoticed.

It took just one wave to shock me into action. It was, I think, the worst configuration of water I have ever seen in open ocean. It passed us by just forty or fifty yards on the port beam and it was those few yards that saved us from an inevitable capsize. The leading face of that wave was as precisely perpendicular as if set by a plumb-line. I don't remember ever seeing anything as clear-cut and vertical as that sheer face of water careering past us at twenty knots or so. I don't remember ever being as impressed by anything watery as I was by that wave. It was by no means a huge wave, perhaps twelve or fifteen feet high, but it was by far the most exquisitely menacing block of water that I have ever set eyes on.

It was also the most communicative of waves. It told me many things. It told me, for example, that to continue fore-reaching at a more or less beam-on attitude to the seas could spell disaster. It made it quite clear that we were now in survival conditions. Above all, that lump of water delivered the unequivocal message that unless I acted quickly I might never again see the fair hills of Banffshire.

24

The phenomenon known as wind sheer ensures that the higher you are from the surface of the water, the stronger the wind. The force applied by a gale will be greater at twenty feet of altitude than at ten feet, and greater at thirty feet than at twenty feet, and so on. What's more, the turbulences and surface frictions caused at sea level by the interaction of wind and water interfere with the passage of air and moderate its sting. In the worst of weather this is one of the compensations of sailing a tiny yacht. Minimum freeboard and a low cabin top keep the bulk of the craft in the confused and less vicious stratum of surface air; this is especially so in the troughs. The shorter and less bulky mast of the small yacht creates considerably less windage than its taller counterpart. When lying a-hull the boom and sail bundle are much lower down too, again minimising exposure to the blast. In a minimal boat you may not be able to get out of the wind, but to a certain extent you can get *underneath* it.

There is no escape, however, from the power and turbulence of the sea itself. Here again the smaller well-found yacht is not altogether at a disadvantage. In bigger seas it is only ever subject to the action of one wave at a time. If properly constructed the hull will be more rigid and, pound for pound, stronger than that of its bigger siblings. A smaller, lighter boat with low freeboard presents less resistance to a breaking wave, riding the punches more easily. This tendency to be pushed sideways, a healthy tendency because it lessens the risk of capsize, increases as the boat's draught reduces. The conventional and probably intuitive wisdom that a deeper draught means greater stability and safety in heavy weather is not necessarily so. A deep keel can trip a boat being pushed sideways by wave action, causing it to roll more easily.

The reduced internal volume of the smaller yacht creates another helpful circumstance: the distance a body can be thrown is severely limited. Most of the injuries sustained by yachtsmen in rough seas are the result of impacts suffered at the final moment of an air-bound trajectory across a wide cabin. The shorter the in-flight distance is, the less the chance of physical damage. Oodles of space below, whether transverse or vertical, may help sales figures at the Boat Show, but could ultimately deliver a cracked head or a broken wrist. Neither is helpful to the single-handed sailor.

While I would not go so far as to argue that the smaller yacht is better suited to heavy weather than a larger one, I don't think that it is at any overall or inherent disadvantage. Size is less relevant than design, preparation and mental attitude. I suspect that the small-boat ocean sailor, less subject to a false sense of security, will in general score better on the last two of these.

Thrown into the mix too is the vexacious question of storm tactics. The principle on which *Mingming* has been developed for survival conditions is to create a kind of capsule; strong, totally watertight, unsinkable and with limited internal space. Add to that a small rig, easily manageable from the hatchway, and you have a reasonable starting point for coping with the worst of weather. This does not imply, however, that all that needs to be done when the going gets rough is to lash the sail bundle, seal the hatch, hunker down and hope for the best; that would be a total and passive surrender to the corked bottle principal. *Mingming* may be designed to survive a bad knockdown or capsize, but I will still use every means at my disposal to avoid the likelihood of either. The forces unleashed during a capsize could well produce collateral damage of some sort, a broken mast being the most likely. I would not discount the possibility either that were *Mingming* to be dumped on her head her coach roof might be split open. While neither of these outcomes would necessarily be terminal, they are best avoided.

If we are sailing a downwind course and can therefore run before the wind from the outset, the normal progression of sail configurations as a storm develops is fairly straightforward. Firstly the self-steering gear is set at about a hundred and sixty-five degrees to the apparent wind, so that we are running about fifteen degrees off square. This keeps us nicely stern on while reducing the chance of an inadvertent gybe. The slightly oblique passage down the face of the waves gives a little more bite and control. As the wind strengthens sail is reduced down until we are running under the squared out sail bundle alone. The junk rig gives infinitesimal control over the amount of sail deployed; if the sail bundle alone does not deliver adequate forward drive I can lift the yard an inch, or two inches, or however much is needed. By the time we are running in a full gale the squared out bundle will be causing too much imbalance. It is now brought inboard and lashed firmly down. We can now run on happily at just a knot or two. *Mingming's* buoyant, foam-filled stern rises effortlessly to the crests bearing down from astern.

If we are sailing a windward course I carry sail for a lot longer. The self-steering is set at forty-five degrees to the apparent wind with, usually, two panels of the mainsail deployed. As the wind increases the sheet is let out until the sail is just feathering. As long as the seas are not dangerously steep or breaking too heavily, this attitude can be held into a severe gale. It is wet, uncomfortable and we certainly take the odd knock or two, but it at least allows us to hold position. As conditions worsen, increasing the risk of capsize, and as long as I have sea room, the next stage is to turn downwind and run off.

Sooner or later, though, the moment will arrive when the wind force and sea state are too extreme to allow us to run before the weather in reasonable safety. This may be possible in a bigger, faster yacht. Here the principle is to sail downwind at high speed, not totally outstripping the advance of the waves, but to a large extent neutralising their destructive power. This is not a strategy that would work with *Mingming*. With a waterline length of little more than sixteen feet, she could never sail fast enough. In any event, to career downwind at the margin of controllability may simply replace one set of risks with another.

Beyond a certain point in the conditions the requirement is therefore for some kind of drogue or sea anchor. This serves two purposes: to control speed and to hold the yacht at a safe attitude to the seas. There are those who favour a large sea anchor – a strong canvas cone or, increasingly these days, a voluminous parachute-style nylon dome, set from the bow and therefore imitating the action of a normal anchor. I don't use one on *Mingming*, for several reasons. Firstly the difficulties of setting and retrieving a sea anchor from the bow of such a small yacht are too extreme to contemplate. Secondly a large single sea anchor asserts its force with a hard and unyielding snubbing action. This can be moderated slightly with the use of a long and stretchy nylon warp, but the boat is nonetheless subject to continual violent shocks. Thirdly the yacht is in any event moving stern first and if thrown backwards risks damaging its rudder. The fact that the boat is moving contrary to its designed direction has an even more significant implication: it is inherently unstable.

With higher freeboard and less underwater volume at the bow, and with the mast well forward of its centre of effort, the boat will be striving the whole time to turn away from wind and sea; the bow always wants to fall off. In a sense the boat is fighting against its anchor, rather than working in harmony with it. This constant yawing, through a wide angle, regularly puts the yacht back into the sort of dangerous attitude it needs to avoid.

My preference is therefore to set any sea anchoring mechanism from the stern, and my contrivance of choice is the Jordan Series Drogue. Don Jordan, an American aeronautical engineer, was commissioned by the US Coastguard to develop the best possible heavy weather safety mechanism for small craft. It took ten years of patient and meticulous research and testing to perfect his drogue. The principle is simple, the action subtle. Scores of ripstop nylon cones, each with a five inch diameter at the mouth, and each one effectively a tiny sea anchor, are threaded and fixed by tapes on to a long warp. The number of cones is determined by the displacement of the yacht. The warp is set from a bridle at the stern and its after end is weighted with chain or a small anchor. The overall length of the drogue, including its bridle, lead, coned area and tail, will vary with the number of cones, but will rarely be less than a hundred metres or so. This ensures that the drogue will be spanning several wave systems simultaneously and is therefore not only subject to the same wave acting on the yacht.

The drogue holds the stern of the boat, its more buoyant end, square on to the advancing seas. As the boat is moving gently forward in its designed direction, it is happier and more stable than if it were anchored from the bow, and so is not given to constant yawing. However the hidden secret of the drogue, and its great beauty, lie in its deceleratory action. Jordan identified that the greatest danger to a small craft was for it to be picked up and accelerated by a wave that then threw it into the trough, or slewed it round and rolled it. His drogue is designed to apply an appropriate contrary force, exactly commensurate with the weight of the boat and the level of acceleration. The faster the yacht is carried forward, the greater the deceleration applied by the drogue. The drogue exerts just the force needed at any given moment, no more and no less. Its action is progressive and therefore soft. This is not to say that it does not impose huge strains on boat and gear, but the stresses build incrementally, rather than by means of a sudden and violent shock.

I built *Mingming's* Jordan Series Drogue prior to our first voyage in 2006. It was, as far as I know, the first time that one had been designed for a yacht of such small displacement. It was well off the lower end of the tables produced by Don Jordan showing the required number of cones for given displacements. Extrapolating from the tables suggested that *Mingming's* drogue might need about eighty-six cones, but I wasn't at all sure about this. Don Jordan himself was by that time in very poor health and not given to answering queries. Fortunately his interest was sufficiently piqued by the light displacement question to confirm that my guess was about right. He has since died.

For four long voyages the drogue had lain packed in its huge nylon bag on the port quarter berth, ready for immediate deployment. For four years it had taken up valuable space and added considerable weight to our load, but I was happy to have it aboard. This was my ultimate insurance policy, my last resort. I hoped I would never have to use it, but I knew well enough that sooner or later the day would come.

That nasty wave, square, unforgiving and prophesying doom, was scarcely past us before I was down below and at work. There was not one shred of doubt in my mind; it was time to launch Mr Jordan's drogue, and launch it fast.

25

For the first time in a month at sea I had to struggle into all that foul-weather gubbins – sea boots and high-bibbed trousers and waterproof jacket, the latter outfit reeking noxiously and forcing me to make a mental note, incongruous under the circumstances, to think about replacing it before our next voyage – then pulled on my harness over the top. I released the inboard end of the drogue from its bag and fed it out on deck through the after portlight. I opened the hatch and let the folding hood forward to give me free passage skywards, fixed one of my harness clips to a strong point at the aft end of the cabin, and climbed out to take the evening air.

I find it impossible to give a stirring description of the outside scene and my slow crawl across the cockpit and onto the after deck. I had no desire to reflect on what was going on around us; there are times when it is better not to know. I simply blanked it all out and concentrated on my hands and my harness clips and my grip and my balance. Once at the pushpit there was difficult work to be done. I had to rotate the pendulum blade of the self-steering gear out of the water and lash it in its vertical non-operational position. I did not dare leave it deployed under the water, in case of damage from the drogue bridle; as yet I had no idea whatsoever as to how steadily we would lie to the drogue. Then I had to un-lash the bridle itself from the after rail and work it aft over the top of the wind vane and pendulum so that it would clear them when set. I was now ready to attach the drogue to its bridle and it was here that I made a stupid, un-seamanlike mistake.

I still can't for the life of me work out what impelled me to be so daft. I can drum up a few excuses: the outlandish conditions, anxiety, over-hastiness, the fact that it was four years since I had built the gear and worked out my system of deployment. Maybe, in the collective, they have some force, but they don't stand up to much scrutiny. I really should have known better.

The bridle was a length of 16mm double braid rope, off the same drum as the warp for the drogue. I was in effect joining rope to rope, the long line of the drogue to the continuous loop of the bridle. My intention had always been to use an anchor bend. This is a knot that tightens nicely on itself, gives a double width of rope at the point of bearing, and therefore minimises any chafe. Without a second's thought I attached the drogue with a nice big loop and a bowline.

Everything was now ready to go. I dropped the bridle over the stern and started feeding out the drogue, pulling it out through the portlight from its bag below. I was pleasantly surprised how quickly and easily I could work it out and into the water. The cones soon came and went, then the long tail, and finally the short length of heavy chain. Within just a few seconds the bridle took up the strain and we pulled round stern on to the seas. I surveyed my handiwork and with a terrible, gut-turning jolt realised what I had done. That loop around the bridle was a sure-fire candidate for chafe; there was a good chance that sooner or later the rope would wear right through and the drogue would disappear into the depths. There was now nothing I could do about it. I could not contemplate trying to retrieve the line and starting again. I could already feel the extraordinary calming effect it was having on *Mingming* in seas that were by now far worse than anything we had ever encountered together. I needed the drogue deployed. In any case, I doubted I could now pull it back by hand. Well, it was good thick rope and with luck would see us through the worst. I crawled back to the hatchway, shifting my harness clips from strong point to strong point, and dropped down into the uncertain haven of the cabin.

For twelve hours we rode to the drogue. Still swaddled in my foul weather gear, in case I had to make another sortie on deck, I made myself comfortable on the cabin sole. A couple of waterproof bags filled with clothes served as a makeshift mattress. My head lay on a pillow propped against the lowest companionway step. My legs were hooked over the food containers lashed at the forward end of the sole. I was tightly held port and starboard; my shoulders were hard against the cabin joinery on each side. I covered myself with a blanket and an unzipped sleeping bag. The position was not altogether foetal, but it was somehow warm and reassuring and womb-like to be squeezed and cosseted in that tight space. There were practical advantages too: my weight was as low down as possible and therefore aiding our stability; thus wedged in I could not be thrown around.

I lay back and closed my eyes and let the tension of the moment drain away and for a moment felt intensely happy. Once again we were hovering at the far edge. The world was now no more than a screaming wind and mountains of water and this tiny cockleshell and her ancient pilot. There was nothing else; all connection with that other world was gone. Here was an existence stripped to its core: the sky, the sea, a boat, a man.

I lay there and let the sounds of the world drift in and out and felt the push and pull and lift and fall of my body on its impromptu bedding. The physical sensation added a new facet to my exhilaration. The interplay of gravity and inertia and the action of the drogue were creating the most intoxicating effect. *Mingming* accelerated forward on each wave crest, but as the drogue softly restrained the hull, my own body kept going, giving a second or two of apparent weightlessness before settling down again. Every few seconds I was floating on air. It was the most subtle of fairground rides. Each time the drogue took up the strain the increased stresses were communicated by a long and rising creak. The drogue warp creaked. The bridle creaked. The chain plates creaked. The hull creaked. Together they harmonised into a great crescendo of a creak, my body levitated for a second or two, and then we all reverted to silence and gravitational normality as the strain came off.

Mingming lay as steadily to the weather as if moored fore and aft, locked into the narrowest of vectors. The gale wound itself up into a right old fury, with seas to match. It no longer mattered much; for us at least the combers had been reduced to a curious impotence. They could rant and they could roar all they liked, but with the drogue set and operational, it was all hollow declamation. We rose and we fell and we pushed forward a little and we fell gently back a little, but our movement was soft-edged and controlled and unthreatening. We had achieved a state of grace. The drogue had handed us a signed and sealed *laissez-passer*, a priceless immunity to the hostilities unfolding all around us.

Hour after hour I lay there, dozing and dreaming, entranced by our easy undulation and the rhythmic cycle of weightlessness. I felt supremely secure but for one nagging doubt: will the drogue chafe through and disappear? From time to time I hauled myself up from the cabin sole and peered out through the sealed after portlight. Everything was fine, except that the pendulum blade of the self-steering that

I had lashed upright so tightly was now flopping back and forth as we rolled, and banging against the vane mechanism. With a curse I exited the hatch and crawled aft to tighten the lashing. Within the hour it was loose again. Once more I made the trip to the after deck and this time realised what was happening. Waves were breaking from astern with such force that they were shifting the whole self-steering gear, pivoting it on the half inch bolt that held it to its brackets. That bolt had been tightened to excess with two large spanners. Well, there was nothing I could do about it. I would have to re-set the gear to its vertical position once conditions eased.

I resumed my vigil on the cabin sole. Full sleep was impossible. We were riding safely, but in a shrieking wind way beyond anything I had met in *Mingming*. Things were getting a little wet too; my dry haven was under assault. The seals of the main hatch were not fully up to the job, and water was also finding its way onto the cabin sole from somewhere under the cockpit. A night in oilskins had left my clothes damp and clammy.

Hour after hour, for a whole night and well into the morning, I lay there half-dozing and day-dreaming. I had by then grown weary of it all and my attention to our movement had long since lapsed. It took a while for me to notice that something had changed. Our movement had become freer. The sound of the world had altered. I checked our compass heading. We had swung through ninety degrees. Then I knew. I looked out aft, though little confirmation was required. It had finally happened. Mr Jordan's drogue was gone.

26

Minimal sailing is about concentration on the essentials. It is about the ruthless stripping away of anything superfluous to the pure act of sailing and survival. In the smallest of minimal boats, hard choices have to be made. There is only so much space. There are severe limits to the weight that can be carried. Every item on board has to justify its presence twofold; its inclusion must be warranted on the grounds both of its own usefulness to the enterprise and of its superiority to any alternative. This does not necessarily mean technological superiority. Fitness for purpose in the world of minimal sailing focuses too on simplicity of construction and ease of repair. As far as is possible, everything on board should keep working, but if it does break down it should be easily fixed.

This tight restriction on what can be carried does not necessarily mean that only one of everything is allowed on board. Far from it. There are some items so fundamental to survival and the completion of a voyage that spares, or at the very least the materials to fabricate spares, are absolutely essential. The amount of weight and space that can be allocated to an item is in direct proportion to its necessity.

My Jordan Series Drogue had for four years taken up a great deal of available space and weight. That had all been justified by its twelve hours of deployment, twelve hours during which it had almost certainly saved us from a capsize or worse. It was now gone and we were once again vulnerable to seas that as yet had shown no sign of relenting. The disappearance of the drogue was a terrible loss, not least given the time and expense involved in its construction. I felt sick at heart, but had only my stupidity to blame. *Let that be a lesson to you* resounded in my head, as we drifted unfettered and dangerously positioned through the continuing maelstrom.

A heavy weather drogue, however, ranks amongst the most necessary of necessaries for the tiny ocean-going yacht, and I had not been so careless as to put to sea with only one at my disposal. Given the huge stresses they create, drogues and their attachments are often liable to failure of some sort; it is wise always to have a second line of defence. Once more I hauled myself on deck and got to work.

With both my harness lines attached to strong points I sat in *Mingming's* reduced cockpit and opened the watertight door to the fill-in compartment built shortly after her purchase. Just inside the door and easily accessible was a mass of lines and shackles and thimbled splices and a heavy-duty swivel and a big, four-handled do-it-yourself-store bag for transporting sand, all joined together into a baroque assembly. This was my home-made sea anchor.

I hauled the bridle inboard. Its central part was badly chafed from the action of the drogue loop, making it unusable. All I could do was attach the rode of the sea anchor directly to the half inch shackle on one of the bridle chainplates. The rode, about thirty metres long, led to a swivel from which four short lines radiated out to the handles of the bag. I dropped the bag over the stern and paid out the rode. With a violent snub *Mingming* jerked round and once more we were lying stern on to the seas.

For six hours, as the storm came slowly off, my little contraption did its work in a messy, jerky way. There is no doubt that it would have been helped by access to the bridle, thereby spreading its load equally to the two quarters, but the contrast with the action of the series drogue could not have been greater. No more smooth braking; on every wave crest we careered forward then were brought up short with a brick wall of a shock. No more lying quietly; as the pressure came on and off we yawed around through a wide and unpredictable arc. Airy weightlessness was replaced with a crude and leaden battering. Well, it was not the most scientific of arrangements, but it got us through the tail end of the blow, and as I hauled it aboard inch by inch I felt an odd affection for it. It had done its best.

I spent the afternoon clearing up. I packed the sea anchor away in its locker. I passed an awkward hour at the after rail, with two big spanners attached by lines, easing the self-steering bolt enough that I could shift the gear back to its proper vertical position, but at the same time not loosening it so much that the heavy mechanism would rotate out of control. I mopped up the water on the cabin sole. I treated myself to a change of clothes, stuffing the rank and damp castoffs into my burgeoning laundry bag. I caught up on sleep. I stared at the chart and at the twenty-three paltry miles between our latest noon positions, twenty-three miles that had not taken us a jot nearer home. I studied the barometer, now back on duty and eager to impress; despite the clearing sky, air pressure was now falling to its lowest of the voyage. I inspected my toilet bucket, now alarmingly cracked and decrepit and scarcely fit for purpose. I raised sail to four panels and as midnight approached reduced again to two; it was blowing up again straight out of the east. An endless line of monstrous swells rolled on beneath us.

27

Ah yes, the sea! What can you say? It rolls on and on and the wind blows. What impels a man to ride those billows, day after day after day? Why this yearning? What madness is it, that finds solace in an indifferent wilderness? Is it return or escape? Is it to touch the heart of life or to caress the cool cheek of death, distantly? What is this thing that hovers, never seen but always there, and draws a man on? What is this lodestone? Why the sea, always the sea?

Since clearing south-west Iceland we had been set back, first by calms and now by storm, and this was to set the pattern for our long struggle homewards. I look at my chart now and remember that grim haul; daily position marks witheringly close; tracks that cross and re-cross; interspersed across the miles a pencilled litany: *becalmed, becalmed, becalmed*; between each calm a welter of wind, once from the south-west, raising hopes, but in the main from the east, always from the east.

For seven days we stop-started our way towards the Faeroes and then were halted, stone-dead, in our tracks. A half-gale came up from the south-east. It was a vicious, pitiless weight of wind and it blew for four days, straight, as it were, into my streaming eyes. There was nothing to be done. The wind was abetted by a transverse current that was now up to a knot and putting paid to any slim hope of progress. Port tack had us heading to the south-west and

Bermuda or maybe our old friend Caracas; starboard tack would bring us to the great cliffs of Suðurø, the Southern Isle. I held position, swinging back and forth over the shallow waters of the Faroes Bank.

For forty days and forty nights we had roamed the desert. I had never felt lonely; loneliness is not, after all, a function of numbers, but the symptom of a mind adrift. In any case, how could I ever feel lonely in the company of such bewitching solitude? Even that solitude had now lost its purchase; I felt an urgency to be home. It was the completeness of the voyage that I was after, the closing of this final stretch of water that would make our circle just. Yes, there was perhaps a tinge of vanity in there, or rather a deep-buried fear that some late slip-up would rob us of a well-made voyage and all its attendant satisfactions.

I was also down to my last two apples. Every day for forty days I had plunged my hand deep into the knapsack that held my hoard of crisp green fruit and pulled one out at random. How I loved that daily apple and all its dribbling flesh! What a balm it was to hold a summer's meadow and the earth and the smell of the earth and the smell of the blossom and all of the earth's leaves and mellow fruitfulness there in the palm of my hand! That daily apple set to rights the imbalance of a life stripped of verdant, growing things. I couldn't bear the thought that there would no apple aboard, that all that pleasure and freshness and association would soon be gone, and so I made a silent pact: I would eat the first apple only when we had broken out of the trap that held us; the second I would keep for the rest of the voyage, and eat only once we had arrived.

Almost on cue the wind swung round to the south, allowing a course that might just take us clear of the Faroes' southern headland. It was nearly midnight, half a day from my usual apple hour, but a misplaced rush of relief and expectation soon had me groping for the penultimate fruit. I sat in the hatchway and gobbled my apple and marvelled at the moon. It was real and rotund and glowed in a black sky. I had almost forgotten night and here it was again, all dressed to kill.

It was a temporary reprieve. Within eight hours it was blowing even harder, once more back at south-east, and I was worried. An ominous sky was linking up with a crackly forecast of a severe depression west of Bailey, almost on our doorstep. Another bad storm was on its way, and here we were in shallow water, with our best drogue lost forever. There was only one prudent course of action. Destroying all the slight progress of the last few days I ran back to the north-west, off the Faroes Bank and into deeper water. A six hour downwind sprint, hurled on by massive combers, was all it took to undo the struggle of days. It was heart-breaking to hurtle back towards Iceland, and with such ease. As soon as I dared I hauled us up to windward to heave to and wait.

We were spared the full blast of that storm, which jinked off to the north-west, but the weather kept us corralled in that narrow sector for three or four more days. The relentless south-easterly still dominated, but it soon lost its sting and left us tumbling around in a mess of cross-swells. Frustration was turning to tedium, and I worked hard not to succumb to the despair of the solitary confinee. I spent several days creating and perfecting a long ode to my toilet bucket, parodying Keats and plumbing new depths of evacuative insight. I studied to excess the flight pattern and landing and take-off procedures of a lesser black-backed gull that had adopted *Mingming*. I developed a philosophical basis for my new system of measuring yacht velocity, based on bubbles per minute, or BPM. Here's an extract from my notes:

BPM is a much more universal measure of progress than mere speed. Speed is of itself a rather limited and unimaginative concept. BPM adds the qualitative aspect missing from, say the measurement of progress in knots. One knot tells you that you have covered a distance of one nautical mile in one hour. How terribly interesting; but does it give you the slightest intimation of how much fun you had while you were doing it? It does not. Does it in any way express the quality of the forward movement? No. Does it give the measurer any latitude to interpret this progress in a pleasingly subjective and creative way? Not at all. The knot is a dead, lifeless form of measurement. I hate it. What I like is measurement by bubbles. The faster the progress, the more effervescent the calibration. It was wonderful! We were doing a thousand bubbles a minute! The great thing is that you don't, of course, have to count them. It's an impressionistic measurement. It's an emotive response, not an exercise with a slide rule. Speed is, after all, no more absolute than anything else. If time and space are not fixed and linear, how on earth can speed be a constant?

On a less whimsical level, I became obsessed with the navigational challenge of weathering Sumbo, the southerly cape of the Faroes. For the second time we were making our stuttering approach, and with a capricious headwind and strengthening current we were forever in and out of the money. I had drawn a circle with a radius of eight nautical miles around the cape. This was the nearest I would allow us to pass. I messed around for hours at every wind shift calculating complex and mostly illusory vectors to reckon our chances of clearing the cape outside this circle and so liberating ourselves from this awful penitentiary.

Our forty-second day at sea came and went. Our six weeks were up, but there we were, still scratching around three hundred and fifty miles from home. The nights were lengthening, and I several times caught the glow of fishing boats at work.

28

At three in the morning of Sunday the ninth of August, our forty-fifth day at sea, the wind swung round to the south-west and, for the moment, stayed there. The gate of the jail opened and out we sailed, well clear of the cape and bounding straight for home.

After breakfast a fishing boat appeared far on our port quarter, heading the same way, then angled in for a closer look. It was one of those sharp-bladed Faroese monsters I knew so well, the *Eysturbugvin*, SA450. Normally I might well have ignored him, but still in the first flush of liberation I felt expansive and magnanimous and in love with life and all of mankind, and so for the first time of the voyage assembled my hand-held VHF radio, loading its batteries and screwing in its aerial, and put out a call to the skipper of my escort, now running parallel with us just fifty metres on our starboard beam. After a few false starts my vocal chords rediscovered their capacity for speech and thus began a long exchange between a hoarse Englishman and a bemused Viking. A synopsis of my voyage evoked some mild respect from this proper seaman. *Yah, this is a long way.* He himself was bound for Peterhead to unload his catch. I chanced my arm, and asked him if he would ask the harbourmaster there to report my position to his Whitehills counterpart. My new friend promised that he would and was as good as his word. The *Eysturbugvin*, out of the little town of Dalur on Sandø, one of the more southerly islands, soon pulled ahead, showing us the way home as she disappeared below the rim of the world.

That moaning, spiteful south-easterly was long since gone, and for that I was most grateful, but within a few hours we were back to that other purgatory of calms and gutless winds. I sat in the hatchway and watched the sea and realised that as far as this voyage was concerned I had seen enough. My head was over-brimming with images. My neural networks had reached capacity. There was nothing more I could willingly absorb. I now needed a different kind of time and space to process all that I had seen and felt. My habitual patience, too, was at its limits. The urgency to be home was mounting, but there we were, drifting to the north, pushed on by a strengthening current. A little breeze came up from the west, but the Schiehallion oil field, well to the west of the Shetlands, was now right in our path, scattering the sea with strange engines and outlandish sculptures, and forcing us to detour around its perimeter. The wind veered and we were now running free and by the early hours of Tuesday the eleventh of August, our forty-seventh day at sea, we had crossed out of deep water and onto soundings.

Ahead lay the Fair Isle Channel, the last difficult node to negotiate. Chance had brought us back there at the top of spring tides, when the currents flow at their fiercest. With a following wind this would not be a problem, but as we drew in closer to the twenty-mile gap between the Orkneys and Fair Isle, with a distant Foula now brooding low on the northern horizon, the wind hauled back to south-west and then almost to south and I knew that we would have our work cut out. We were back to grey and mucky weather, with poor visibility from time to time, and now there was traffic about, mostly flat-bed oil rig supply ships plying east and west, and the occasional fishing boat at work; the world felt cramped and crowded, what with all this jostling for space in a narrow strait. With the flood tide under us we could hold our course, just. It was the approaching ebb that worried me; would we get picked up and carried willy-nilly to the more dangerous north side of the channel and the cliffs of Fair Isle itself? Night fell. The tide turned. We sailed on through the water but made no progress over the sea bed seventy metres or so beneath. I plotted our position every hour. The crosses edged closer and closer and at the height of the flow reversed a little. We were being set backwards, but still holding tight to the pencilled line of my ideal course. A light flashed far on the starboard bow: North Ronaldsay.

The release, when it came, was comprehensive. The new flood tide combined with a backing of the wind to the west. It was not any old westerly, this one; within the shortest time it was a rollicking Force 6, a beautiful and perfectly positioned blast that had us haring through the last few miles of the channel at the most extravagant speed of our whole voyage. Yes, that wind and tide fair spat us out into the North Sea and the blackest of nights. We were racing, and my heart sang, for I knew that only the cruellest mischance could stop us now. I hauled us round to the south. Our course was straight for Whitehills. On we leaped in a boisterous beam sea, rolling and roistering along with three thousand miles behind us and a clear run for home.

It took just one more day and one more night to close the final gap. Our luck more than held; that wild, westerly wind saw us well into the Moray Firth, and then gave way to a subdued northerly that wafted us easily through the last few miles. Dawn stole softly in on the morning of Thursday the thirteenth of August. We had been at sea for forty-eight days and lived a lifetime of adventure, yet here were the hills of Banffshire, every last contour just as it was, here were the tight-packed roofs of Banff and Macduff, here were those self-same wind turbines and fields and hedgerows and, as we moved in closer, the little light that marks the entrance to Whitehills Harbour.

I called Brenda, now on her way to work through a press of Londoners, and found that I was still remembered, and still in favour. I called up Jim Abel, the relief harbourmaster. He was expecting us, and sent out Martin Wibner in his sloop *Calloo* to tow us the last few yards between wall and rock. And so we came safely into harbour and, for a while at least, lived happily ever after.

The isle of Foula...
'ebony cliffs backed by white-hot liquid gold'.

Approaching the southern end of Jan Mayen.

Close in to Eggoya, Jan Mayen's central headland.

Sailing along the base of Mount Beerenberg, Jan Mayen's seven thousand foot volcano.

'The ice floes glowed.'

'...a rim of spun sugar...'

'...huge and precious stones...'

'...the thinnest of cornices projecting far out over the water.'

'...here were the most extraordinary shapes and arrangements.'

'It was a scene of the most heart-warming desolation.'

Approaching Straumnes, Iceland's north-west headland.

Entering Aðalvík.

Leaving Aðalvík, with the headland Ritur astern.

Sailing through the Denmark Strait
in the lee of the Snaefellsjökull.

Riding to the Jordan Series Drogue.

Mingming *back at Whitehills after forty-eight days at sea.*

The author photographed just a few hours after arrival.
(Courtesy of George Boardman.)

APPENDIX ONE

MINGMING – THE BARE FACTS

Mingming is a Mark II Corribee, designed by Robert Tucker, and built by Newbridge Boats Ltd in Poole, Dorset in 1980. Her hull number is 8064. She is one of the few factory-built junk-rigged Corribees built at that time, distinguishable by their two small portlights in place of the usual Corribee window, and the re-engineered fore-hatch to act as partners for the keel-stepped mast. Fin and bilge keel versions were produced; *Mingming* is the latter. Her principal dimensions are:

Length overall	20ft 9in
Length waterline	16ft 3in
Beam	7ft 2in
Draught	2ft 2in
Displacement	2000lbs
Sail area (mainsail)	216sq ft

She also has a nylon multi-purpose genoa of c.50sq ft and a terylene jib of c.25sq ft.

The main sea-going modifications and additions are:

- Foam-filled sections fore and aft behind watertight bulkheads.

- Raised bridge deck.
- Washboards replaced with solid mahogany fixture and sealing portlight.
- Sliding hatch replaced with watertight escape hatch. This hatch protected by timber coamings and a folding hood.
- Cockpit volume reduced by large watertight compartment.
- Hull and coach roof lined with one-inch thick Plastazote foam and carpet.
- Bowsprit attached to pulpit with U-bolts, to carry headsails.
- Redesigned stainless steel masthead fitting.
- Heavy duty stainless steel yard sling.
- Yard heavily leathered to reduce mast chafe.
- Boom served with rope in mast area to reduce chafe.
- Top batten extended with carbon-fibre tube to allow for six-part mainsheet.
- LED navigation lights (USCG approved to two nautical miles) powered by small solar panel and gel battery.
- Windpilot Pacific Light self-steering gear.
- Home-designed and –built remote control for self-steering gear.
- Tiller lines leading to de-mountable whipstaff for internal steering.
- Two fifteen-foot Douglas fir sculls doubling as jury spars and jury steering oars.
- Two ten-foot ash sweeps operated on stainless steel thole pins in mahogany blocks.
- Jordan Series Drogue (86 cones on 12mm double braid line, breaking strain 3340Kg).
- Sea anchor made from Travis Perkins sand bag.
- Gunmetal chainplates to take drogue bridle fixed to each quarter with three half-inch bolts.

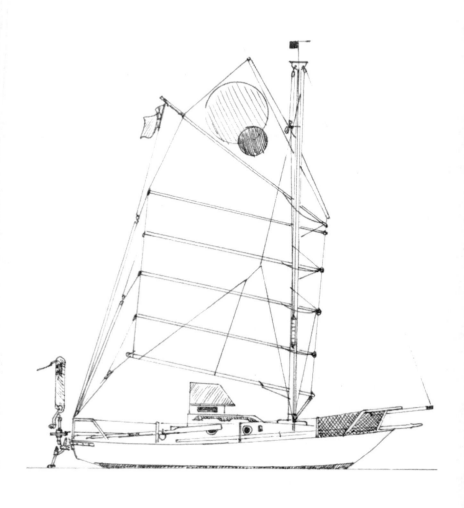

Mingming

APPENDIX TWO

TYPICAL STORES LIST FOR PROJECTED FORTY-TWO DAY VOYAGE
(c.80 days' food and c.100 days' fluids)

Dinner Food

Pre-cooked rice meals x 250 gm	55
Pre-cooked pasta meals x 220gm	10
Dried Potato x 350gm	5
Assorted tins fish/mussels/oysters	60
Assorted tins vegetables	60

Desserts

Assorted long-life desserts	40
Large plastic jars preserved fruit	3

Snack Food

Large homemade Xmas cakes	2
Homemade flapjacks	64
Trek bars/muesli bars	70
Chocolate slabs x 250gm	12
Small Kitkat	30
Home-assembled trail mix	5Kg
Jar dried Swiss bouillon for hot drinks	1

Breakfast Food
Muesli x 750gm   10

Lunch Food
Rye/Pumpernickel Bread x 500 gm   10
Assorted hard cheese   5Kg
Spreadable butters   1Kg
Jars squeezy jam/honey /marmite   5

Fresh Food
Green apples   40
Green bananas   20
Fresh loaves (long life)   2

Fluids
Water   55L
Long-life whole milk   10L
Assorted flavoured soy drinks   3L
Lime juice   1.5L
Ribena   .75L

Navigation
Sextant (Ebbco)
Sight reduction tables and sheets
Pencils/sharpener
Compass
Dividers
Parallel rules/Portland RIB plotter
Charts/pilots/almanac
Log books/notebooks
Pens (waterproof ink)
Handheld GPS x2
Handheld VHF
Shortwave radio receiver

Hand-bearing compass
Chronometer
Binoculars

Bosun's stores
Assorted tools
Rigging knives, fids, marlin spikes
Spare timber, aluminium tubing, plywood
Spare sailcloth
Assorted sailmaker's needles, threads, palm
Supply lanolin, beeswax, tallow, WD40
Assorted balls tarred twine
Assorted stainless steel screws, bolts, shackles
Assorted copper boat nails
Assorted blocks
Several rolls gaffer tape, electrical tape
Assorted glues
Tubes filler, Sikaflex
Spare lines, warps, various diameters
Supply shock cord, various diameters
Spare hose clips, plugs

Miscellaneous
Stills cameras x2
Video camera
Fully charged camera batteries
Spare camera cards
Matches
Currency
Ship's papers
Insurance papers
Passport
Courtesy flags
Spare specs

Sunglasses
Alarms
Spare alarm batteries
LED wind-up torches
LED headlamp
Kitchen rolls x10
Meths 2L
Dry hand wash
Eye shade
Ear plugs
Assorted flares
Intrepid Mk8 abandonment suit